# THE
# EVERYTHING®
## DUTCH OVEN
## COOKBOOK

Dear Reader,

One of the first things I received from my mother when I moved into my first college apartment was a sturdy Dutch oven. She taught me how to make pot roasts, chicken-fried steak, casseroles, and soups with this one very practical and versatile vessel. I learned from her that a good Dutch oven is a cook's best friend! When I got married I started to add to my Dutch oven collection, and over time that collection has grown as my need for dependable cookware has increased. Today the collection stands at five in various shapes and sizes for all kinds of jobs in my very busy kitchen. I can't imagine the holidays or special-occasion cooking without them!

In this book I hope you will find recipes, tips, information, and ideas that will help you unlock the magic of Dutch oven cooking in your own kitchen! A Dutch oven is an investment in good cooking, good food, and good times. For many years the humble Dutch oven was considered a little old-fashioned and out of date, but it is making a comeback as people realize that the old tools are the best tools. Take the time to learn what a Dutch oven can do for you, and you will not be disappointed!

*Kelly Jaggers*

# Welcome to the EVERYTHING® Series!

These handy, accessible books give you all you need to tackle a difficult project, gain a new hobby, comprehend a fascinating topic, prepare for an exam, or even brush up on something you learned back in school but have since forgotten.

You can choose to read an Everything® book from cover to cover or just pick out the information you want from our four useful boxes: e-questions, e-facts, e-alerts, and e-ssentials.

We give you everything you need to know on the subject, but throw in a lot of fun stuff along the way, too.

We now have more than 400 Everything® books in print, spanning such wide-ranging categories as weddings, pregnancy, cooking, music instruction, foreign language, crafts, pets, New Age, and so much more. When you're done reading them all, you can finally say you know Everything®!

## QUESTION

Answers to
common questions

## FACT

Important snippets
of information

## ALERT

Urgent
warnings

## ESSENTIAL

Quick
handy tips

**PUBLISHER** Karen Cooper

**MANAGING EDITOR** Lisa Laing

**COPY CHIEF** Casey Ebert

**ASSISTANT PRODUCTION EDITOR** Jo-Anne Duhamel

**ACQUISITIONS EDITOR** Hillary Thompson

**DEVELOPMENT EDITOR** Brett Palana-Shanahan

**EVERYTHING® SERIES COVER DESIGNER** Erin Alexander

Visit the entire Everything® series at *www.everything.com*

# THE EVERYTHING®
# DUTCH OVEN COOKBOOK

Kelly Jaggers

Adams Media
New York  London  Toronto  Sydney  New Delhi

*To Carol and Howard: Never give up, never surrender.*

Adams Media
An Imprint of Simon & Schuster, Inc.
57 Littlefield Street
Avon, Massachusetts 02322
Copyright © 2016 by Simon & Schuster, Inc.

An Everything® Series Book.
Everything® and everything.com® are registered trademarks of Simon & Schuster, Inc.

ADAMS MEDIA and colophon are trademarks of Simon and Schuster.

For information about special discounts for bulk purchases, please contact Simon & Schuster Special Sales at 1-866-506-1949 or business@simonandschuster.com.

The Simon & Schuster Speakers Bureau can bring authors to your live event. For more information or to book an event contact the Simon & Schuster Speakers Bureau at 1-866-248-3049 or visit our website at www.simonspeakers.com.

Photographs by Kelly Jaggers

Manufactured in the United States of America

10  9  8  7  6  5  4  3  2

Library of Congress Cataloging-in-Publication Data has been applied for.

ISBN 978-1-44059761-9
ISBN 978-1-4405-9762-6 (ebook)

Always follow safety and commonsense cooking protocol while using kitchen utensils, operating ovens and stoves, and handling uncooked food. If children are assisting in the preparation of any recipe, they should always be supervised by an adult.

Contains material adapted from *The Everything® One-Pot Cookbook, 2nd Edition* by Pamela Rice Hahn, copyright © 2009, 1999 by Simon & Schuster, Inc., ISBN 978-1-59869-836-7; *The Everything® Potluck Cookbook* by Linda Larsen, copyright © 2009 by Simon & Schuster, Inc., ISBN 978-1-59869-990-6; *The Everything® Soup, Stew, & Chili Cookbook* by Belinda Hulin, copyright © 2009 by Simon & Schuster, Inc., ISBN 978-1-60550-044-7; and *The Everything® Cast-Iron Cookbook* by Cinnamon Cooper, copyright © 2010 by Simon & Schuster, Inc., ISBN 978-1-4405-0225-5.

# Contents

# Introduction

THE DUTCH OVEN IS perhaps the most versatile cooking vessel in the kitchen. A Dutch oven is more than just your grandmother's favorite heavy stew pot; it can be used to fry, roast, bake, sauté, simmer, braise, and boil, and it can be used on the stovetop, in the oven, and even on the campfire! For hundreds of years the Dutch oven has been an indispensable part of kitchens and campgrounds the world over. Their versatility and durability make them, if properly cared for, a treasure to be handed down from generation to generation. Do you want to make loaves of crusty artisan bread? Do you want to make fried foods that come out crisp and golden? Do you want to make tender roasts, creamy casseroles, and moist cakes? Then you need a Dutch oven!

It is not certain how the Dutch oven got its name, but some people think the name comes from the method used to make the pots. For many years cast-iron cooking vessels were made in baked clay or loam molds, which created pots with a rough surface. In 1704 a man from England named Abraham Darby traveled to Holland and inspected a Dutch casting process that used dry sand molds for making brass vessels. Darby went home to England and began experimenting with the process, eventually perfecting a process that used baked sand molds that produced cast-iron pots with a much smoother texture. The pots he cast were shipped across Europe and eventually to the American colonies and all over the world.

Darby's Dutch ovens are different in a few ways from the modern Dutch oven. Darby's Dutch ovens were designed for cooking over a fire, either outside or in the kitchen hearth. They had legs to hold the base of the pot out of the cooking fire so foods would not burn on the bottom. Over time the lids evolved to develop a lip for holding hot coals on the top so foods would be surrounded by heat for even baking and cooking. While you can still find Dutch ovens that are similar to those early pots—they are often sold as "camp ovens"—today's Dutch ovens are designed with modern cooking appliances in mind. The bottoms of the pots are smooth for use on stoves and cooktops, and the lids are dome shaped. Almost any recipe you can make in your oven, slow cooker, or pressure cooker can be made in your Dutch oven.

Dutch ovens come in a variety of shapes and sizes, and can be either deep or shallow. They can be cast iron or aluminum, enamel coated or uncoated, and may be made with or without legs. Some Dutch ovens are perfect for camping, while others have a sleek design perfect for the modern kitchen. A Dutch oven makes a great gift for a birthday, housewarming, or wedding. If you have a child about to leave the nest, a Dutch oven—along with a copy of this book—is a gift that will keep on giving. It is safe to say that a kitchen isn't complete without at least one Dutch oven!

## Acknowledgments

First I want to thank my husband, Mark, for doing all you do. From finding my mistakes to tasting recipes, you are my hero. I love you more than you can ever know. To Hillary at Adams Media, thank you for this opportunity, and for being so very helpful. I could not have done this without your help! To Lisa at Adams Media, thank you for always thinking of me! I love working with you!

I would like to thank my friends Torie and Jennifer for your constant support. You two are the best! To my work crew Tanisha, Jodi, Sonya, and Novia, thank you for doing what you do, and for being so good to me! You make what we do so much fun!

# CHAPTER 1

# Dutch Oven Cooking Basics

A Dutch oven is one of the best investments you can make for your kitchen. In one vessel you can make fried foods, slow-simmered soups and stews, tender roasts, golden-brown breads, cakes, cobblers, and so much more. Because of the way the Dutch oven is constructed, heat is evenly distributed throughout the pot, creating an even, gentle cooking environment. The lid helps hold in the heat and steam, so braised and roasted foods are juicy and tender, and breads baked inside a Dutch oven come out with a crisp crust.

# Types and Styles of Dutch Ovens

Dutch ovens—also called cast-iron pots, round pots, stock pots, and French ovens—come in a variety of shapes, sizes, and materials. Deciding which type of Dutch oven is right for you largely depends on how you plan to use it. It is not uncommon to have several Dutch ovens in different materials for different uses in the kitchen. No matter what kind you decide to buy, remember that a good Dutch oven will have a well-fitting lid and sturdy handles, and the metal walls and bottom should be an even thickness. Go to a few home stores and take a look at what is available. It is best to see the Dutch ovens in person, hold them, carry them, and decide which size and weight are best for you.

## Sizes

Dutch ovens come in a variety of sizes. From small 2-quart sizes good for side dishes and small meals to 12-quart behemoths that are suitable for cooking massive meals for large groups, there is sure to be a size for most any job. For the average home cook a 5- to 8-quart Dutch oven will do the job for most recipes.

**FACT**

Remember, Dutch ovens can be very heavy—especially if they are made from cast iron—so it is a good idea to shop for them in person. Lift them and see how they feel. Can you lift the oven easily, or is it hard to manage? If you struggle to lift the Dutch oven while it is empty, consider how much more difficult it will be filled with food. Trying to carry a boiling-hot Dutch oven that is too heavy can be dangerous!

In general Dutch ovens are sized using two measurements: the width of the pot's opening and the volume of the Dutch oven in quarts. While every manufacturer is different—and you should check the dimensions when shopping—in general a 2-quart Dutch oven is about 8 inches wide; a 6-quart is about 12 inches wide; and a 10-quart is about 14 inches wide. If you plan to use your Dutch oven for a lot of frying be sure to find one that is approximately 5 to 6 inches deep to ensure you have enough room for the oil to expand after food is added.

For this book a 6- or 8-quart Dutch oven will work for most recipes. Sizes are provided in this book as a guide, but as long as all the food fits in your oven you can cook most of the recipes contained here.

## Shapes

Dutch ovens come in a variety of shapes—round, oval, and even square. Each shape has its benefits and drawbacks. In general, round Dutch ovens will suit almost all needs perfectly. This shape is easy to fit on a stovetop burner, will fit in a standard oven, and can hold a lot of food. An oval Dutch oven is good for longer pieces of meat, such as whole racks of ribs and large leg joints. These are best used in the oven as their shape makes it hard to evenly heat on a burner. The less common square Dutch oven is good for baking breads and roasting meat in the oven. They can also be used on the stovetop but are not usually suitable for deep-frying.

## Camp Ovens

Camp ovens are similar to the original Dutch ovens produced in the 1700s. They have three short legs to hold the base of the pot out of hot coals, and the lid is lipped so coals and ash are held on top. These Dutch ovens are for use outdoors over campfires, and are available in most sporting goods stores. These Dutch ovens are almost always made from bare cast iron, so you will need to thoroughly season the pot before using.

## Materials

Dutch ovens typically come in three materials—cast iron, stainless steel, and anodized aluminum. Which material you choose will depend on a number of factors including cost, ease of use, and durability. A good-quality Dutch oven can last a lifetime, and it can be an investment, but a well-constructed Dutch oven made from quality materials will more than make up for any initial cost.

### Cast Iron

Cast iron is the "gold standard" for many cooks. It heats slowly and evenly, and it holds the heat well and retains the heat for a long time. It also recovers the heat quickly when cool foods are added when browning or deep-frying, and is very versatile. Cast iron is less likely to have major hot and cool spots, so foods brown and cook evenly. The iron must be seasoned or coated, and special care is required to protect the iron from rust.

### Bare versus Enameled Cast Iron

Enameled cast iron is coated with enamel and is very durable. Because it is coated it is resistant to rust and has some nonstick properties, making it easy to clean and maintain. The enamel coating cannot withstand extremely high heat and should never be used on the grill or over open flames. When cooking with enameled cast iron it is best to avoid high heat on the stovetop and temperatures higher than 450°F in the oven. To get your enameled Dutch oven to temperature it is best to heat it slowly over medium heat before cooking. This may take a little longer, but the slow heating will give you all the benefits of high heat. Deep-frying is not recommended in enameled cast iron. Because enameled pots come in a variety of colors, many people choose to display them. They can be a beautiful addition to any kitchen!

**QUESTION**

**How do I season my new cast-iron Dutch oven?**
Hand wash your new Dutch oven and lid with warm water and a mild detergent, then dry the oven completely with a towel. Lightly coat the Dutch oven and the lid inside and out with vegetable oil or lard and place in a cold oven. Heat the oven to 500°F and bake for 1 hour. The oven may smoke so be sure to open a window and turn on a vent fan. Turn off the oven and let pot and lid cool. Check the color. If it is dark gray or brown but not black, repeat the oiling and baking process a second time.

Bare cast iron must be seasoned before use, and once seasoned it will have a naturally nonstick cooking surface. Care must be taken with cleaning a bare cast-iron Dutch oven so the seasoning is not stripped off, and you should only use wood or heatproof rubber tools to avoid scratching the surface. The pot can withstand very high temperatures, and can be used out on the grill or over open flame. It also is ideal for deep-frying. Although you can cook in a bare cast-iron Dutch oven over high heat, it is best to heat the pan over medium heat first, then increase the heat to high. Some bare cast-iron Dutch ovens come preseasoned, but it is still a good idea to season the pot again at home.

### Stainless Steel

Stainless steel has many benefits. It heats quickly, is nonreactive to acids in foods, and it is easy to clean. Stainless steel Dutch ovens can withstand heat up to 500°F, and can be placed on a grill over moderate heat, but you should avoid direct flame. Even though stainless steel can be used to cook over high heat, it is best to slowly heat the pan starting at medium and adjusting to high. Stainless holds heat moderately well, and does a fairly good job of heating evenly, but you will still need to watch the temperature when using it for deep-frying or searing.

### Anodized Cast Aluminum

Aluminum Dutch ovens are probably the most affordable option on the market. They are lightweight, heat very quickly, and are easy to clean. Aluminum pots are sensitive to changes in temperature and recover slowly when cool foods are added during browning and deep-frying, so it is difficult to cook evenly in them. Aluminum is also reactive to acids in foods, so the pots are not recommended for tomato-based sauces. Some aluminum Dutch ovens have a nonstick coating. This coating will limit the heat the pan can withstand, and with time it may flake or chip.

## Caring for Your Dutch Oven

A properly maintained Dutch oven can last for years. Each type of Dutch oven requires different care and cleaning, so be sure you are familiar with your Dutch oven's needs. No matter what kind of Dutch oven you have it is never a good idea to stack it with other pots and pans. The abrasion of the other pots can mar the finish of the Dutch oven—even chip an enamel coating or scratch the seasoning. If you absolutely must stack a Dutch oven due to space constraints line the inside of the Dutch oven with a soft cloth or towel to protect the surface.

## Enameled Cast Iron

Enameled cast iron is very easy to clean. Just a little hot water and soap should work in most cases. Never put your enameled cast-iron Dutch oven in the dishwasher. The high heat and harsh detergents can chip and crack the enamel. If you find the interior of the enamel has discolored you can pour in a solution of 1 teaspoon bleach to 1 pint of water. Let it stand for one hour and then rinse and dry.

## Non-Enameled Cast Iron

As with enameled cast iron, you should never put a non-enameled cast-iron pot in the dishwasher. Bare cast iron that is well seasoned only requires a little hot water to clean it. If there is a stubborn spot pour a little water into the Dutch oven and heat it to a boil, then use a wooden spoon or heatproof rubber spatula to gently work the food away. Once the Dutch oven is clean place it on the stove over medium heat until the water has evaporated away to prevent rusting. Allow the Dutch oven to cool completely before storing.

## Stainless Steel

Stainless steel Dutch ovens are dishwasher safe, so they are easy to clean. Stainless can discolor if not completely cleaned before reheating, and the stainless can scratch if abrasive cleaners or scrubbing pads are used to clean them. Stainless steel that has discolored spots can be cleaned with lemon juice or vinegar. Just dampen a towel with the cleaner of your choice and gently rub the discolored area.

## Anodized Aluminum

Anodized aluminum is dishwasher safe, but be sure that your detergents do not contain bleach or citrus acids. While most aluminum cookware can be cleaned in the dishwasher, it is best to hand wash these pieces. The harsh detergents in the dishwasher can corrode the metal and cause it to oxidize. It is also best to avoid using harsh acids, detergent with a citrus base, or bleach in aluminum as they too can cause oxidization. If your Dutch oven has a nonstick interior coating you should never use abrasive cleaners or scrubbing pads.

**What should I do if my aluminum Dutch oven oxidizes?**
Oxidization is not harmful, so do not think you need to discard any cooking utensils that have oxidized. If you find that your aluminum Dutch oven or any other aluminum cookware develops a dark color or white powdery spots, you can clean the metal with a paste of cream of tartar and a little warm water. Using a rag, scrub the oxidized surface of your cookware with the paste. If the pot is heavily oxidized you may need to spend a little time and elbow grease scrubbing the paste into the metal. Once you are finished rinse well with warm water. You may need to repeat this process several times to restore the metal.

## Essential Tools

The right tools make any job easier, and that applies doubly to cooking. Luckily, you probably already have the tools you need to master Dutch oven cooking in your home kitchen. Most Dutch ovens are durable and can withstand most utensils, but as a rule it is best to avoid metal utensils in your Dutch oven, especially if it has a nonstick coating or if you are using newly seasoned cast iron. Enamel is much more forgiving of metal utensils, but the surface can develop marks with repeated use. In general it is best to use wood or heatproof plastic and rubber utensils to preserve your Dutch oven's cooking surface.

**ESSENTIAL**

Tools for Dutch oven cooking that are handy to have include sturdy oven mitts, short and long tongs, slotted spoons, spiders or a wire mesh tool for removing deep-fried foods, deep-fry thermometer for monitoring oil temperatures, and an instant-read thermometer for checking the internal temperatures of food.

If you are using a camp oven there are specific tools you can purchase for outdoor cooking. Cooking over a campfire, or over red hot coals, can be tricky and these tools will make your job easier and safer. You might want to purchase a lid lifter for lifting a lid that is holding hot coals, a coal holder to set your coals in before placing your Dutch oven on top to keep them in place, and a kickstand for storing a hot lid as it cools. From time to time you may need to replace parts of your camp oven. Check with your manufacturer. Most of them sell fairly inexpensive replacement parts online or in sporting goods stores.

# Cooking Techniques

Your Dutch oven is a versatile cooking tool, and it is a good idea to become familiar with all it can do for you in the kitchen. Once you are familiar with what it can do, you can easily use it to make recipes that call for other kinds of pans, cookware, and dishes. As with everything else, become familiar with your Dutch oven's manual. The manual will tell you the heat limits of your oven and what temperatures are best for stovetop cooking.

## Slow Cooking

Your Dutch oven makes a great slow cooker! You can slow cook on the stove or in the oven, or start your food on the stove and transfer it to the oven. The Dutch oven provides gentle, consistent heat so meats will braise evenly and stews will cook uniformly. Never leave your Dutch oven unattended when slow cooking on the stove or in the oven. Any recipe that calls for a slow cooker can be made in a Dutch oven. Most foods slow cooked in a Dutch oven will be ready in 2–4 hours, depending on what you are preparing.

## Deep-Frying

Dutch ovens make deep-frying easy at home! They heat up evenly, and most of them are able to recover the oil temperature quickly when foods are added. When selecting a Dutch oven for deep-frying you should look for a deep pot that allows for a minimum 3-inch air gap at the top of the pot once 2 to 3 inches oil have been added. This will allow room for the food and for expanding oil. This will also help prevent a boil-over or a grease fire. When you are deep-frying always drop food away from you, drop it slowly, and drop the food close to the oil to avoid splashes, which can cause burns and also cause a fire. Invest in a good oil thermometer to monitor your oil's temperature while frying for best results. Look for a thermometer that is instant-read, that comes with a clip to attach it to your Dutch oven, and, if possible, look for digital.

## Casseroles

Who needs an army of casserole dishes when you have a Dutch oven? The Dutch oven is ideal for making most casseroles, and due to its versatility you can often prep pasta, make sauces, or brown meats all in the same vessel you will be baking in, saving time now and when washing up later! It also goes from stove to oven to table with ease, and heavy cast-iron Dutch ovens will keep food warmer longer due to the metal's ability to retain heat. While coated and seasoned Dutch ovens are naturally nonstick, it never hurts to add a little nonstick cooking spray as insurance. Stainless steel and aluminum without a nonstick coating will need a nonstick cooking spray to help foods release after baking.

**ALERT**

Your Dutch oven can get very, very hot! It is important to take some precautions when handling a hot Dutch oven. Buy a pair of heatproof oven mitts that cover at least part of your forearms. This will help protect your arms when reaching into a hot oven, and when carrying your Dutch oven from stove to oven, or from oven to table. Also, be aware that most Dutch ovens do not have cool touch handles, so always use an oven mitt when touching a heated Dutch oven.

## Baking

You might think of cobbler or cornbread when you think baking in your Dutch oven, but it can do so much more. The heavy, tight-fitting lid holds in steam, making it the perfect vessel to bake crusty loaves of rustic bread. You will need to preheat the Dutch oven before baking bread, and take care not to open the lid before indicated in the recipe to hold in the steam. Besides bread, the Dutch oven is good for baking flaky biscuits, buttery cinnamon rolls, bubbling pot pies, tender cakes, large cookies, gooey brownies, creamy custards, and roasted fruits. Your Dutch oven also makes deep dish pizza that is better than ordering from your local pizza joint!

# Tips for Success

There are a few cooking basics that will help you achieve the best possible result when working with a Dutch oven. You may already know these, but it never hurts to have a refresher. Anything worth doing is worth doing well, and any food worth eating deserves your time and attention. It is important to take the time you need to cook, not be rushed, and read through your recipe at least once before you start. The following tips will also help you make delicious meals that will keep people coming back for more!

## Browning Meats

When cooking meats in your Dutch oven for soups, stews, or roasts it is always a good idea to brown them first. Browning does two things. First, it makes the meat look more appealing. We eat with our eyes first. You may have the best beef stew in town, but if you have gray hunks of meat floating around in the bowl it will look much less appetizing. Second, it improves the flavor of your food. Browning helps caramelize the natural sugars and proteins in the meat, and that browning adds richness and additional umami—or savory flavor—to your finished dish. Take the time to brown the meat well on all sides, and do not crowd the pan or you will steam the meat rather than brown it. If the meat sticks to the Dutch oven while browning do not force it to release. Once it is well browned it will release naturally.

## Temperatures

Invest in an oven thermometer, an instant-read meat thermometer, and an oil thermometer. These will be the most important tools you can use for successful cooking. An oven that is not properly calibrated can be off by as much as 50°F! That is a huge difference. Check your oven's temperature every time you bake to be sure the temperature is accurate. The same goes with an oil thermometer. Keeping your oil at a steady temperature will ensure that your food is cooked properly and will keep you from having to deal with burned oil, which will ruin the flavor of your food. Finally, an instant-read thermometer will ensure that your foods are cooked to a safe temperature and are ready to eat.

## Uniformly Sized Food

For stews and casseroles you should make sure your meats and vegetables are cut into uniform sizes. This will ensure that the dish is cooked evenly and each bite will be perfect! Remember, smaller pieces of meat and vegetable will cook more quickly than larger ones, so making sure your sizes are even is import for consistency. As a general rule, for soups and casseroles you should use a small dice, about ¼ inch to ½ inch. For stew you want your food more chunky, so aim for ½ inch to 1 inch. Roasts can also be divided into smaller pieces (for example, a 3-pound roast can be cut into three 1-pound roasts) to speed up cooking time. Be sure to check the smaller roasts approximately 45 minutes before the cooking time needed for a 3-pound roast to avoid overcooking.

## Storage and Safety

Taking care of your tools, and taking care with the food you prepare, are important for long-term cooking success. Dutch ovens should be cooled, cleaned, and completely dry before storing. For Dutch ovens made of cast iron it is a good idea to heat the oven over medium heat after washing and drying to be sure all the moisture has evaporated. Cool the Dutch oven and store as usual. If you must stack your Dutch oven be sure to use a towel or soft cloth between the pots to protect their finish. Check with your Dutch oven's manufacturer about care and cleaning. This chapter is a guide, but the instructions that may have come with your Dutch oven will contain further details about temperature limits, cleaning instructions, and how to properly use the oven. When in doubt contact the manufacturer with questions. The customer service departments are usually happy to help!

**CHAPTER 2**

# Breakfast Dishes

# Overnight French Toast

*This is the perfect dish to serve overnight guests since most of the preparation is done the evening before. Your guests will wake up to the irresistible aroma of French toast, and you can relax with a cup of coffee!*

**PREP TIME:** 10–12 hours
**COOK TIME:** 45 minutes

**INGREDIENTS | SERVES 8**

1 (13-ounce) loaf French bread, cut into 1" slices
8 large eggs
2 cups half and half
1 cup whole milk
¼ cup maple syrup
2 teaspoons vanilla extract
¾ teaspoon cinnamon, divided
½ teaspoon nutmeg, divided
¼ teaspoon salt
2 sticks unsalted butter, cubed and chilled
½ cup sugar
½ cup packed light brown sugar
2 tablespoons all-purpose flour
1 cup chopped pecans

1. Spray a 6- or 8-quart Dutch oven with nonstick spray and layer bread slices into the bottom of the pot. Not all bread will fit. Save leftover slices for garlic toast or croutons.

2. In a medium bowl add eggs and whisk until the yolks are broken. Add half and half, milk, maple syrup, vanilla, ½ teaspoon cinnamon, ¼ teaspoon nutmeg, and salt and whisk until thoroughly combined.

3. Pour egg mixture evenly over bread slices. Cover the Dutch oven with the lid and refrigerate overnight, or at least 4 hours.

4. In the work bowl of a stand mixer fitted with the paddle attachment, or in a large bowl with a hand mixer, combine ¼ teaspoon cinnamon, ¼ teaspoon nutmeg, butter, sugar, brown sugar, flour, and pecans. Blend on medium speed until completely combined. Cover and chill overnight.

5. Heat oven to 350°F.

6. Once the oven is hot, remove the Dutch oven from the refrigerator and remove the lid. Sprinkle pecan mixture evenly over the top of bread and bake 40–50 minutes, or until casserole is golden brown and puffed all over. Remove from the oven and cool 5 minutes before serving.

# Savory Breakfast Bread Pudding

*Do you want to make bread pudding, but your bread isn't stale? No problem! Just cube the bread, spread it out on a sheet pan, and toast it at 350°F for 10–12 minutes, or until the bread is golden brown and dry.*

**PREP TIME:** 10 minutes
**COOK TIME:** 1 hour

**INGREDIENTS | SERVES 8**

1 pound breakfast sausage, mild or spicy

6 cups cubed stale white or whole-wheat bread

2 cups shredded Cheddar cheese, divided

4 large eggs

3 cups whole milk

2 tablespoons maple syrup

¼ teaspoon salt

¼ teaspoon freshly cracked black pepper

1. Heat oven to 350°F.

2. In a 6- or 8-quart Dutch oven over medium heat add breakfast sausage. Cook, breaking into crumbles, until cooked through and browned, about 8–10 minutes. Remove the Dutch oven from heat and carefully drain as much of the fat as you can.

3. Add bread and 1½ cups shredded cheese, and mix well.

4. In a medium bowl whisk together eggs, milk, maple syrup, salt, and pepper until well combined. Pour egg mixture over bread and allow the mixture to stand 10 minutes at room temperature to absorb.

5. Sprinkle remaining cheese over the top of the casserole and bake 40–50 minutes, or until bread pudding is golden brown and puffed all over. Allow to cool 5 minutes before serving.

## Vegetarian Sausage

You can make this casserole with frozen vegetarian sausage patties if you or your guests don't like meat. Just thaw the patties in the microwave and chop them into chunks. Add 2 tablespoons oil to the Dutch oven and sauté the sausage chunks until they are crisp around the edges. Proceed with the recipe as directed.

# Oven Omelet

*This recipe can be served as the main dish for a Sunday brunch or as the centerpiece for a vegetarian luncheon.*

**PREP TIME:** 10 minutes
**COOK TIME:** 40 minutes

**INGREDIENTS | SERVES 8**

3 tablespoons unsalted butter, melted
18 large eggs
1 teaspoon salt
⅛ teaspoon pepper
1 cup sour cream
1 cup whole milk
2 tablespoons Dijon mustard
1½ cups shredded Colby cheese
¼ cup grated Parmesan cheese

1. Heat oven to 325°F. Pour melted butter into a 6- or 8-quart Dutch oven and spread on the bottom.

2. In a large bowl, combine eggs with salt, pepper, and sour cream and whisk until well combined. Add milk and mustard and beat until blended.

3. Stir in Colby cheese and pour into prepared Dutch oven. Sprinkle with Parmesan cheese and bake 35–45 minutes, or until eggs are puffed, set, and lightly browned.

# Classic Breakfast Grits

*This is a basic, slow cooked grits recipe that is a staple of the Southern breakfast table.*

**PREP TIME:** 5 minutes
**COOK TIME:** 2 hours

**INGREDIENTS | SERVES 6**

5 cups water, plus more as needed
½ teaspoon salt
1 cup stone-ground grits
2 tablespoons salted butter
Hot sauce, optional

1. In a 4-quart Dutch oven bring water to a boil over high heat. Add salt, then reduce heat to medium.

2. Stirring constantly, gradually add grits. Reduce heat to medium-low and cook grits, stirring often, to prevent grits from sticking to the bottom of the Dutch oven. Cook until grits are creamy and soft, about 1½–2 hours. If grits become too thick add additional water ¼ cup at a time as needed. Grits should have the consistency of thick pancake batter.

3. Stir in butter and season with hot sauce and additional salt, if desired.

# Dutch Oven Frittata

*This recipe is a great place to use your favorite fresh herbs. Use whatever you like, or use a mixture of chives, flat-leaf parsley, rosemary, and tarragon. Serve slices of this frittata with a dollop of crème fraîche or sour cream for an elegant touch.*

**PREP TIME:** 10 minutes
**COOK TIME:** 20 minutes

**INGREDIENTS | SERVES 8**

1 pound smoked bacon, chopped

1 medium onion, peeled and finely chopped, about ¾ cup

1 (10-ounce) bag chopped frozen spinach, thawed and drained well

12 large eggs

1 cup shredded Gruyère cheese

2 tablespoons chopped fresh herbs

¼ teaspoon salt

¼ teaspoon freshly cracked black pepper

1. Heat oven to broil.

2. To a 6-quart Dutch oven over medium-high heat, add chopped bacon. Cook, stirring often, until bacon has rendered its fat and is crisp, about 8 minutes. Remove bacon from the pan to a paper towel–lined plate to drain, and pour off all but 2 tablespoons of drippings.

3. Return the Dutch oven to medium-high heat and add chopped onion. Cook, stirring often, until onions have softened, about 3 minutes. Add spinach and cook until spinach is hot, about 3 minutes. Return bacon to the pan and stir to combine.

4. In a medium bowl whisk eggs until all the yolks are broken. Stir in shredded cheese, fresh herbs, salt, and pepper. Add beaten egg mixture to the Dutch oven and reduce heat to medium-low. Cover and cook until the bottom of eggs are set and top is just starting to firm up, about 3–5 minutes.

5. Remove the lid and place the Dutch oven under the broiler and cook 3–4 minutes, or until top of the frittata is lightly browned and eggs are firm. Serve immediately.

# Veggie Dutch Oven Frittata with Goat Cheese

*This dish is a fantastic way to showcase fresh, seasonal vegetables from the farmers' market or your local co-op. Be creative and use the vegetables you love best!*

**PREP TIME:** 10 minutes
**COOK TIME:** 20 minutes

**INGREDIENTS | SERVES 8**

2 tablespoons unsalted butter

1 medium zucchini or yellow squash, diced, about 1 cup

1 medium onion, peeled and chopped, about ½ cup

1 pint sliced mushrooms

1 clove garlic, peeled and minced

½ teaspoon fresh thyme leaves, or ¼ teaspoon dry thyme

½ teaspoon salt

½ teaspoon freshly cracked black pepper

¼ teaspoon crushed red pepper flakes

8 large eggs

4 ounces goat cheese, crumbled, divided

1. In a 6-quart Dutch oven over medium-high heat, add butter. Once butter is melted and starts to foam add zucchini or squash, onion, and mushrooms. Cook until squash and mushrooms are tender and onion is translucent, about 8 minutes. Add garlic, thyme, salt, pepper, and red pepper flakes and cook until thyme and garlic are fragrant, about 1 minute.

2. In a medium bowl whisk eggs until all the yolks are broken. Stir in ¾ of goat cheese. Add beaten egg mixture to the Dutch oven and reduce heat to medium-low. Cover and cook until bottom of eggs are set and top is just starting to firm up, about 3–5 minutes.

3. Remove the lid and place the Dutch oven under the broiler 3–4 minutes, or until top of the frittata is lightly browned and eggs are firm. Sprinkle top with the reserved goat cheese and serve immediately.

# Ham and Cheese Soufflé

*This soufflé is easier to serve than others because it will stand without falling.*

**PREP TIME:** 8–24 hours
**COOK TIME:** 60 minutes

**INGREDIENTS | SERVES 6**

3 cups cubed French bread

2 cups chopped cooked ham

2 (4-ounce) cans sliced mushrooms, drained

2 cups shredded Havarti cheese

1 cup shredded Cheddar cheese

6 large eggs, beaten

2 cups milk

½ cup sour cream

½ teaspoon salt

1 teaspoon dry mustard

¼ cup Dijon mustard

3 tablespoons all-purpose flour

¼ cup melted unsalted butter

¼ cup grated Parmesan cheese

1. The day before, spray 6- or 8-quart Dutch oven with nonstick cooking spray. Combine bread, ham, mushrooms, and both cheeses in the Dutch oven and toss to mix, then spread into an even layer.

2. In large bowl, beat eggs with milk, sour cream, salt, dry mustard, Dijon mustard, flour, and melted butter until combined. Pour over bread and cheese mixture. Cover and refrigerate 8–24 hours.

3. When ready to bake, heat oven to 350°F. Sprinkle with Parmesan cheese and bake 50–60 minutes until puffed and deep golden brown.

## Make-Ahead Tips

This type of soufflé is more like a strata, or layered bread and cheese topped with an egg custard. You can make several of them ahead of time if you're serving a crowd, then bake them one after the other so a hot soufflé is always available. Flavor them in different ways: chicken and peas or sausage and green bell pepper are good combinations.

# *Chilaquiles con Huevos* (Tortillas in Salsa with Eggs)

*Chilaquiles are a popular Mexican dish served for breakfast or brunch. Popular garnishes for Chilaquiles include fresh avocado slices, sour cream, fresh chopped onion and cilantro, and hot sauce.*

**PREP TIME:** 10 minutes
**COOK TIME:** 25 minutes

**INGREDIENTS | SERVES 6**

Vegetable or peanut oil for frying

12 corn tortillas, cut into 1" strips

½ teaspoon salt

2 tablespoons unsalted butter

6 large eggs, beaten

2 cups red chili pepper sauce, or red salsa

1 cup shredded queso quesadilla or Monterey jack cheese

## Tortilla Chips

In a hurry? You can make this dish with store-bought tortilla chips rather than frying your own. Just substitute about 3 cups of tortilla chips for the homemade tortilla chips in this recipe. For best results use thick chips, and if you can find tortilla strips that is even better. This trick will cut your prep time in half!

1. Add 2" oil to a 6-quart Dutch oven and place over medium-high heat. Once oil reaches 350°F add tortilla strips and fry until strips are golden brown and crisp, about 3 minutes. Remove tortilla strips from oil and season with salt. Set aside. Drain oil from the pan.

2. Heat oven to broil.

3. Return the Dutch oven to medium heat and add butter. Once butter foams add beaten eggs and scramble until the curds are soft set, about 5–8 minutes. Remove eggs from the pan and set aside.

4. Return tortilla strips to the pan along with red chili pepper sauce and simmer until tortilla strips are softened, about 3 minutes. Top with scrambled eggs and shredded cheese.

5. Place the Dutch oven under the broiler until cheese is melted and bubbling, about 3 minutes. Serve immediately.

# *Migas* Tex-Mex Style

*Migas originated in Spain and are a popular way to use up day-old bread. The Tex-Mex version uses crisp corn tortillas in place of the bread, and also includes fresh vegetables and cheese. Serve this dish with fresh salsa and Refried Beans (Chapter 7).*

**PREP TIME:** 15 minutes
**COOK TIME:** 20 minutes

**INGREDIENTS | SERVES 6**

3 tablespoons vegetable oil

12 corn tortillas, cut into wedges

½ teaspoon salt

1 medium green bell pepper, diced, about ½ cup

1 medium onion, peeled and diced, about ½ cup

1 medium tomato, seeded and diced, about ½ cup

6 large eggs, beaten

½ cup shredded queso fresco

2 tablespoons chopped fresh cilantro

1. Add oil to a 6-quart Dutch oven and place over medium-high heat. Once oil is hot and starts to shimmer add tortilla wedges and fry until wedges are golden brown and crisp, about 3–5 minutes. Remove tortilla wedges from the pan and season with salt. Set aside.

2. Add bell peppers and onion to the Dutch oven and sauté until they soften, about 5 minutes. Add tomato and cook until heated through, about 1 minute.

3. Add tortilla wedges and beaten eggs to the Dutch oven and cook until eggs are set to your liking. Garnish with queso fresco and cilantro. Serve immediately.

# Oven-Baked Blueberry Pancake

*You don't have to use blueberries here. You can substitute diced strawberries, fresh raspberries, rehydrated dried fruit such as raisins or cranberries, chopped nuts, or chocolate chips!*

**PREP TIME:** 15 minutes
**COOK TIME:** 30 minutes

**INGREDIENTS | SERVES 6**

1½ cups all-purpose flour

⅓ cup sugar

2 teaspoons baking powder

¼ teaspoon baking soda

¼ teaspoon cinnamon

¼ teaspoon salt

1 cup buttermilk

2 large eggs, beaten

¼ cup (4 tablespoons) unsalted butter, melted and cooled

1 teaspoon vanilla

1 cup fresh blueberries

Powdered sugar, for garnish

Maple syrup, for garnish

## Do Your Berries Sink?

If you find that fresh berries sink to the bottom of your baked pancakes, quick breads, or muffins you can toss them in a tablespoon of all-purpose flour before adding them to the batter. The flour will help the berries to stay suspended in the batter. This trick also works with nuts and chocolate chips!

1. Heat oven to 375°F. Place a 4-quart Dutch oven into oven to preheat.

2. In a large bowl combine flour, sugar, baking powder, baking soda, cinnamon, and salt. Whisk until mixture is thoroughly combined.

3. In a separate bowl whisk together buttermilk, eggs, butter, and vanilla until thoroughly combined. Add the wet ingredients into the dry and mix until just combined. Add in blueberries and fold until they are evenly distributed.

4. Remove the Dutch oven from the oven and spray lightly with nonstick cooking spray. Add pancake batter and evenly spread the mixture into the Dutch oven.

5. Bake 25–30 minutes or until the pancake springs back when lightly pressed in the center and a toothpick inserted into the center of pancake comes out clean. Allow to cool 5 minutes before serving. Garnish each slice with a dusting of powdered sugar and a drizzle of maple syrup.

# Devil's Food Cake Doughnuts

*Nothing beats fresh doughnuts for breakfast, and these are sure to please the chocolate lover in your life! You can garnish the glazed doughnuts with sprinkles, chopped toasted nuts, or toasted coconut for a festive touch.*

**PREP TIME:** 2 hours 30 minutes
**COOK TIME:** 30 minutes

**INGREDIENTS | YIELDS 18 DOUGHNUTS**

3 tablespoons unsalted butter, at room temperature

½ cup sugar

½ cup packed light brown sugar

3 large eggs

2 cups all-purpose flour

1½ cups bread flour

½ cup plus 2 tablespoons Dutch-processed cocoa powder, divided

1 tablespoon baking powder

½ teaspoon salt

¾ cup buttermilk

¼ teaspoon powdered unflavored gelatin

⅓ cup cooled coffee

¼ cup corn syrup

1 teaspoon vanilla

1 pound powdered sugar

Oil, for frying

1. In the work bowl of a stand mixer fitted with the paddle attachment, beat butter, sugar, and brown sugar on low speed until crumbly, about 2 minutes. Add eggs, one at a time, beating well after each addition.

2. In a separate bowl, combine flour, bread flour, ½ cup cocoa powder, baking powder, and salt. Whisk until well combined.

3. Working in three additions, add flour mixture into butter mixture alternately with buttermilk, starting and ending with flour mixture. Mix 10–15 seconds per addition, or until a soft dough forms. Cover and refrigerate 2 hours or overnight.

4. Turn the dough out onto a well-floured work surface and gently pat into a ¼"-thick circle. Cut with a floured 2½" doughnut cutter. Cover with a towel and allow the doughnuts and holes to rest 10 minutes.

5. While dough rests prepare the glaze. In a measuring cup combine gelatin with 1 tablespoon of coffee. Let stand 5 minutes to allow gelatin to soften and bloom (expand), and then melt in microwave 8–10 seconds. Combine gelatin mixture with remaining coffee, corn syrup, vanilla, cocoa powder, and powdered sugar and whisk until smooth. Cover with plastic until ready to use.

6. In an 8-quart deep Dutch oven heat 2" oil to 375°F. Gently add two or three doughnuts at a time, frying 1½ minutes per side, or until doughnuts are puffed and buoyant. The doughnut holes will need 1 minute per side. Transfer doughnuts to a wire rack to cool about 3 minutes, then dip the tops of the doughnuts into the chocolate glaze. Let the glaze set, about 20 minutes.

# Apple Fritters

*These fritters are just like the fritters you find in doughnut shops. Part yeast doughnut, part apple dumpling, these fritters have lots of tender apples and crisp edges that will keep you coming back for more!*

**PREP TIME:** 1 hour 30 minutes
**COOK TIME:** 45 minutes

**INGREDIENTS | YIELDS 12**

½ cup water, heated to 110°F

2½ teaspoons dry active yeast

1 medium Granny Smith apple, peeled, cored, and diced

¼ cup sugar, divided

½ teaspoon cinnamon

2 tablespoons vegetable shortening

2 teaspoons salt

⅛ teaspoon mace or nutmeg

1 tablespoon nonfat dry milk

1 large egg

2 cups bread flour

¼ teaspoon powdered unflavored gelatin

⅓ cup water

¼ cup corn syrup

1 teaspoon vanilla

1 pound powdered sugar

Oil, for frying

1. In the work bowl of a stand mixer combine the heated water and yeast. Allow to sit 10 minutes. In a small bowl combine the apples with 2 tablespoons sugar and cinnamon. Set aside. In the same bowl as the yeast mixture mix the remaining sugar, shortening, salt, mace or nutmeg, dry milk, egg, and bread flour. Mix with the dough hook on low speed 3 minutes. Dough should be sticky but should not cling to your finger. Mix on medium speed 6 minutes, or until the dough is smooth and forms a ball around the dough hook. Cover the bowl with a damp towel and allow the dough to double in bulk, about 1 hour.

2. Turn the dough out onto a floured surface and press the dough into a 12" × 18" rectangle with the heel of your hand. Spread the apple mixture onto the dough, fold in half and cut into 12 pieces. Using a butter knife gently chop the fritters so they look lumpy and misshapen with bits of apple peeking out. Cover the fritters with a damp towel and let rest 20 minutes.

3. Prepare the glaze. In a small microwave-safe bowl combine the gelatin and water. Stir and allow to stand 10 minutes. Then place the bowl in the microwave and heat for 8–10 seconds or until the gelatin melts. Do not boil. Combine the melted gelatin in a large bowl with the corn syrup, vanilla, and powdered sugar. Whisk until smooth. Cover with plastic wrap and set aside.

4. Heat at least 3" oil in an 8-quart deep Dutch oven to 375°F. Cook the fritters one or two at a time until they are golden brown, about 2 minutes per side. Transfer cooked fritters to a wire rack to drain. Dip the warm fritters into the glaze, coating all sides, and transfer to a cooling rack to drain. Let the glaze set 30 minutes before eating.

# Refrigerator Biscuit Doughnuts

*Sometimes you need doughnuts and you need them in a hurry. When that happens turn to large, flaky refrigerator biscuits. This shortcut means you are never more than about 20 minutes away from warm doughnuts!*

**PREP TIME:** 10 minutes
**COOK TIME:** 10 minutes
**INGREDIENTS | YIELDS 8**

Oil, for frying
½ cup sugar
1 teaspoon cinnamon
1 (16-ounce) can large flaky biscuits

### Jam-Filled Doughnuts

For jam-filled doughnuts use the regular-sized flaky biscuits and fry them whole then cool completely. To fill, use a piping bag filled with your favorite jam fitted with a medium star tip. Push the tip into the side of the doughnut and squeeze about 1 tablespoon of filling into the doughnut. Dust with powdered sugar and enjoy!

1. Heat at least 3" oil in an 8-quart deep Dutch oven to 350°F.

2. In a small bowl, combine sugar and cinnamon and set aside.

3. Place biscuits on a lightly floured work surface and lightly flatten with your fingers. With a 1½" round cookie or biscuit cutter, cut out a hole from middle of each biscuit.

4. Fry biscuits two or three at a time until golden on each side, about 1½ minutes per side. Fry doughnut holes about 1 minute per side. Remove biscuits from hot oil and drain on wire rack over a sheet pan until cool enough to handle. Toss in cinnamon and sugar mixture. Enjoy immediately.

# Easy Baked Cheese Grits

*Make your friends and family happy by making this cheesy crowd pleaser for your next breakfast, brunch, or even dinner! If you like, you can substitute half the cheese called for with smoked Gouda.*

**PREP TIME:** 10 minutes
**COOK TIME:** 55 minutes

**INGREDIENTS | SERVES 6**

4 cups water

1 stick unsalted butter

½ teaspoon salt

1 cup quick-cooking grits

½ teaspoon freshly cracked black pepper

1 cup shredded sharp Cheddar cheese

½ cup shredded Gruyère cheese

2 tablespoons shredded Parmesan cheese

2 large eggs

¼ cup heavy cream

1. Heat oven to 350°F.

2. In a 4-quart Dutch oven over medium-high heat add water, butter, and salt. Bring mixture to a boil.

3. Stirring constantly, gradually add grits. Reduce heat to medium-low and cook grits until they are slightly thickened, about 5 minutes. Remove from heat. Stir in pepper and the shredded cheeses.

4. In a small bowl beat eggs with heavy cream. Stir into cooked grits.

5. Bake grits 45–50 minutes, or until grits feel firm to the touch in the center. Cool 10 minutes before serving.

# Eggs Baked in Creamy Grits

*This recipe calls for quick-cooking grits, but you can use traditional grits; simply cook them 10 additional minutes on the stove. Please, do not use instant grits as they will not be creamy out of the oven.*

**PREP TIME:** 10 minutes
**COOK TIME:** 45 minutes

**INGREDIENTS | SERVES 6**

4 cups water

1 cup heavy cream

1 teaspoon salt, divided

2 cups quick-cooking grits or polenta

1 tablespoon unsalted butter

1 cup shredded sharp Cheddar cheese

6 large eggs

½ teaspoon freshly cracked black pepper

¼ cup fresh chopped chives, optional

## Quick versus Regular Grits

In terms of taste, there is little difference between traditional grits and quick-cooking grits. Quick grits are ground a little finer than traditional grits and therefore cook more rapidly. The texture is a bit different, but not at all unpleasant. With quick grits you can have them ready to serve in about 5 minutes rather than the 25 minutes it can take for regular grits. On a busy morning, or after a long day at work, quick grits are a cook's best friend!

1. Heat the oven to 350°F.

2. In an 8-quart deep Dutch oven combine the water, heavy cream, and ½ teaspoon salt. Heat the mixture over high heat and allow to come to a rolling boil. Reduce heat to medium-low and slowly whisk in grits. Once all grits are added turn heat up to medium and cook, stirring constantly with a wooden spoon or heatproof spatula, 5 minutes, or until grits have absorbed all the liquid.

3. Remove grits from heat and add butter and cheese. Stir until melted and completely combined.

4. Place the cover on the Dutch oven and bake grits 15 minutes. Remove the pot from the oven and remove the lid. Carefully make 6 indentions in grits using back of large ladle or spoon. Crack 1 egg into each indention. Sprinkle eggs with remaining salt and pepper.

5. Bake, uncovered, until egg whites have set but yolks are still slightly soft in the center, about 12–15 minutes. Garnish with fresh chives, if desired. Serve hot.

# Hash Brown Breakfast Casserole

*Ready-shredded hash browns make this dish easy to make any day of the week. If you want to use fresh potatoes be sure to wring out as much moisture as you can; otherwise the casserole will be too watery.*

**PREP TIME:** 15 minutes
**COOK TIME:** 55 minutes

**INGREDIENTS | SERVES 8**

2 pounds breakfast sausage, mild, spicy, or a mixture of both

1 tablespoon unsalted butter

1 medium onion, peeled and chopped, about ½ cup

1 (20-ounce) bag shredded hash browns

½ teaspoon smoked paprika

½ teaspoon freshly cracked black pepper

¼ teaspoon salt

½ cup shredded pepper jack cheese

½ cup shredded Cheddar cheese

4 large eggs

1 cup whole milk

½ cup heavy cream

1. Heat oven to 350°F.

2. Heat a 4-quart Dutch oven over medium-high heat. Add sausage and cook, breaking sausage into crumbles, until cooked through and browned, about 8–10 minutes. Remove sausage from the Dutch oven and drain off all but 2 tablespoons of sausage drippings.

3. Add butter to the Dutch oven and once it foams add onion. Cook, stirring constantly, until onion is translucent, about 3 minutes. Remove the pot from heat and add cooked sausage, hash browns, paprika, pepper, salt, and both cheeses. Stir to combine.

4. In a medium bowl beat eggs with milk and cream. Pour egg mixture evenly over hash brown mixture.

5. Bake 30–40 minutes, or until casserole is golden brown on top and the center of casserole is set. Cool 5 minutes before serving.

# Spicy Breakfast Potatoes

*This makes a good side to scrambled, poached, or fried eggs. Add some crisp bacon or sausage patties to make this a complete meal!*

**PREP TIME:** 15 minutes
**COOK TIME:** 25 minutes

**INGREDIENTS | SERVES 6**

¼ cup vegetable oil

2 large Russet potatoes, scrubbed and cut into ½" cubes

1 medium onion, peeled and chopped, about ½ cup

1 medium red bell pepper, chopped, about ½ cup

½ teaspoon salt

½ teaspoon chili powder

¼ teaspoon smoked paprika

¼ teaspoon cumin

¼ teaspoon cayenne pepper

¼ teaspoon freshly cracked black pepper

1. Heat a 6-quart Dutch oven over medium-high heat. Add oil and once it shimmers add potatoes. Cook, stirring frequently, until potatoes begin to soften and are starting to crisp, about 15 minutes.

2. Add onion and bell pepper and cook 5 minutes, then add remaining ingredients and cook until potatoes are golden brown and tender inside, another 3–5 minutes. Serve hot.

# Sausage Gravy for Biscuits

*This gravy is perfect for fresh buttermilk biscuits, and it is also good on fried potatoes, like Spicy Breakfast Potatoes (see recipe in this chapter). You can make this vegetarian by using 4 tablespoons oil or butter and omitting the sausage.*

**PREP TIME:** 5 minutes
**COOK TIME:** 25 minutes

**INGREDIENTS | SERVES 6**

1 pound breakfast sausage

½ cup all-purpose flour

2 cups whole milk

1 cup half and half

1 teaspoon freshly cracked black pepper

½ teaspoon salt

1. Heat a 4-quart Dutch oven over medium-high heat. Add sausage and cook, breaking sausage into crumbles, until cooked through and browned, about 8–10 minutes.

2. Sprinkle all-purpose flour evenly over sausage and cook, stirring constantly, until flour has absorbed sausage drippings and is just turning a light golden brown color, about 3 minutes.

3. Reduce heat to medium-low and slowly whisk in milk and half and half. Adding liquid slowly will help prevent lumps. Add pepper and salt, then raise heat to medium and cook, stirring constantly, until mixture comes to a boil and thickens, about 8 minutes. Serve immediately.

# Fruity Steel-Cut Oats

*This recipe makes steel-cut oats an easy option for any day of the week! You can use any dried fruit you like, or use fresh fruit if you prefer.*

**PREP TIME:** 8–10 hours
**COOK TIME:** 15 minutes

**INGREDIENTS | SERVES 8**

8 cups filtered water

2 cups steel-cut oats

¼ teaspoon salt

1 cup orange juice

½ cup dried cranberries

¼ cup golden raisins

Maple syrup or brown sugar, for garnish

1. In an 8-quart Dutch oven add water, oats, and salt. Bring mixture to a boil and cook 1 minute, then turn off heat and cover with the lid. Let stand overnight in the refrigerator.

2. In a microwave-safe bowl combine orange juice, dried cranberries, and raisins. Microwave 1 minute then cover and refrigerate overnight.

3. The next morning drain the dried fruit and discard liquid. Remove lid from oats and stir in soaked fruit. Place the Dutch oven over medium heat and bring oats to a boil. Turn off heat and add maple syrup or brown sugar. Enjoy warm or at room temperature.

# Quinoa Porridge

*This vegan breakfast porridge is hearty, warming, and filling. Feel free to add toasted nuts, fresh fruit, or jam as a topping.*

**PREP TIME:** 5 minutes
**COOK TIME:** 35 minutes

**INGREDIENTS | SERVES 8**

4 cups quinoa, rinsed and drained

4 cups water

2 cups full-fat coconut milk

½ cup packed light brown sugar

¼ teaspoon cardamom

¼ teaspoon cinnamon

¼ teaspoon salt

1. In a 6-quart Dutch oven add all the ingredients and bring to a simmer over medium heat.

2. Put lid on the pot and reduce heat to low. Cook 20 minutes and then remove lid and simmer until liquid is absorbed and quinoa is tender. Serve warm.

**CHAPTER 3**

# Breads and Rolls

# Flaky Dutch Oven Biscuits

*These biscuits are perfect as a side dish for soup, stew, or as an addition to the breakfast table. Brush these with a little honey butter when they come out of the oven for extra decadence!*

**PREP TIME:** 35 minutes
**COOK TIME:** 20 minutes

**INGREDIENTS | YIELDS 12**

2 cups all-purpose flour
1 tablespoon plus 1 teaspoon baking powder
2 teaspoons sugar
1 teaspoon salt
8 tablespoons unsalted butter, cubed and chilled
½ cup buttermilk

## Biscuit Scraps

If you have any scraps left from making buttermilk biscuits don't throw them away. You can refrigerate them for up to 3 days and use them for dumplings, wrap them around hot dogs for pigs in blankets, or cut them into small pieces and deep-fry them for quick doughnut holes!

1. Heat oven to 425°F and lightly spray a 14-inch Dutch oven with nonstick cooking spray.

2. In a large bowl whisk together flour, baking powder, sugar, and salt.

3. With your fingers rub butter into flour until mixture resembles coarse sand studded with pea-sized pieces of butter.

4. Add buttermilk to flour mixture and mix until the dough forms a shaggy ball. Turn dough out onto a lightly floured surface and press dough into a rough rectangle. Fold dough in half and press out again. Repeat this process 4 more times, then wrap dough in plastic and chill 20 minutes.

5. Once dough has chilled roll it out on a lightly floured surface until it is ½" thick. With a round biscuit cutter, cut 12 biscuits from dough and place in a single layer in the Dutch oven. If you do not get 12 biscuits from the first roll, re-roll the scraps. Do not roll them out a third time.

6. Bake biscuits 20–25 minutes, or until the biscuits are golden brown on top and cooked through. Serve warm.

# Quick Buttermilk Drop Biscuits

*These fluffy biscuits are super-quick to make—less than 10 minutes to get them into the oven—and are usually the first thing on the table to disappear!*

**PREP TIME:** 15 minutes
**COOK TIME:** 25 minutes

**INGREDIENTS | YIELDS 12**

2 cups all-purpose flour
1 tablespoon baking powder
½ teaspoon baking soda
1 teaspoon salt
1 teaspoon sugar
1½ sticks unsalted butter, divided
1 cup buttermilk

### Garlic and Cheese, Please!

Make these fluffy drop biscuits even more savory with Cheddar cheese and garlic. Just mix 1 cup of shredded sharp Cheddar cheese and ½ teaspoon of garlic powder into the dry ingredients and proceed as directed. The finished biscuits are reminiscent of a popular seafood chain, but better because you made them at home!

1. Heat oven to 375°F and lightly spray a 14-inch Dutch oven with nonstick cooking spray.

2. In a large bowl combine flour, baking powder, baking soda, salt, and sugar. Whisk to combine.

3. Cube 8 tablespoons (1 stick) of butter and add it to flour mixture. With your fingers rub butter into flour until mixture resembles coarse sand studded with pea-sized pieces of butter.

4. Add buttermilk to flour mixture and mix until the dough is just combined. This dough will be sticky.

5. Using a large disher or two spoons, scoop dough into 12 biscuits and place in one layer in the Dutch oven.

6. Bake biscuits 20–25 minutes, or until they are cooked through. Melt remaining butter and brush the tops of the biscuits, then turn on the broiler and broil 2–4 additional minutes, or until biscuits are golden brown. Serve warm.

# Ham and Cheese Biscuit Spirals

*These buttery biscuit spirals make a great lunch with a green salad, but can also be served on a brunch buffet or as an afternoon snack. If you like you can use roast beef, turkey, or chicken lunch meat here.*

**PREP TIME:** 1 hour 10 minutes
**COOK TIME:** 20 minutes
**INGREDIENTS | YIELDS 8**

1½ cups all-purpose flour

1 tablespoon baking powder

1 teaspoon sugar

1 teaspoon salt

6 tablespoons unsalted butter, cubed and chilled

⅓ cup buttermilk

1 tablespoon mayonnaise

2 teaspoons mustard

¼ teaspoon freshly cracked black pepper

½ cup shredded Gouda cheese

6 ounces thin-sliced ham lunch meat, patted dry and roughly chopped

1 large egg, beaten

1. In a large bowl whisk together flour, baking powder, sugar, and salt.

2. With your fingers rub butter into flour until mixture resembles coarse sand studded with pea-sized pieces of butter.

3. Add buttermilk to flour mixture and mix until the dough forms a shaggy ball. Turn dough out onto a lightly floured surface and press dough into a rough rectangle. Fold dough in half and press out again. Repeat this process 4 more times, then wrap dough in plastic and chill 20 minutes.

4. Once dough has chilled roll it out on a lightly floured surface until it is roughly a 12" × 14" rectangle. It should be roughly ¼" thick.

5. In a small bowl combine mayonnaise, mustard, and pepper. Brush this mixture on dough, then sprinkle cheese and ham evenly over top. Carefully begin rolling the long edge of the dough toward you, making sure not to roll the spiral too tightly. Wrap dough in plastic wrap and chill 30 minutes to make slicing easier.

6. Heat oven to 425°F and lightly spray a 14-inch Dutch oven with nonstick cooking spray.

7. Once chilled, remove the plastic and slice dough into 8 even pieces, using a serrated knife, and arrange in the prepared Dutch oven. Brush each spiral with beaten egg and bake 20–22 minutes, or until golden brown all over and cheese is bubbling. Serve warm.

# Quick Biscuit Cinnamon Rolls

*When you want cinnamon rolls but you don't want to wait for yeast dough to rise, give this recipe a try. The rolls are soft, buttery, and will satisfy your cravings in a hurry!*

**PREP TIME:** 20 minutes
**COOK TIME:** 25 minutes

**INGREDIENTS | SERVES 12**

½ cup plus 2 tablespoons packed light brown sugar, divided

2 cups all-purpose flour

1 teaspoon baking powder

½ teaspoon baking soda

¼ teaspoon salt

12 tablespoons (1½ sticks) unsalted butter, divided

½ cup sour cream, at room temperature

¼ cup whole milk, at room temperature

1 teaspoon cinnamon

1 ounce cream cheese, at room temperature

½ teaspoon vanilla

1 cup powdered sugar

1. Heat oven to 350°F and lightly spray a 2- or 4-quart Dutch oven with nonstick cooking spray.

2. In a medium bowl add 2 tablespoons brown sugar, flour, baking powder, baking soda, and salt. Whisk to combine. Dice 2 tablespoons of butter into small cubes and rub it into flour mixture until it looks like coarse sand.

3. Melt 4 tablespoons butter and combine it with sour cream and milk in a small bowl. Pour milk mixture into flour and stir until just combined. Set aside while you prepare filling.

4. In a small bowl combine ½ cup brown sugar, cinnamon, and 4 tablespoons butter until it forms a smooth paste. Set aside.

5. Turn out dough on a lightly floured work surface. Press it into a rough square that is ¼" thick. Spread filling evenly over dough. Carefully roll dough along the long edge into a log, then slice the log into 1" rolls.

6. Place rolls into the prepared Dutch oven leaving a little room between rolls for them to expand while baking. Bake 20–25 minutes, or until rolls are golden brown, puffed, and spring back when gently pressed in the center. Allow rolls to cool 5 minutes before frosting.

7. For the frosting, whisk together remaining butter, cream cheese, and vanilla until smooth. Slowly add in powdered sugar until frosting is your preferred thickness. Frost rolls while still warm. Serve warm or at room temperature.

# Blueberry Maple Scones

*These drop scones make a wonderful breakfast or an energizing snack
in the afternoon with a cup of coffee or strong tea.*

**PREP TIME:** 20 minutes
**COOK TIME:** 25 minutes

**INGREDIENTS | YIELDS 12**

2½ cups all-purpose flour

¾ teaspoon baking soda

¾ teaspoon baking powder

½ teaspoon salt

¼ cup sugar

½ cup unsalted butter, cubed and chilled

⅓ cup maple syrup

⅔ cup buttermilk

1 teaspoon vanilla

1 cup fresh blueberries

1 large egg, beaten

¼ cup light brown sugar

## What about Frozen Blueberries?

Fresh blueberries are best when they are in season, as off-season blueberries can be disappointing, sour, and mushy. Frozen berries are a good option when the blueberries in your local market are not at their peak. Frozen blueberries are picked and frozen at the peak of the season, giving them a better, sweeter flavor. If you are using frozen blueberries in scones, quick breads, and other baked goods it is best to thaw them first and drain off the liquid. This will prevent the berries from making your baked goods soggy. Save the liquid for making glazes and smoothies.

1. Heat oven to 350°F and lightly spray a 10-inch Dutch oven with nonstick cooking spray.

2. In a medium bowl combine flour, baking soda, baking powder, salt, and sugar. Whisk until well combined. Add cubed butter and, with your fingers, rub butter into flour mixture until it resembles coarse sand studded with pea-sized pieces of butter. Set aside.

3. In a small bowl whisk together maple syrup, buttermilk, and vanilla until well combined. Pour mixture into dry ingredients and stir until just moistened, about 6 strokes.

4. Add blueberries and stir to distribute, about 4–5 strokes. Do not overmix.

5. Scoop 12 mounds of dough into the prepared Dutch oven using a large disher or two spoons. Brush biscuits with beaten egg then sprinkle brown sugar over the top.

6. Bake 15–18 minutes, or until scones are golden brown and spring back when gently pressed in the center. Cool 10 minutes before serving.

# Golden Brown Dinner Rolls

*These rolls slathered with butter are the perfect addition to a hearty meal, but they also make excellent slider buns. Split, toast, and fill these rolls with Italian Beef for Sandwiches (Chapter 8), leftover roast, or thick slices of ham.*

**PREP TIME:** 1 hour 45 minutes
**COOK TIME:** 35 minutes

**INGREDIENTS | YIELDS 12**

2 teaspoons active dry yeast
1 tablespoon sugar
¼ cup water, heated to 110°F
½ cup whole milk
½ cup heavy cream
1 large egg
2 tablespoons unsalted butter, melted
2 cups all-purpose flour, plus more as needed
2 cups bread flour
½ teaspoon salt

## Active Dry versus Instant Yeast

Have you ever wondered what the difference between active dry and instant yeast is? Well, for the most part they are interchangeable. Active dry yeast is sold in jars or packets, and requires a little sugar and warm water to activate. Instant yeast can be added directly to the dry mix without activating, and it works more quickly in most recipes. If a recipe says to "let the dough double in bulk, about 1 hour," that time will likely be 20–30 minutes when using instant. When making slow-rising dough, or dough that needs to sit overnight in the refrigerator to develop additional flavor, use active dry yeast as it works more slowly.

1. In a small bowl combine yeast, sugar, and water. Let stand until yeast is foamy, about 10 minutes.

2. Add yeast mixture to the work bowl of a stand mixer along with remaining ingredients. Mix dough on low speed 3 minutes then test the hydration of the dough. The mixture should be sticky, but dough should not cling to your fingers. Add additional all-purpose flour or water, 1 tablespoon at a time, until dough reaches the correct consistency.

3. Increase the mixer to medium speed for 8 minutes. Turn dough out onto a lightly floured work surface and form a smooth ball. Transfer dough to a lightly oiled bowl, cover with a damp towel, and let dough double in bulk, about 1 hour.

4. Heat oven to 350°F and spray a 12-inch Dutch oven with nonstick cooking spray.

5. Once dough has risen, turn it out onto a lightly floured work surface and press out the gas with the heel of your hand. Divide dough into 12 pieces and shape each into a ball. Arrange dough balls in the Dutch oven and cover with lid. Let dough stand 30 minutes, or until dough balls are risen and do not spring back when you press a finger lightly into the side.

6. Uncover rolls and bake 20–25 minutes, or until rolls are golden brown on top and sound hollow when gently tapped. Let rolls cool 15 minutes before serving.

# Honey Wheat Rolls

*Honey gives these rolls a slightly sweet flavor that pairs well with savory dishes. For added texture you can add a tablespoon of wheat germ or wholemeal flour to these rolls.*

**PREP TIME:** 1 hour 40 minutes
**COOK TIME:** 35 minutes

**INGREDIENTS | YIELDS 12**

2½ teaspoons active dry yeast
¼ cup honey, divided
½ cup water, heated to 110°F
1 cup whole milk
4 tablespoons unsalted butter, melted
1 large egg
½ teaspoon salt
3 cups bread flour
1 cup whole-wheat flour, plus more as needed

1. In a small bowl combine the yeast, 1 tablespoon honey, and water. Let stand until the yeast is foamy, about 10 minutes.

2. Add yeast mixture to the work bowl of a stand mixer along with remaining ingredients. Mix dough on low speed 3 minutes then test the hydration of dough. The mixture should be sticky, but dough should not cling to your fingers. Add additional whole-wheat flour or water, 1 tablespoon at a time, until dough reaches correct consistency.

3. Increase the mixer to medium speed for 8 minutes. Turn dough out onto a lightly floured work surface and form a smooth ball. Transfer dough to a lightly oiled bowl, cover with a damp towel, and let dough double in bulk, about 1 hour.

4. Heat oven to 350°F and spray a 12-inch Dutch oven with nonstick cooking spray.

5. Once dough has risen, turn it out onto a lightly floured work surface and press out the gas with the heel of your hand. Divide dough into 12 pieces and shape each into a ball. Arrange dough balls in the Dutch oven and cover with lid. Let dough stand 30 minutes, or until dough balls are risen and do not spring back when you press a finger lightly into the side.

6. Uncover rolls and bake 20–25 minutes, or until rolls are golden brown on top and sound hollow when gently tapped. Let rolls cool 15 minutes before serving.

# Pecan Sticky Rolls

*Pecan lovers are going to love these gooey, sticky, buttery rolls. These are best when they are fresh from the oven, but leftover rolls can be reheated in a 350°F oven for 5–10 minutes.*

**PREP TIME:** 2 hours
**COOK TIME:** 50 minutes

**INGREDIENTS | YIELDS 12**

2 teaspoons active dry yeast
¼ cup sugar
¼ cup water, heated to 110°F
1 cup whole milk
1 large egg
1 cup (2 sticks) unsalted butter, melted, divided
4 cups all-purpose flour, plus more as needed
1 teaspoon salt, divided
1 cup packed light brown sugar, divided
¼ cup honey
1 cup chopped pecans, divided
1 teaspoon cinnamon
½ teaspoon vanilla

1. In a small bowl combine active dry yeast, sugar, and water. Let stand until yeast is foamy, about 10 minutes.

2. Add yeast mixture to the work bowl of a stand mixer along with milk, egg, 4 tablespoons butter, flour, and ¾ teaspoon salt. Mix on low speed 3 minutes then test the dough. It should be sticky, but should not cling to your fingers. Add additional flour or water, 1 tablespoon at a time, until it reaches the correct consistency.

3. Increase to medium speed for 8 minutes. Turn dough out onto a lightly floured surface and form a smooth ball. Transfer to a lightly oiled bowl, cover with a damp towel, and let dough double in bulk, about 1 hour. Spray a 12-inch Dutch oven with nonstick cooking spray.

4. In a medium bowl combine 8 tablespoons butter, ½ cup brown sugar, ¼ teaspoon salt, and honey and mix. Spread into the bottom of the Dutch oven, then sprinkle ½ cup pecans over it. Set aside.

5. Combine remaining butter, brown sugar, pecans, cinnamon, and vanilla in a small bowl. Stir.

6. Once dough has risen, turn it out onto a floured surface and with the heel of your hand form an 18" × 15" rectangle. Spread filling evenly over dough, then roll dough along the long edge into a log. Pinch the seam to seal, and carefully slice log into 12 rolls.

7. Arrange rolls in the Dutch oven and cover with lid. Let stand 30–60 minutes.

8. Heat oven to 350°F. Uncover rolls and bake 35–45 minutes, or until golden brown on top. Let rolls cool 15 minutes before serving. Enjoy warm.

# Overnight Cinnamon Rolls

*These cinnamon rolls are great for overnight guests, brunch with friends, or a big holiday breakfast. Be sure not to substitute instant yeast in this recipe since the rolls will be held overnight in the refrigerator.*

**PREP TIME:** 8–12 hours
**COOK TIME:** 45 minutes

**INGREDIENTS | YIELDS 12**

2 teaspoons active dry yeast
¼ cup sugar
¼ cup water, heated to 110°F
1 cup half and half
1 large egg
12 tablespoons (1½ sticks) unsalted butter, melted, divided
4 cups all-purpose flour, plus more as needed
½ teaspoon salt
½ cup packed light brown sugar
2 tablespoons corn syrup
1 teaspoon cinnamon
1 teaspoon vanilla, divided
1 cup powdered sugar

1. In a small bowl combine active dry yeast, sugar, and water. Let stand until yeast is foamy, about 10 minutes.

2. Add yeast mixture to the work bowl of a stand mixer along with half and half, egg, 4 tablespoons butter, flour, and salt. Mix on low speed 3 minutes then test the dough. It should be sticky, but should not cling to your fingers. Add additional flour or water, 1 tablespoon at a time, until it reaches the correct consistency.

3. Increase to medium speed for 8 minutes. Turn dough out onto a lightly floured surface and form a smooth ball. Transfer to a lightly oiled bowl, cover with a damp towel, and let double in bulk, about 1 hour.

4. Prepare filling by combining 4 tablespoons butter, brown sugar, corn syrup, cinnamon, and ½ teaspoon vanilla in a small bowl. Stir and set aside.

5. Spray a 12-inch Dutch oven with nonstick cooking spray. Turn dough out onto a floured surface and using the heel of your hand form an 18" × 15" rectangle.

6. Spread filling over dough, then roll dough into a log. Pinch the seam to seal, and then carefully slice log into 12 rolls. Arrange rolls in the Dutch oven, cover with lid, and place in refrigerator overnight.

7. The following morning heat oven to 350°F. Prepare frosting by combining remaining butter, vanilla, and powdered sugar in a separate small bowl until smooth. Cover with plastic and set aside.

8. Remove rolls from refrigerator and let stand at room temperature 1 hour. Bake rolls 35–45 minutes, or until golden brown on top. Let rolls cool 10 minutes then spread frosting over tops of rolls.

# Crusty No-Knead Bread

*This recipe produces a crusty loaf of bread that will look and taste like you bought it at an artisan bakery. No one needs to know how easy it was to make!*

**PREP TIME:** 20 hours
**COOK TIME:** 35 minutes

**INGREDIENTS | YIELDS 1 LOAF**

3 cups all-purpose flour
1¾ teaspoons salt
½ teaspoon yeast
1½ cups water

## No-Knead Method

Most bread recipes call for a good, hearty kneading either with a stand mixer or by hand to help form gluten, the proteins that give bread its structure. With no-knead breads the ingredients are gently mixed into a very wet dough that is left to stand for 12–24 hours, then formed into a ball and baked. The combination of the wet dough and the long rise produce the gluten in this bread, and when the loaf is baked in a Dutch oven you will get a crisp crust and a chewy crumb.

1. In a large bowl whisk together flour, salt, and yeast. Add water and mix until a shaggy ball forms. Cover the bowl with plastic wrap and set aside 18 hours at room temperature (around 70°F).

2. Carefully transfer dough onto a heavily floured sheet of baking parchment, making sure not to de-gas dough too much, and gently shape into a ball. Cover loosely with plastic wrap sprayed lightly with nonstick cooking spray and let dough rise at room temperature 2 hours. The dough is ready when a finger poked into the side of the ball leaves a dimple in the dough.

3. Place a 6- or 8-quart Dutch oven in a cold oven, then set the oven to 450°F.

4. Once oven has reached 450°F, carefully remove the hot Dutch oven. Peel the plastic wrap from dough, slide your hand under dough ball, and drop it into the Dutch oven. It may look messy and slightly deflated, but that is okay. Cover the Dutch oven with the lid and return to oven 25 minutes.

5. After 25 minutes remove lid and bake an additional 10–15 minutes, or until bread is golden brown and sounds hollow when tapped. Remove bread from the Dutch oven to a rack to cool.

# Sweet Cornbread

*This moist and tender cornbread has a mildly sweet flavor that goes perfectly with a piping hot bowl of stew or some spicy Texas Red Chili (Chapter 5).*

**PREP TIME:** 10 minutes
**COOK TIME:** 35 minutes

**INGREDIENTS | SERVES 10**

1 cup yellow cornmeal
1 cup all-purpose flour
2 tablespoons sugar
1 tablespoon baking powder
1 tablespoon nonfat dry milk
½ teaspoon salt
¾ cup buttermilk
1 large egg
1 tablespoon honey
5 tablespoons unsalted butter, melted, divided

1. Heat oven to 350°F and place a 10-inch Dutch oven in to heat.

2. In a large bowl combine cornmeal, flour, sugar, baking powder, nonfat milk, and salt.

3. In a medium bowl add buttermilk, egg, honey, and 4 tablespoons melted butter and whisk until completely combined. Pour wet ingredients into dry ingredients and mix until just combined and no large lumps of dry ingredients remain, about 10–12 strokes.

4. Carefully remove the Dutch oven from oven and brush remaining butter inside the pot. Pour in cornbread mixture and return to oven 25–30 minutes, or until cornbread is golden brown and a toothpick inserted into the center comes out clean. Cool 10 minutes before serving.

# Ham and Cheese Cornbread

*The American cheese will satisfy younger tastes. Adults might prefer it made with Swiss or Cheddar cheese. You can use either chopped cooked ham or thinly sliced boiled ham.*

**PREP TIME:** 10 minutes
**COOK TIME:** 25 minutes

**INGREDIENTS | SERVES 4–8**

2 tablespoons unsalted butter or bacon grease

1 large yellow onion, peeled and thinly sliced

1 clove garlic, peeled and minced

¼ teaspoon chili powder

½ cup unsalted peanuts, chopped

½ teaspoon freshly cracked black pepper

1 (10-ounce) package cornbread mix

1 large egg, beaten

½ cup milk

½ pound cooked ham

3 slices American cheese

Pimiento-stuffed olives, optional, for garnish

1. Heat oven to 350°F.

2. Melt butter or bacon grease in a 12-inch Dutch oven over medium heat. Add onion, garlic, and chili powder, and sauté until onion slices are transparent, about 5 minutes. Remove from heat and stir in peanuts and pepper. Stir to mix well.

3. Once the Dutch oven has cooled, add cornbread mix, egg, and milk; combine with onion and peanut mixture. Spread evenly over the bottom of the Dutch oven and top with ham.

4. Bake 15 minutes, or until cornbread is still moist but a toothpick comes out clean. Top with cheese and return to oven; bake an additional 5 minutes, or until cheese is melted. Garnish with olive slices if desired.

# Jalapeño Cheddar Hushpuppies

*Legend has it that hushpuppies were invented by fishermen as a means to hush a hungry puppy during a fish fry. A staple of the South, these hushpuppies will also hush a table full of hungry humans!*

**PREP TIME:** 15 minutes
**COOK TIME:** 25 minutes

**INGREDIENTS | SERVES 8–12**

1 teaspoon vegetable oil

½ medium onion, peeled and finely chopped

1 medium jalapeño, seeded and minced

1 clove garlic, peeled and minced

Vegetable or peanut oil, for frying

1 cup all-purpose flour

¾ cup yellow cornmeal

2 tablespoons sugar

½ teaspoon salt

½ teaspoon baking powder

½ cup buttermilk

8 tablespoons (1 stick) unsalted butter, melted and cooled

1 large egg

½ cup shredded sharp Cheddar cheese

## Hushpuppy Additions

Hushpuppies don't have to be relegated to side dish status. With a few creative additions the humble hushpuppy can be the star of a cocktail party, part of an appetizer buffet, or a welcome addition to brunch. Some fancy hushpuppy additions include cooked, finely chopped shrimp, lump crabmeat, diced ham, crumbled breakfast sausage, or crispy smoked bacon. Just ⅓ to ½ cup of any of these, or any addition you like, will elevate your hushpuppies to the next level!

1. In a small skillet heat 1 teaspoon oil over medium heat. Add onion, jalapeño, and garlic and cook, stirring often, until vegetables begin to soften, about 3 minutes. Remove pan from heat and let vegetables cool.

2. Heat 3" oil in a deep Dutch oven, making sure to have a 3" air gap at the top of the pot, to 350°F.

3. In a medium bowl combine flour, cornmeal, sugar, salt, and baking powder. Whisk until dry ingredients are thoroughly mixed.

4. In a separate bowl add buttermilk, butter, and egg and whisk to combine.

5. Add liquid ingredients to dry ingredients and stir until dry ingredients are just moistened, about 8 strokes. Add cooked vegetables and cheese and fold to combine, about 5–8 strokes. Do not overmix. A few lumps are fine.

6. Scoop mixture by the rounded tablespoonful into hot oil. Cook, turning occasionally, until hushpuppies are golden brown all over, about 4 minutes. Drain cooked hushpuppies on a wire rack over a sheet pan. Serve warm.

# Monkey Bread

*This bread is popular with kids, and it is a good way to get them involved in the kitchen. Little ones will enjoy dipping the biscuits in butter and sugar, and you will enjoy how easy this bread is to make!*

**PREP TIME:** 10 minutes
**COOK TIME:** 50 minutes

**INGREDIENTS | SERVES 12**

1 cup sugar

1 teaspoon cinnamon

¼ teaspoon allspice

8 tablespoons (1 stick) salted butter, melted and cooled

½ teaspoon vanilla

4 (7.5-ounce) cans flaky biscuits

1. Heat oven to 350°F and spray a 4-quart Dutch oven with nonstick cooking spray.

2. Mix sugar, cinnamon, and allspice in a large bowl. Set aside.

3. In a medium bowl add butter and vanilla and mix to combine.

4. Remove biscuits from can and cut each biscuit into 4 pieces.

5. Dunk each biscuit piece into butter mixture, then roll in cinnamon mixture. Place biscuit pieces in the prepared Dutch oven. Pour any remaining butter over biscuits, then bake 40–45 minutes, or until golden brown and puffed. Cool 10 minutes before serving. If you prefer, you can turn Monkey Bread out onto a serving plate. Enjoy warm.

# Cheesy Bacon Pull-Apart Bread

*Planning a party for the big game? Looking for a fun treat for a tailgate party, birthday party, or simply want a decadent afternoon snack? This pull-apart bread will keep you, and your guests, coming back for more!*

**PREP TIME:** 15 minutes
**COOK TIME:** 50 minutes

**INGREDIENTS | SERVES 12–14**

½ pound thick-cut smoked bacon, cooked crisp and crumbled

1 cup shredded sharp Cheddar cheese

½ cup shredded pepper jack cheese

1 recipe Golden Brown Dinner Rolls dough (see recipe in this chapter)

8 tablespoons (1 stick) salted butter, melted and cooled

1. Heat oven to 350°F and lightly spray a 12-inch Dutch oven with nonstick cooking spray.

2. In a medium bowl combine bacon with shredded cheeses. Toss to evenly combine.

3. Divide dinner roll dough into 24 balls. Dip each ball in melted butter, then roll each in shredded cheese and bacon mixture. Place coated dough balls in the Dutch oven. Pour any remaining butter over dough, and top with any remaining cheese and bacon mixture.

4. Bake 35–45 minutes, or until bread is golden brown and sounds hollow when tapped. Cool 15 minutes before serving.

# Biscuit Topping for Savory Stews

*Use this topping as an alternative topping for pastry crusts on pot pies or as an addition to hearty stew recipes.*

**PREP TIME:** 15 minutes
**COOK TIME:** 20 minutes

**INGREDIENTS | YIELDS 12–24**

1½ cups all-purpose flour

2 teaspoons baking powder

¼ teaspoon baking soda

½ teaspoon salt

½ teaspoon sugar

8 tablespoons (1 stick) unsalted butter, cubed and chilled

¾ cup buttermilk

1. In a large bowl combine flour, baking powder, baking soda, salt, and sugar. Whisk to combine.

2. Add butter to flour mixture, and with your fingers rub butter into flour until mixture resembles coarse sand studded with pea-sized pieces of butter.

3. Add buttermilk to flour mixture and mix until dough is just combined. This dough will be sticky.

4. Using a large disher or two spoons, scoop dough into 12–24 biscuits on top of stew or pot pie filling 20 minutes before it has finished baking. Cook until biscuits are golden brown on top.

# All-Butter Pastry Crust for Pot Pies

*All-butter crusts have a lovely melt-in-the-mouth feel and bake up golden brown on top of a pot pie or stew.*

**PREP TIME:** 50 minutes
**COOK TIME:** 0 minutes

**INGREDIENTS | YIELDS 1 CRUST**

1¼ cups all-purpose flour
1 teaspoon sugar
½ teaspoon salt
8 tablespoons (1 stick) unsalted butter, cubed and chilled
3–4 tablespoons ice water

## Vegan Pastry Crust

When making a vegan pastry crust you can use either vegetable shortening or a vegan butter that is suitable for baking in place of dairy butter. Avoid vegan butters that have a high water content as they will lead to a mushy crust that is difficult to work with. If you like you can mix half vegetable shortening and half vegan butter for a crust that is easy to work with and also has a buttery flavor.

1. In a large bowl sift together flour, sugar, and salt.

2. Add butter and, using your fingers, rub it into flour until mixture looks like coarse sand studded with pea-sized pieces of butter.

3. Add 2 tablespoons water and mix until dough forms a rough ball. Add more water, 1 tablespoon at a time, if needed.

4. Turn dough out onto a lightly floured surface and form a disk. Wrap in plastic and chill at least 30 minutes or up to 3 days.

5. Remove dough from the refrigerator 10 minutes before rolling out. Roll out on a lightly floured surface to ⅛" thick, about a 12" circle, turning dough often to make sure it does not stick. Dust surface with additional flour if needed. Cover with plastic wrap and chill until ready to bake. If your Dutch oven is larger than 12 inches you can roll crust a little thinner to accommodate up to a 14-inch Dutch oven. If it is smaller just use a knife to cut away the excess crust.

# Dutch Oven Pizza Crust

*The Dutch oven is perfect for making deep dish pizzas. The steady, even heat means the crust will be browned and crusty on the bottom while the toppings stay gooey and cheesy! This crust works best in a 12-inch Dutch oven.*

**PREP TIME:** 1 hour 15 minutes
**COOK TIME:** 18–25 minutes

**INGREDIENTS | YIELDS 1 (12") CRUST**

1 cup all-purpose flour

2 tablespoons semolina flour

¼ teaspoon baking powder

½ teaspoon salt

½ teaspoon dry active yeast

½ cup beer, lager or bock preferred, heated to 100°F

1 teaspoon olive oil

## Pizza Spices

Want to elevate a jarred sauce, or maybe gussy up a frozen pizza? Look no further than this herb blend! You can add this to jarred sauce, sprinkle it on frozen pizza, or even use it to season pasta dishes. Mix 1 teaspoon dry oregano, 1 teaspoon ground fennel, ½ teaspoon dry thyme, and ¼ teaspoon crushed red pepper flakes. Use as little or as much as you like. Adding this simple seasoning in any amount will up your pizza game!

1. In the work bowl of a stand mixer with the hook attachment, combine flour, semolina flour, baking powder, and salt.

2. In a small bowl combine yeast and beer. Once yeast is bubbling and foamy, about 10 minutes, add it to dry mixture along with olive oil.

3. Mix on low speed 3 minutes. The dough should be fairly sticky but form a smooth ball. If dough seems dry add water 1 tablespoon at a time until no dry flour remains. Increase speed to medium and mix 5 minutes.

4. Turn dough out on a lightly floured surface and form it into a smooth ball. Place in a greased bowl, turn once to coat, and cover with plastic wrap. If you are using right away allow dough to double in bulk, about 1 hour. If using the next day refrigerate overnight, then allow to come to room temperature.

5. Roll out the dough into a 14" circle and line the inside of a 12-inch Dutch oven, making sure the crust comes at least 1" up the sides of the pot. Fill the crust with your desired toppings and bake for 18–25 minutes, or until the toppings are bubbling and the crust is golden brown.

# CHAPTER 4

# Appetizers and Dips

# Spinach Artichoke Dip

*This dip is rich and creamy, and perfect as an appetizer or as a take-along dish for a potluck party. Serve with grilled or toasted bread brushed with a little olive oil or butter, or warm tortilla chips.*

**PREP TIME:** 20 minutes
**COOK TIME:** 40 minutes

**INGREDIENTS | SERVES 8–12**

1 (10-ounce) package chopped frozen spinach, thawed and drained well

1 (12-ounce) bag frozen artichoke hearts, thawed and chopped

1 (8-ounce) block cream cheese, at room temperature

½ cup mayonnaise

¼ cup sour cream

½ cup shredded Parmesan cheese

½ cup shredded jack cheese

¼ teaspoon garlic powder

¼ teaspoon crushed red pepper flakes

½ cup panko bread crumbs

1 tablespoon unsalted butter, melted and cooled

1. Heat oven to 375°F and spray a 2-quart Dutch oven with nonstick cooking spray.

2. In a large bowl combine spinach, artichoke hearts, cream cheese, mayonnaise, sour cream, Parmesan cheese, jack cheese, garlic powder, and red pepper flakes until well mixed. Spread mixture into the prepared Dutch oven.

3. In a small bowl combine bread crumbs and butter and toss until evenly coated.

4. Spread bread crumbs on top of cream cheese mixture and bake 30 minutes, or until bread crumbs are golden brown and dip is bubbling. Cool 10 minutes before serving.

## Frozen versus Canned Artichoke Hearts

When it comes to artichoke hearts, does it matter if you get canned or frozen? Well, it depends on what you are making. Frozen artichoke hearts tend to have a more natural flavor, and look more like steamed fresh artichokes, where canned or jarred artichoke hearts have a tangy, brined flavor. For dips, gratins, and soups it is best to use frozen. For salads and antipasto platters go with canned or jarred.

# Creamy Baked Seafood Dip

*Seafood lovers will flip for this dip, which is packed with lump crab and shrimp. Feeling extra fancy? Substitute cooked lobster for some of the crab or shrimp!*

**PREP TIME:** 20 minutes
**COOK TIME:** 45 minutes

**INGREDIENTS | SERVES 8–12**

1 tablespoon unsalted butter

1 medium red bell pepper, seeded and chopped

1 medium onion, peeled and chopped

1 clove garlic, peeled and minced

1 teaspoon seafood seasoning such as Old Bay

1 (8-ounce) block cream cheese, at room temperature

1 cup mayonnaise

½ cup shredded Parmesan cheese

½ cup shredded jack cheese

8 ounces fresh lump crabmeat, drained

½ pound peeled cooked shrimp, chopped

½ cup panko bread crumbs

1 tablespoon butter, melted and cooled

1. Heat oven to 375°F and spray a 2-quart Dutch oven with nonstick cooking spray.

2. In a medium skillet melt butter over medium heat. Once butter starts to foam add bell pepper and onion. Cook, stirring constantly, until vegetables soften, about 3 minutes. Add garlic and seafood seasoning and cook until garlic is fragrant, about 30 seconds. Remove pan from the heat and set aside.

3. In a large bowl combine cream cheese, mayonnaise, Parmesan cheese, and jack cheese until well mixed. Add in cooked vegetables, crab, and shrimp and mix well. Spread mixture into prepared Dutch oven.

4. In a small bowl combine bread crumbs and melted butter and toss until evenly coated.

5. Spread bread crumbs on top of cream cheese mixture and bake 30 minutes, or until bread crumbs are golden brown and dip is bubbling. Cool 10 minutes before serving.

# Onion and Garlic Jam

*This "jam" is naturally sweet because the sugars in the onions caramelize during the long cooking time.*

**PREP TIME:** 10 minutes
**COOK TIME:** 35 minutes

**INGREDIENTS | SERVES 12**

2 tablespoons olive oil
1 tablespoon unsalted butter
4 cups chopped onions
4 cloves garlic, peeled and minced
1 teaspoon salt
¼ cup brown sugar
3 tablespoons tarragon vinegar
2 teaspoons chopped fresh tarragon leaves

1. In 4- or 6-quart Dutch oven add olive oil and butter over medium heat. Once butter is melted add onions, garlic, and salt. Cook mixture, stirring, until the onions are translucent. Reduce heat to low and cook, stirring occasionally, until onions are deep golden brown, about 20–25 minutes.

2. Add sugar, vinegar, and tarragon leaves, and cook, stirring often, 10 minutes.

3. Transfer mixture to a resalable container and store in refrigerator up to 4 days.

# Sausage and Cheese Dip

*This dip isn't fancy, but it is sure to be a crowd pleaser! Feel free to substitute chorizo, taco meat, or vegetarian crumbles for the sausage if you prefer.*

**PREP TIME:** 10 minutes
**COOK TIME:** 20 minutes

**INGREDIENTS | SERVES 12**

1 pound hot breakfast sausage
1 medium onion, peeled and chopped
1 (10-ounce) can diced tomatoes and green chilies, undrained
1 pound processed American cheese (such as Velveeta), cut into ½" cubes

1. Heat a 4-quart Dutch oven over medium heat. Add breakfast sausage and cook, breaking sausage into crumbles, until cooked through, about 8–10 minutes.

2. Add onion and cook until tender, about 5 minutes. Remove from heat and carefully drain off most of the fat.

3. Return the Dutch oven to heat and add diced tomatoes and green chilies with the juice and cubed cheese. Reduce heat to medium-low and cover the Dutch oven. Cook, stirring frequently, until cheese is melted. Serve immediately.

# Chili con Queso

*This cheese dip is a staple at Tex-Mex restaurants, but can also be found on the menu for football-watching parties, potluck parties, and holiday gatherings. You can reheat this dip on the stove over low heat if it starts to get cold.*

**PREP TIME:** 10 minutes
**COOK TIME:** 20 minutes

**INGREDIENTS | SERVES 8–12**

3 tablespoons unsalted butter

1 medium onion, peeled and chopped

1 jalapeño, seeded and minced

2 serrano peppers, seeded and minced

2 cloves garlic, peeled and minced

½ teaspoon cumin

¼ cup all-purpose flour

2 cups half and half

8 ounces shredded medium Cheddar cheese

4 ounces diced American cheese

1. In a 4-quart Dutch oven heat butter over medium heat until it foams. Add onion, jalapeño, and serrano peppers and cook until vegetables are tender, about 3 minutes. Add garlic and cumin and cook until fragrant, about 30 seconds.

2. Add flour and cook until it has absorbed butter and is starting to turn slightly golden brown, about 3 minutes. Slowly whisk in half and half, then reduce heat to medium-low and cook until it begins to simmer and thicken slightly, about 8–10 minutes.

3. Turn off heat and stir in cheeses in three batches, making sure the first addition is melted before adding the next. Serve immediately.

## Make It Meaty!

If you are looking to make this dip a little heartier to keep a hungry crowd happy you can add a variety of different meats to it: 1 cup of taco-seasoned ground beef, seasoned shredded chicken, cooked pork chorizo, or chopped Beer-Braised Beef Brisket (Chapter 8) or Braised Pork Shoulder (Chapter 10) are just a few ideas for meaty mix-ins that will make this dip more of a meal. Top your hearty dip with some fresh diced avocado, diced tomatoes, chopped cilantro, and hot sauce!

# Cheesy Corn Dip

*You can use fresh cut corn for this dip if it is in season, but frozen cut corn is easy and always available in the store. Don't use canned corn as it will be a little too mushy.*

**PREP TIME:** 15 minutes
**COOK TIME:** 45 minutes

**INGREDIENTS | SERVES 8–12**

1 (8-ounce) block cream cheese

1 cup mayonnaise

2 cups shredded Cheddar cheese, divided

1 cup shredded jack cheese

1 teaspoon Worcestershire sauce

½ teaspoon dry mustard

½ teaspoon onion powder

½ teaspoon dry dill

¼ teaspoon garlic powder

¼ teaspoon salt

1 (10-ounce) can diced tomatoes and green chilies, drained

1 tablespoon unsalted butter

1 medium onion, peeled and chopped

1 medium red bell pepper, seeded and chopped

1 (10-ounce) bag frozen corn, thawed

1. In a large bowl combine cream cheese, mayonnaise, 1 cup Cheddar cheese, jack cheese, Worcestershire sauce, dry mustard, onion powder, dill, garlic powder, and salt. Mix until everything is thoroughly combined. Fold in diced tomatoes and green chilies and set aside.

2. Heat oven to 350°F.

3. In a 4-quart Dutch oven over medium heat add butter. Once it foams add onion and bell pepper. Cook, stirring often, until they begin to soften, about 5 minutes. Add corn and toss to coat then remove the pot from heat and add vegetables to cream cheese mixture. Fold to combine.

4. Pour the mixture back into the Dutch oven and spread it evenly. Top with remaining Cheddar cheese and bake 30 minutes, or until dip is bubbling and cheese is golden brown on top. Cool 10 minutes before serving.

# Jalapeño Popper Dip

*This dip is addictive! It takes all the best things about jalapeño poppers and transforms them into a creamy, cheesy dip perfect for warm tortilla chips!*

**PREP TIME:** 15 minutes
**COOK TIME:** 45 minutes

**INGREDIENTS | SERVES 8**

3 tablespoons unsalted butter, divided
1 large onion, peeled and chopped
4 medium jalapeños, seeded and minced
2 cloves garlic, peeled and minced
12 strips of bacon, cooked crisp and crumbled
½ teaspoon cumin
2 (8-ounce) packages cream cheese, at room temperature
1 cup mayonnaise
2 cups shredded sharp Cheddar cheese
1 cup grated Parmesan cheese, divided
½ cup pickled jalapeños, chopped
1 cup panko bread crumbs
¼ teaspoon paprika

1. Heat oven to 350°F.

2. In a 4-quart Dutch oven over medium heat add 2 tablespoons butter. Once butter becomes foamy add onion, jalapeños, garlic, bacon, and cumin. Sauté until onions begin to soften, about 5 minutes. Remove the Dutch oven from heat to cool slightly.

3. In a medium bowl add cream cheese and mayonnaise and mix until smooth. Add sautéed onion mixture, Cheddar cheese, ½ cup of the Parmesan cheese, and chopped pickled jalapeños and mix so all the ingredients are evenly distributed.

4. Spread mixture into the Dutch oven.

5. Melt remaining tablespoon butter and mix it with panko bread crumbs until evenly coated. Toss paprika and remaining Parmesan cheese with bread crumbs and spread this mixture evenly over the dip. Bake 30 minutes, or until topping is golden brown and dip is bubbling around the edges. Cool 10 minutes before serving.

# Bacon-Wrapped Jalapeño Poppers

*These baked poppers are a nice change of pace from the traditional fried poppers. The poppers can be made up the day before and baked when you are ready to serve.*

**PREP TIME:** 10 minutes
**COOK TIME:** 30 minutes

**INGREDIENTS | SERVES 12**

6 strips thick-cut bacon, cut in half

4 ounces cream cheese, at room temperature

½ cup shredded sharp Cheddar cheese

½ teaspoon smoked paprika

¼ teaspoon garlic powder

¼ teaspoon onion powder

¼ teaspoon salt

¼ teaspoon freshly cracked black pepper

6 large jalapeños, cut in half lengthwise and seeded

## Par-Cooking Bacon

Par-cooking means to cook something partially. For any dish where bacon is used to wrap the finished product it is always a good idea to par-cook it. This will ensure that your bacon is completely cooked through, and it will also help render some of the fat and keep the bacon from being too fatty or rubbery. Your finished product will have a lovely blanket of perfectly cooked bacon.

1. Heat oven to 400°F and lightly spray a 14-inch Dutch oven with nonstick cooking spray.

2. Place bacon pieces on a microwave-safe plate covered by a double layer of paper towels. Cover with another sheet of paper towel and microwave bacon 1–1½ minutes, or until bacon fat has begun to render but bacon is still soft. Set aside to cool.

3. In a medium bowl combine cream cheese, Cheddar cheese, paprika, garlic powder, onion powder, salt, and pepper. Blend until mixture is thoroughly combined.

4. Spoon filling mixture into hollowed-out jalapeños. Wrap bacon around jalapeños and secure with a toothpick. Place jalapeños into bottom of the Dutch oven in a single layer and bake 20–25 minutes, or until bacon is crisp and filling is hot and bubbling. Cool 5 minutes before serving.

# Sweet and Spicy Cocktail Sausages

*This appetizer, with its combination of sweet and savory flavors, is always a hit with guests. The bonus is it is very simple to prepare. Win-win!*

**PREP TIME:** 5 minutes
**COOK TIME:** 30 minutes

**INGREDIENTS | SERVES 12**

2 (14-ounce) packages smoked cocktail sausages, drained and patted dry
1 cup Thai sweet chili sauce
¼ cup hot pepper jelly
2 tablespoons orange juice
2 tablespoons lime juice
1 tablespoon light soy sauce

1. Heat oven to 350°F.

2. Combine all ingredients in a 4-quart Dutch oven and stir well.

3. Cover with lid and bake 10 minutes, then remove lid and increase heat to 400°F and bake 20–25 minutes, or until sauce has become sticky and sausages are browned. Serve hot.

# Tipsy Meatballs

*Beer adds rich and smooth flavor to this updated appetizer recipe.*

**PREP TIME:** 10 minutes
**COOK TIME:** 1 hour

**INGREDIENTS | SERVES 8–10**

2 medium onions, peeled and chopped
1 (16-ounce) package frozen meatballs
1 (12-ounce) can beer
1 cup ketchup
½ cup chili sauce
2 tablespoons mustard
¼ cup pickle relish

1. Place onions in a 4- or 6-quart Dutch oven, then add meatballs.

2. In medium bowl, combine remaining ingredients and pour over meatballs.

3. Cover and cook over medium-low heat 1 hour, or until meatballs are hot and tender. Serve with toothpicks.

# Grape Jelly Meatballs

*Need these meatballs in a hurry? Feel free to substitute your favorite*
*frozen or ready-cooked meatballs in this recipe!*

**PREP TIME:** 1 hour 15 minutes
**COOK TIME:** 40 minutes

**INGREDIENTS | SERVES 8–12**

½ pound smoked bacon, cut into 1" pieces

1 pound ground beef

½ cup panko bread crumbs

½ medium onion, peeled and chopped

1 large egg

1 teaspoon salt

½ teaspoon ground fennel

½ teaspoon oregano

½ teaspoon smoked paprika

¼ teaspoon freshly cracked black pepper

4 tablespoons unsalted butter, divided

1 cup tomato-based chili sauce

1 cup grape jelly

1. In the work bowl of a food processor add bacon. Pulse until bacon is ground but not a paste, about 20–30 pulses.

2. In a large bowl add ground bacon, ground beef, bread crumbs, onion, egg, salt, fennel, oregano, paprika, and pepper. Gently mix until everything is evenly combined. A hand mixer with the dough hook attachment is ideal for this job.

3. Scoop meat mixture into 1½" meatballs and place on a parchment-lined baking sheet. Refrigerate, uncovered, 1 hour.

4. Heat a 6- or 8-quart Dutch oven over medium-high heat. Once hot add 1 tablespoon butter. Once it has melted and begins to foam add ¼ of the meatballs and brown well on all sides. Transfer to a paper towel–lined platter to drain. Repeat with remaining butter and meatballs.

5. Reduce heat to medium-low and add chili sauce and grape jelly to the Dutch oven. Once jelly has melted and sauce is combined add browned meatballs and gently toss to coat. Simmer, uncovered, 30 minutes, or until meatballs are cooked through and sauce is reduced and sticky. Serve warm.

# Stuffed Grape Leaves

*This dish is often used as an appetizer, but it's also good as a light supper. Serve it with Cucumber-Yogurt Salad (see sidebar).*

**PREP TIME:** 20 minutes
**COOK TIME:** 1 hour

**INGREDIENTS | SERVES 4–6**

1 pound lean ground lamb
1 cup uncooked long-grain rice
¼ teaspoon ground cinnamon
¼ teaspoon ground allspice
½ teaspoon salt
½ teaspoon freshly cracked black pepper
1 (1-pound) jar grape leaves
Water or chicken broth as needed
Juice of 2 medium lemons

## Cucumber-Yogurt Salad

To make this delicious salad: In a serving bowl, mix together 3 cups drained plain yogurt and 2–3 peeled, seeded, and thinly sliced cucumbers. Add 12 fresh chopped mint leaves, 2 minced garlic cloves, and ¼ teaspoon salt to a small bowl, and crush them together. Stir the mint mixture into the salad. Add more salt, if needed. Chill until ready to serve.

1. In a bowl, mix together lamb, rice, cinnamon, allspice, salt, and pepper.

2. Drain grape leaves. Use any small leaves to line the bottom of Dutch oven treated with nonstick spray. Lay each larger leaf on a flat surface, vein-side up; trim off any stem.

3. Spoon some of lamb mixture onto center of each grape leaf. To form each roll, fold the stem end over the filling, then fold the sides over each other, and fold down the tip. Carefully place each roll, seam-side down, in the Dutch oven. Place rolls close together to prevent them from unrolling while they cook. You may end up with several layers of rolls, depending on the size of the Dutch oven.

4. Place a plate over rolls and then add enough water or broth to cover the plate. Bring to a boil over medium-high heat, then reduce heat, cover, and simmer 30 minutes.

5. Add lemon juice; cover and continue to simmer for an additional 30 minutes. Stuffed grape leaves are done when they're tender when pierced with a fork. You can serve them warm, at room temperature, or cool.

# Korean Hot Wings

*Because of the small bones and ratio of skin to meat in chicken wings, they make great chicken stock. Store the wing tips in a gallon-sized sealable bag in your freezer and turn them into chicken stock.*

**PREP TIME:** 1 hour 15 minutes
**COOK TIME:** 25 minutes

**INGREDIENTS | SERVES 4**

3 tablespoons soy sauce

1 tablespoon water

1 teaspoon brown sugar

1 tablespoon white wine

Juice from 1 medium lemon

1 tablespoon chili paste

2 tablespoons honey

2 serrano peppers, seeded and thinly sliced

2 pounds chicken wings, split at joint, without tips

1 teaspoon salt

½ teaspoon ground pepper

2 tablespoons cornstarch

2 cups plus 1 tablespoon canola, corn, or peanut oil

2 cloves garlic, sliced

1 (2" piece) fresh ginger, peeled and matchsticked

1. Combine soy sauce, water, brown sugar, and white wine in a small bowl. Heat in the microwave until sugar is dissolved. Add lemon juice, chili paste, honey, and serrano slices and let rest at room temperature 1 hour or in the refrigerator 3 days.

2. Rinse chicken wings and pat dry. Place in a large bowl and sprinkle with salt, pepper, and cornstarch to coat. Let set 5 minutes. Place a wire rack over a baking sheet. Place 2 cups oil in a 6- or 8-quart Dutch oven over medium heat. The oil is hot when a sprinkle of cornstarch causes oil to bubble instantly.

3. Use tongs to slip 4 pieces of chicken into the Dutch oven. Cook on the first side 2 minutes and the second side 1 minute. Place the wings on wire rack to drain and repeat with remaining wings. Bring oil back to temperature between batches.

4. Add remaining 1 tablespoon oil to a skillet over medium-low heat. Add garlic and ginger and cook 30 seconds. Add sauce and stir continually, 30 seconds. Add chicken wings and stir 3 minutes until heated through and evenly coated. Serve warm.

# Salt and Pepper Shrimp

*Szechuan pepper is milder than black pepper, and produces a tingly numbing sensation when eaten. Spice shops and Asian markets often carry a Szechuan salt and pepper blend that is perfect for this recipe!*

**PREP TIME:** 10 minutes
**COOK TIME:** 15 minutes
**INGREDIENTS | SERVES 8**

Oil, for frying
1 pound large ($21/30$) tail-on shrimp
1 cup cornstarch
2 teaspoons Szechuan salt and pepper blend
1 jalapeño or serrano pepper, seeded and minced
1 tablespoon finely chopped cilantro

## Make It Yourself!

Can't find a Szechuan salt and pepper blend? No problem, make it yourself! Combine ¼ cup salt and 2 teaspoons Szechuan peppercorns in a dry wok or skillet. Cook over low heat until the peppercorns are fragrant and the salt has started to brown, about 10 minutes. Cool the mixture completely then grind in a spice grinder, food processor, or with a mortar and pestle. This mix can be used for seasoning Asian dishes or as a topping for fried foods.

1. In a deep Dutch oven add 2" oil, making sure there is at least a 3" air gap at the top of the pot. Heat the oil to 350°F.

2. Dredge shrimp in the cornstarch, tapping off any excess, and immediately place into hot oil. Fry 4–5 shrimp at a time. Cook until shrimp are golden brown, about 2 minutes. Transfer to a paper towel–lined plate to drain and immediately sprinkle with a good amount of Szechuan salt and pepper. Repeat with remaining shrimp.

3. Garnish with hot peppers and cilantro. Serve immediately.

# Fried Green Tomatoes

*If you have any leftover batter, try dredging some pickle slices in it and frying them. They'll cook in about 1½ minutes and are just as tasty as fried green tomatoes.*

**PREP TIME:** 15 minutes
**COOK TIME:** 15 minutes

**INGREDIENTS | SERVES 6–8**

1½ cups all-purpose flour
½ cup cornmeal
½ teaspoon salt, plus 1 pinch
¼ teaspoon ground black pepper
¼–½ cup milk
3–4 large green tomatoes
Oil, for frying
¾ cup ranch dressing

1. Mix together flour, cornmeal, ½ teaspoon salt, and pepper in a large bowl. Pour ¼ cup milk into bowl and stir to combine. If mixture looks dry, add more milk until you get a thick batter.

2. Slice tomatoes into ¼" slices. Pat dry with paper towels.

3. In a 6-or 8-quart deep Dutch oven add 1" of oil, making sure there is a 3" air gap at the top of the Dutch oven. Heat oil to 350°F over medium-high heat.

4. Working with 3–4 tomato slices at a time, dip each tomato slice into batter and let excess drip off. Slide slices into hot oil so they're not touching. Cook each side for 1½–2 minutes. Remove them and place on a rack set over paper towels to keep fried tomatoes from getting soggy. Repeat with the remaining tomato slices.

5. While they're still hot, sprinkle with a pinch of salt. Serve with ranch dressing as a dipping sauce.

# Fried Ravioli Appetizer

*This recipe works best with ravioli that are about 1½"–2" across. Larger ravioli won't cook through and smaller ravioli will break up while frying.*

**PREP TIME:** 10 minutes
**COOK TIME:** 15 minutes

**INGREDIENTS | SERVES 8–10**

1 large egg
½ cup panko bread crumbs
1 teaspoon dried oregano
1 teaspoon garlic powder
¼ teaspoon freshly ground black pepper
½ teaspoon salt
2 tablespoons shredded Parmesan cheese
1 package frozen ravioli, thawed
Oil, for frying
1 cup marinara sauce, warmed

1. Whisk egg in a small bowl. In a separate bowl combine panko, spices, and cheese.

2. Dip each ravioli in egg with one hand, then dip ravioli in panko mixture with the other hand. Place prepared ravioli onto a sheet pan while you heat the oil.

3. Place a 6- or 8-quart Dutch oven over medium heat and fill it with 2" of vegetable oil, making sure there is a 3" air gap at the top of the pot. Once oil reaches 350°F carefully drop 5–6 ravioli in oil and cook 2 minutes on each side, or until lightly golden. Repeat with the remaining ravioli.

4. Remove ravioli from the Dutch oven and drain on paper towels. Serve with a bowl of warmed marinara sauce for dipping.

# Rice and Cheese Balls

*This old-fashioned recipe is a great accompaniment to a grilled steak.*

**PREP TIME:** 5–9 hours
**COOK TIME:** 25 minutes

**INGREDIENTS | SERVES 8**

1 tablespoon olive oil
½ cup peeled, minced onion
1 tablespoon all-purpose flour
½ teaspoon salt
½ teaspoon dried thyme leaves
⅛ teaspoon cayenne pepper
½ cup buttermilk
1½ cups shredded Muenster cheese
2 cups cold cooked rice
1 large egg, beaten
¾ cup seasoned dry bread crumbs
Oil, for frying

1. In 6-quart Dutch oven heat olive oil over medium heat. Add onion and cook until tender, about 5 minutes. Add flour, salt, thyme, and cayenne; cook and stir until bubbly.

2. Add buttermilk and cook until thickened, about 3 minutes, then remove from heat and stir in shredded cheese. Add rice and mix well. Chill 4–8 hours.

3. Roll chilled rice mixture into 1½" balls. Dip into beaten egg and roll in bread crumbs to coat. Place balls on a parchment-lined baking sheet and chill 1 hour. Wash and thoroughly dry out the Dutch oven.

4. When ready to eat, add 2" oil to the Dutch oven with at least a 3" air gap at the top of the pot and heat to 350°F. Add balls, 5 at a time, and fry until golden brown. Drain on paper towels and serve. You can keep balls warm in a 250°F oven until all are fried.

**CHAPTER 5**

# Soup, Stew, and Chili

# Beer Cheese Soup

*This soup is rich and comforting, and makes a perfect meal on a chilly night. If you want you can add diced smoked sausage after the soup has been blended to make this soup heartier!*

**PREP TIME:** 10 minutes
**COOK TIME:** 45 minutes

**INGREDIENTS | SERVES 8**

4 tablespoons unsalted butter

1 stalk celery, finely chopped

1 medium carrot, peeled and finely chopped

1 small onion, peeled and finely chopped

1 teaspoon salt

⅓ cup all-purpose flour

2 cups low-sodium chicken broth

2 cups half and half

1 cup lager-style beer

8 ounces processed American cheese, cut into ½" cubes

8-ounce block sharp Cheddar cheese, shredded

½ teaspoon hot sauce

½ teaspoon freshly cracked black pepper

## Blending Hot Soups

The blender is the best way to make your soups velvety and smooth, but you need to take a few safety precautions. First, let your hot soup cool for 5–10 minutes before blending. Second, never fill your blender container more than half full. Finally, be sure to vent the lid. The reason for these steps is that hot soup expands in the blender and can explode out of it, which can be dangerous and very messy!

1. In a 6- or 8-quart Dutch oven over medium-high heat melt butter. Once it foams add celery, carrot, and onion. Season with salt and cook until vegetables are tender, about 8 minutes.

2. Sprinkle flour over vegetables and cook until flour is moistened and is just turning golden brown in color, about 5 minutes.

3. Reduce heat to low and slowly whisk in chicken broth, making sure to whisk out any lumps of flour. Whisk in half and half and gently stir in beer. Increase heat to medium and cook, stirring constantly, until soup just comes to a boil and thickens, about 12 minutes.

4. Reduce heat to low and add processed American cheese and stir until it has completely melted. Add Cheddar cheese in three batches, whisking well to make sure the first batch has completely melted before adding the next. Remove the Dutch oven from heat and allow the soup to cool 10 minutes.

5. Working in batches, purée soup in blender until smooth. Return soup to the Dutch oven and warm soup over medium-low heat until hot and steamy. Season with hot sauce and black pepper before serving.

# Portuguese Caldo Verde

*Kale provides the green in this soup. If kale isn't available, you can substitute collard greens but it will change the flavor somewhat.*

**PREP TIME:** 1 hour 10 minutes
**COOK TIME:** 1 hour 15 minutes
**INGREDIENTS | SERVES 6–8**

1 pound kale
1 tablespoon extra-virgin olive oil
1 large yellow onion, peeled and thinly sliced
½ pound linguiça or kielbasa, sliced
4 large russet potatoes, peeled and diced
4 cups chicken broth
2 (15-ounce) cans cannelloni beans, rinsed and drained
½ teaspoon salt
½ teaspoon freshly cracked black pepper

1. Trim the large ribs from kale. Slice into thin strips. Place kale strips into a bowl of cold water and soak 1 hour; drain well.

2. Add oil to a 6-quart Dutch oven over medium-high heat. Once the oil is hot and starts to shimmer, add the onions and sauté until tender, 8–10 minutes.

3. Add linguiça or kielbasa and potatoes and sauté 3–5 minutes.

4. Add chicken broth, drained kale, and beans. Bring to a boil. Lower heat, cover with the lid, and simmer 1 hour. Season with salt and pepper.

# Sausage, Bacon, and Bean Feast

*The simple step of sautéing the vegetables as you fry the bacon and sausage
gives this dish that simmered-all-day, comfort food flavor.*

**PREP TIME:** 10 minutes
**COOK TIME:** 25 minutes

**INGREDIENTS | SERVES 6–8**

1 (8-ounce) package bacon, cut
into pieces

8 ounces ground pork sausage

3 large carrots, peeled and
finely chopped

2 stalks celery, finely chopped

1 large yellow onion, peeled and
finely chopped

2 cloves garlic, peeled and minced

1 bay leaf

½ teaspoon dried thyme, crushed

3 cups chicken broth

2 (15-ounce) cans cannelloni beans,
rinsed and drained

½ teaspoon salt

½ teaspoon freshly cracked
black pepper

1 teaspoon hot sauce, optional

1. Add bacon and sausage to a 4- or 6-quart Dutch oven and fry over medium heat until some of the fat begins to render from meat, about 5 minutes. Add carrots and celery; sauté along with meat, stirring occasionally. When meat is cooked through, drain all but 1–2 tablespoons of the rendered oil. Add onion and sauté until transparent, about 5 minutes. Add garlic and sauté 30 seconds.

2. Add bay leaf, thyme, broth, and beans. Stir to combine. Bring to a boil and then lower heat and simmer, covered, 15 minutes.

3. Discard bay leaf and add salt and pepper immediately before serving. Add hot sauce to enhance the flavor, if desired.

# Butternut Squash Soup with Kielbasa and Wild Rice

*If you prefer, you can substitute cooked pork, chicken, or turkey for the kielbasa.*

**PREP TIME:** 10 minutes
**COOK TIME:** 2 hours 30 minutes

**INGREDIENTS | SERVES 6–8**

1 (1½–2-pound) butternut squash

2 tablespoons extra-virgin olive oil, divided

6 cups chicken broth, divided

1 large yellow onion, peeled and diced, divided

1 cup uncooked wild rice

1 pound kielbasa, cut into ¼" slices

1 (12- or 16-ounce) package frozen whole kernel corn, thawed

½ teaspoon salt

½ teaspoon freshly cracked black pepper

Water, as needed

1 cup heavy cream

1 tablespoon chopped fresh parsley

### Microwave-Roasted Butternut Squash

Instead of baking the butternut squash, you can cook it in the microwave. Wash the squash, slice in half lengthwise, remove the seeds, and place it cut-side down in a shallow microwave-safe pan. Add water to about ¾" deep. Microwave on high for 8–10 minutes, or until the squash is tender.

1. Heat oven to 400°F.

2. Cut squash in half and remove the seeds. Place squash halves skin-side down on a baking sheet and drizzle with 1 tablespoon olive oil; bake 1 hour. Remove from oven and let cool completely. Peel squash and add it to a blender or food processor along with 2 cups chicken broth; purée until smooth and set aside.

3. Add remaining 4 cups broth and ½ diced onions to a 6- or 8-quart Dutch oven and bring to a simmer over medium heat. Stir in rice; cook 1 hour, or until rice is tender and most of liquid is absorbed, stirring occasionally with a fork. Remove rice from the pan and set aside.

4. Add remaining 1 tablespoon oil to the Dutch oven and bring it to temperature over medium heat. Add kielbasa slices and brown 3 minutes. Add remaining onions and corn; season with salt and pepper and sauté 3 minutes.

5. Add squash purée; reduce heat to medium-low, cover, and simmer 20 minutes, checking occasionally and adding water, if needed. Skim off any fat on the surface, stir in the rice, and continue to cook 10 minutes.

6. Remove from heat and stir in the cream. Taste for seasoning and add more salt and pepper if desired. Serve garnished with parsley.

# Split Pea with Ham Soup

*Don't throw away your leftover ham bones! They can add a lot of flavor to stocks and soups, and make the perfect base for a pot of country-style split pea soup!*

**PREP TIME:** 10 minutes
**COOK TIME:** 3 hours 45 minutes

**INGREDIENTS | SERVES 8**

1 pound dried green split peas
2 quarts water
1 meaty ham bone
1 cup chopped onion
1 clove garlic, peeled and minced
½ teaspoon salt
¼ teaspoon dried thyme
¼ teaspoon freshly cracked
black pepper
1 bay leaf
1 cup chopped celery
1 cup chopped carrot

1. Add dried peas to a 6-quart Dutch oven and cover with water. Bring peas to a boil and cook 2 minutes, then turn off heat, cover the pot, and let peas soak 1 hour.

2. Add ham bone, onion, garlic, salt, thyme, pepper, and bay leaf to soaked peas. Bring soup to a boil, then reduce heat to medium-low, cover, and simmer 2 hours, stirring occasionally. Remove bay leaf and discard.

3. Remove ham bone from soup and carefully remove meat and dice it. Add diced ham, celery, and carrot to soup and allow soup to simmer 40–45 minutes more, or until carrots and celery are very tender. Serve warm.

## No Ham Bone?

This soup is a great way to use up a left-over ham bone, but if you do not have one handy you can substitute a ham hock. Ham hocks, the knuckle of the pig, are available fresh at most Asian markets or at a full-service butcher's shop. The hock is very fatty, so soup made with a ham hock will be very rich, and very tasty!

# *Frijoles a la Charra* (Pinto Bean Soup)

*Also known as "charro beans," this soup is popular as an appetizer or a side dish with grilled meat. Add some beer in place of the water for cooking and you will have frijoles borrachos, or drunken beans.*

**PREP TIME:** 8–10 hours
**COOK TIME:** 2 hours 20 minutes

**INGREDIENTS | SERVES 8**

1 pound dried pinto beans
½ pound bacon, chopped
1 large onion, peeled and chopped
2 cloves garlic, peeled and minced
1 jalapeño, seeded and minced
2 teaspoons cumin
1 teaspoon coriander
½ teaspoon smoked paprika
2 quarts water
¼ cup roughly chopped cilantro
½ teaspoon salt

## Tips for Speedy Beans

When time is short, or you forgot to soak your dried beans, you can still have a delicious pot of beans. Simply use 4 (15-ounce) cans of low-sodium pinto beans in place of the dried. Rinse the beans well under cold water and proceed with the recipe as normal. The beans may be a little mushier than dried beans soaked overnight, but they will taste just as good!

1. Rinse and sort dried beans in a colander, then transfer to a large bowl, cover with cold water, and let beans soak overnight in the refrigerator.

2. Heat a 6- or 8-quart Dutch oven over medium heat. Add bacon and cook, stirring often, until bacon is browned and fat has completely rendered, about 10 minutes. Add onion and cook, stirring often, until tender, about 5 minutes. Add garlic, jalapeño, cumin, coriander, and smoked paprika and cook until garlic and spices are fragrant, about 2 minutes.

3. Strain beans and shake off any excess water. Add beans to the Dutch oven and toss to coat in onion and spices. Add water and cilantro and bring mixture to a boil. Once soup comes to a boil reduce heat to low, cover, and let simmer 2 hours, stirring occasionally, until beans are tender. Season with salt and serve hot.

# Guinness Stew

*A staple of Irish pub menus, this stew is a one-pot meal perfect for lunch or dinner. This stew tastes better the second day, so feel free to make this a day in advance and reheat over medium-low heat before serving.*

**PREP TIME:** 15 minutes
**COOK TIME:** 2 hours 30 minutes

**INGREDIENTS | SERVES 8**

2 pounds boneless beef chuck steak, trimmed, cut into 2" cubes

2 tablespoons all-purpose flour

¼ teaspoon cayenne

¼ teaspoon salt

¼ teaspoon freshly cracked black pepper

1½ tablespoons vegetable oil, divided

1 medium onion, peeled and chopped

1 clove garlic, chopped

¼ teaspoon dry thyme

1 cup Guinness beer, divided

1 cup beef stock

1 bay leaf

2 large carrots, peeled and cut into 1" pieces

2 medium Russet potatoes, scrubbed and cut into 1" pieces

¼ cup chopped parsley

1. In a medium bowl add beef, flour, cayenne, salt, and pepper. Toss until beef is thoroughly coated. Set aside.

2. In a 6- or 8-quart Dutch oven over medium heat add half the oil. Once oil is hot add half the beef and brown well on all sides. Transfer beef to a bowl and repeat with remaining oil and beef.

3. Add onion, garlic, and thyme to the Dutch oven and cook until onions are tender, about 5 minutes, then add half the Guinness and scrape off all the browned bits from the bottom of the Dutch oven.

4. Add remaining Guinness, beef stock, bay leaf, carrots, potatoes, and browned beef along with any juices that have accumulated in the bowl. Bring mixture to a boil, then reduce heat to low, cover with a lid, and simmer 2–2½ hours, or until meat is tender. Discard bay leaf and serve hot with fresh parsley as a garnish.

# Lamb and Spring Vegetable Stew

*Ask for meat from the leg, the shoulder, or top round. These cuts can handle the long stewing period and they tend to be some of the cheaper cuts available.*

**PREP TIME:** 10 minutes
**COOK TIME:** 1 hour 55 minutes

**INGREDIENTS | SERVES 4**

2 tablespoons olive oil

1 large onion, peeled and chopped

1 clove garlic, peeled and minced

1 pound lean, boneless lamb, cut into cubes

Pinch salt

Pinch pepper

¼ cup dry white wine

4 cups chicken stock

1 bay leaf

1 sprig fresh thyme

2 pounds small red potatoes, scrubbed

8 ounces baby carrots

8 ounces button mushrooms, halved

8 ounces radishes, stems and roots trimmed

8 ounces frozen peas

1. Heat oven to 350°F. Place a 6- or 8-quart ovenproof Dutch oven over medium heat and add oil and onion. Cook 8–10 minutes. Add garlic and stir continually 1 minute.

2. Season lamb lightly with salt and pepper. Add lamb cubes and cook 2 minutes on each side, turning as needed, until all of the meat is browned.

3. Add wine to the pan and scrape the bottom. Add chicken stock, bay leaf, thyme, potatoes, carrots, and mushrooms. Bring contents to a boil and then cover pot. Bake 1 hour.

4. Add radishes, replace the lid, and bake 30 minutes. Add peas, replace the lid, and bake 10 minutes. Remove bay leaf and thyme sprig.

5. Season with salt and pepper as needed and serve while warm.

# Vegetable Barley Soup

*Vegetarians and meat eaters alike will enjoy this robust soup bursting with vegetables and barley. Leftovers make a great lunch the next day!*

**PREP TIME:** 15 minutes
**COOK TIME:** 35 minutes

**INGREDIENTS | SERVES 8**

2 tablespoons unsalted butter or vegetable oil

1 medium onion, peeled and chopped

1 medium green bell pepper, seeded and chopped

1 medium carrot, peeled and chopped

1 stalk celery, chopped

1 pint sliced mushrooms

1 Russet potato, peeled and cut into ½" cubes

1 cup frozen corn

1 cup frozen cut green beans

1 (14-ounce) can low-sodium diced tomatoes, undrained

2 pints vegetable broth

2 pints water

1 cup pearl barley

1 bay leaf

1 teaspoon salt

1 teaspoon ground fennel

½ teaspoon dried thyme

½ teaspoon freshly cracked black pepper

1. Heat a 6- or 8-quart Dutch oven over medium heat. Add butter or oil, and once hot add onion, bell pepper, carrot, celery, and mushrooms. Sauté until vegetables begin to soften, about 5 minutes.

2. Add remaining ingredients and bring to a boil over medium-high heat, then reduce heat to low, cover with a lid and simmer 30 minutes, or until barley is tender and potato is cooked through. Discard bay leaf before serving.

## Toasted Barley

If you want, you can toast the barley before adding it to the soup to give the barley a nutty flavor. In a medium skillet add 1 tablespoon butter or oil over medium heat. Add the barley and cook, stirring constantly, until the barley is golden brown. Once toasted, you can add to the soup and cook as usual. Cooked toasted barley is also good in salads, stuffing, and stews.

# Cock-a-Leekie

*This is the Scottish version of a chicken soup. Feel free to add carrots to the soup if you desire more vegetables with your meal. Serve it alongside or over buttered biscuits for true comfort food goodness.*

**PREP TIME:** 15 minutes
**COOK TIME:** 1 hour 30 minutes

**INGREDIENTS | SERVES 6–8**

3–4 pounds bone-in chicken pieces

1 pound beef shanks, sawed into 1" cubes

4 slices thick-cut bacon, diced

4 cups chicken broth

1 tablespoon dried thyme

1 bay leaf

Water, as needed

¾ cup pearl barley

1½ cups leeks (white part only), well-rinsed and chopped

½ teaspoon salt

½ teaspoon freshly cracked black pepper

2 tablespoons chopped fresh parsley

## Matzo Balls

Matzo balls are good in almost any chicken soup. To make 6 servings, mix 2 tablespoons chicken fat, 2 large eggs, ½ cup matzo meal, 1 teaspoon salt, and 2 tablespoons chicken broth. Cover and refrigerate at least 20 minutes. Roll the mixture into 12 balls. Cook, covered, in boiling water or broth 30–40 minutes.

1. Add chicken, beef shanks, bacon, broth, thyme, and bay leaf to a 6- or 8-quart Dutch oven. Add enough water to cover the meat. Bring to a boil over medium-high heat; cover, reduce heat, and simmer 1 hour, or until chicken is cooked through and tender.

2. Use a slotted spoon to remove chicken and beef shanks from the pot. Set aside and allow to cool. Bring broth to a boil over medium heat. Add barley. Boil 10 minutes, stirring occasionally.

3. While the barley cooks, remove the chicken from the bones. Discard skin and bones, and shred the chicken. Next, remove the beef from the bones, discarding bones and any fat.

4. Add leeks to pan. Reduce heat, cover, and simmer 10 minutes. Add chicken and beef to pan. Cover and simmer 5 minutes to bring meat to temperature. Add salt and pepper and garnish with chopped parsley.

# Gumbo

*For the broth, backwoods cooks save up chicken gizzards and necks until they have 2 pounds of each, then simmer them in 3–4 quarts of water. You can find filé powder at www.thespicehouse.com if your local grocery store doesn't carry it.*

**PREP TIME:** 15 minutes
**COOK TIME:** 1 hour 10 minutes

**INGREDIENTS | SERVES 6–8**

4 tablespoons lard or peanut oil

4 tablespoons all-purpose flour

4 stalks celery, chopped

1 large yellow onion, peeled and diced

1 medium green bell pepper, seeded and diced

3 cloves garlic, peeled and minced

1 (15-ounce) can diced tomatoes

¼ teaspoon dried thyme

¼ teaspoon dried basil

3 bay leaves

2 tablespoons filé powder

2 tablespoons Worcestershire sauce

1 teaspoon hot sauce, or to taste

8 cups chicken broth

1 pound smoked sausage, sliced

2 cups shredded cooked chicken

¼ teaspoon salt

¼ teaspoon freshly cracked black pepper

4½ cups cooked long-grain rice

1. Add lard or oil and flour to a 6- or 8-quart Dutch oven over medium heat. Cook, stirring constantly so it doesn't burn, 15 minutes, or until the mixture (roux) is the color of peanut butter.

2. Stir in celery, onion, green pepper, garlic, and tomatoes; cook, stirring constantly, until vegetables are tender. Add remaining ingredients except sausage, chicken, salt, pepper, and rice and simmer covered over medium heat 30–45 minutes, or until mixture thickens.

3. Stir in sausage, chicken, salt, and pepper, and simmer uncovered an additional 15 minutes. Serve hot over a heaping ½ cup of rice per serving.

## Cooked Rice

For 4½ cups of cooked rice, rinse and drain 1½ cups of uncooked rice and add to a large saucepan along with 2½ cups of water and salt to taste. Cover and let set 30 minutes. Bring to a boil over high heat, reduce heat to medium-low, and cook covered 15 minutes. Turn off the heat. Leave covered 10 minutes or until ready to serve, for up to 1 hour.

# Old-Fashioned Chicken and Dumplings

*Chicken and dumplings are, for many, the definition of comfort food. For this recipe the Biscuit Topping for Savory Stews (Chapter 3) doubles as tender, fluffy dumplings!*

**PREP TIME:** 15 minutes
**COOK TIME:** 1 hour 25 minutes

**INGREDIENTS | SERVES 8**

1 (4-pound) chicken, cut into 8 pieces
1 medium onion, peeled and chopped
2 stalks celery, chopped
1 medium carrot, peeled and chopped
½ teaspoon salt
½ teaspoon freshly cracked black pepper
½ teaspoon poultry seasoning
1 bay leaf
2 quarts water
2 quarts chicken stock
3 tablespoons unsalted butter
3 tablespoons all-purpose flour
½ cup half and half
1 recipe Biscuit Topping for Savory Stews (Chapter 3)

### Flat Dumplings

If you prefer flat, noodle-like dumplings to fluffy biscuit-like dumplings here is the recipe for you. Mix 1 cup all-purpose flour, 1 tablespoon butter, 2 teaspoons baking powder, and ½ teaspoon salt in a bowl. Add 2 beaten eggs and ½ cup whole milk and form a dough. Roll out to ⅛" thick, cut into 1" strips, and add to the pot. Cover and cook 10 minutes, then remove the lid and cook 10 minutes more.

1. In an 8-quart Dutch oven add chicken, onion, celery, carrot, salt, pepper, poultry seasoning, bay leaf, water, and chicken stock. Bring to a boil over high heat, then reduce heat to low, cover with lid, and simmer until chicken is cooked through and tender, about 40 minutes.

2. Remove chicken from the pot and once cool enough to handle, pull chicken meat from the bones. Return meat to the pot and keep soup warm over low heat.

3. In a medium saucepan over medium heat add butter. Once it foams add flour and cook, stirring constantly, until flour is cooked through and smooth, about 3 minutes. Reduce heat to low and add ½ cup soup liquid, whisking well to prevent lumps. Slowly add 1 additional cup soup liquid and half and half, whisking constantly. Once all the liquid is added whisk flour mixture into soup, increase heat to medium and allow soup to come to a boil and thicken, about 10 minutes.

4. Once soup has thickened, reduce heat to medium-low and drop golf ball–sized scoops of Biscuit Topping for Savory Stews into the soup. Do not stir. Immediately cover with the lid and let dumplings steam 10 minutes, then test for doneness by inserting a toothpick into a dumpling. If toothpick comes out clean they are ready. If not ready, cover and cook 3–5 additional minutes. Serve hot.

# Texas Red Chili

*Texans are particular about their chili. It can't have beans or tomatoes, and it should be simmered low and slow so the meat is melt-in-your-mouth tender. This recipe should do any Texan proud!*

**PREP TIME:** 40 minutes
**COOK TIME:** 2 hours 50 minutes

### INGREDIENTS | SERVES 8

2 dried Anaheim chilies

2 dried New Mexico chilies

1 tablespoon chili powder

1 teaspoon cumin

1 (12-ounce) can lager- or bock-style beer, divided

2 pounds chili meat made from chuck roast

1 medium onion, peeled and chopped

2 cloves garlic, peeled and minced

1 tablespoon brown sugar

½ teaspoon salt

½ teaspoon freshly cracked black pepper

2 cups beef broth

2½ cups water, divided

¼ cup corn masa

1 tablespoon lime juice

1 teaspoon hot sauce

1. Heat oven to 350°F.

2. Cut dried chilies and remove the stem and seeds. Place chilies on a baking sheet and roast 8–10 minutes, or until fragrant. Place hot chilies into a heatproof bowl and cover with hot water. Let chilies soak until tender, about 30 minutes.

3. Drain chilies and place into the container of a blender along with chili powder, cumin, and half the beer. Purée until smooth, about 1 minute. Set aside.

4. In an 8-quart Dutch oven over medium-high heat brown chili meat. Once browned add onion, garlic, brown sugar, salt, and pepper and cook until onions are just tender, about 10 minutes.

5. Add chili paste, reserved beer, beef broth, and 2 cups water and bring to a boil, then reduce heat to low, cover, and simmer until the meat is tender, about 1½ hours.

6. Remove lid, raise heat to medium, and let chili cook 30 minutes.

7. In a small bowl, mix masa with remaining water and whisk mixture into the chili, then add lime juice and hot sauce.

8. Bring to a boil to thicken, about 5 minutes. Serve hot.

# Lamb Chili

*Serve this chili with a tossed salad that includes avocado slices, papaya pieces, and goat cheese. A little drizzle of extra-virgin olive oil is the only dressing it needs.*

**PREP TIME:** 10 minutes
**COOK TIME:** 1 hour 50 minutes
**INGREDIENTS | SERVES 6–8**

2 pounds ground lamb

3 tablespoons extra-virgin olive oil

1 large yellow onion, peeled and diced

4 cloves garlic, crushed

2 tablespoons chili powder

1 tablespoon whole cumin seeds

¼ teaspoon dried oregano, crushed

2 medium jalapeño or red peppers, seeded and diced

2 medium green bell peppers, seeded and diced

1 (28-ounce) can diced tomatoes

1 (8-ounce) can tomato sauce

1 tablespoon Worcestershire sauce

2 (15-ounce) cans red kidney beans, rinsed and drained

½ teaspoon salt

½ teaspoon freshly cracked black pepper

Water, if necessary

1. Add lamb, oil, onion, garlic, chili powder, and cumin seeds to a 6- or 8-quart Dutch oven over medium heat. Sauté until meat is brown and onion is transparent, about 5 minutes, and then add remaining ingredients. Add water, if needed, so that all the ingredients are covered by liquid.

2. Continue to cook on medium about 15 minutes to bring all the ingredients to temperature, then lower heat, cover, and simmer 1½ hours. Check the pot periodically to stir chili and to make sure that it doesn't boil dry. Add more water, if necessary.

## Make Your Own Chili Powder

To make your own chili powder just add 5 dried poblano peppers, 1 dried ancho chili pepper, ⅜ teaspoon ground cumin, ¾ teaspoon dried oregano, and 1 teaspoon garlic powder to a spice grinder, food processor, or blender. Process until fine. Add cayenne pepper to taste if you wish to make it hotter. Store in the freezer in a tightly covered container and it'll keep indefinitely.

# Cincinnati Chili

*Cincinnati Chili is served like a sauce over cooked pasta, and then topped with onion and cheese.*

**PREP TIME:** 10 minutes
**COOK TIME:** 45 minutes

**INGREDIENTS | SERVES 8**

2 pounds lean ground beef

3 large yellow onions, peeled and diced, divided

3 cloves garlic, peeled and minced

1 (16-ounce) can tomato sauce

1 cup beef broth

2 tablespoons chili powder

2 tablespoons semisweet chocolate chips

2 tablespoons red wine vinegar

2 tablespoons honey

1 tablespoon pumpkin pie spice

1 teaspoon ground cumin

½ teaspoon ground cardamom

¼ teaspoon ground cloves

½ teaspoon salt

½ teaspoon freshly cracked black pepper

2 (15-ounce) cans kidney beans, rinsed and drained

1 pound cooked pasta of your choice

4 cups shredded American or Cheddar cheese

1. Add ground beef and ¾ of diced onions to a 4½-quart Dutch oven over medium-high heat; stir-fry until beef is browned and the onion is transparent, about 10 minutes. Drain off and discard any excess fat. Stir in garlic and stir-fry 30 seconds.

2. Add tomato sauce, broth, chili powder, chocolate chips, vinegar, honey, pumpkin pie spice, cumin, cardamom, cloves, salt, and pepper; mix well. Bring to a simmer; lower heat to maintain the simmer, and cook at least 30 minutes to let the flavors mix.

3. Shortly before serving, add kidney beans and cook until heated through.

4. Serve meat sauce over cooked pasta, then top chili with remaining diced onions and a generous amount of grated cheese.

# White Bean Chicken Chili

*To save time you can use shredded breast meat from a rotisserie chicken in this recipe.*

**PREP TIME:** 10 minutes
**COOK TIME:** 45 minutes

**INGREDIENTS | SERVES 8**

2 tablespoons unsalted butter

1 medium onion, peeled and chopped

2 cloves garlic, peeled and minced

1 teaspoon cumin

½ teaspoon oregano

2 (4-ounce) cans diced green chilies

3 (4-ounce) skinless, boneless chicken breasts

2 cups chicken stock

2 cups water

3 (14.5-ounce) cans great northern beans, drained and rinsed

¼ cup roughly chopped cilantro

1 cup shredded pepper jack cheese

1 cup roughly crushed tortilla chips

1. In an 8-quart Dutch oven over medium heat add butter. Once it foams add onion and cook until translucent, about 3 minutes. Add garlic, cumin, and oregano and cook until fragrant, about 1 minute.

2. Add remaining ingredients except cheese and tortilla chips, bring to a boil over high heat, then reduce heat to low, cover, and simmer until chicken is cooked through, about 30 minutes.

3. Carefully remove chicken from the Dutch oven, increase heat to medium, and let the chili reduce by ¼. While chili reduces, shred chicken with two forks and then return meat to the Dutch oven. Serve in bowls with a garnish of cheese and tortilla chips.

# Pumpkin Soup

*Canned pumpkin actually packs more nutrients than raw fresh pumpkin, so this is one shortcut you absolutely shouldn't feel guilty about! Serve with cornbread or peanut butter sandwiches.*

**PREP TIME:** 10 minutes
**COOK TIME:** 30 minutes

**INGREDIENTS | SERVES 4–6**

2 tablespoons unsalted butter

1 stalk celery, finely diced

1 large carrot, peeled and finely diced

1 medium yellow onion, peeled and minced

1 medium apple, peeled, cored, and minced

1 (15-ounce) can pumpkin purée

3 cups chicken broth

1 (10-ounce) package frozen whole kernel corn, thawed

½ cup diced cooked ham

½ teaspoon salt

½ teaspoon freshly cracked black pepper

3 tablespoons toasted pumpkin seeds, shelled

1. Melt butter in a 4- or 6-quart Dutch oven over medium heat. Add celery and carrot and sauté 3–5 minutes, or until tender. Add onion and apple; sauté until onion is transparent, about 5 minutes.

2. Stir in pumpkin and chicken broth. Bring to a boil; reduce heat and simmer 10 minutes. Use a stick blender to purée the soup if you wish.

3. Add corn and ham and simmer 8 minutes, or until corn is tender. Season with salt and pepper and garnish with pumpkin seeds.

## Pumpkin Soup Variations

Omit the corn in this Pumpkin Soup recipe and stir in ½ cup of peanut butter and a little brown sugar instead. Or, season the soup by adding 1 teaspoon smoked paprika, ⅛ teaspoon ground cumin, and a pinch of cayenne pepper. Turn any variation into a cream soup by stirring in ½ cup of heavy cream, or more to taste.

# Clam and Potato Chowder

*Bacon is the secret to the rich, smoky flavor in this chowder. Use a good-quality smoked bacon here for the best flavor.*

**PREP TIME:** 10 minutes
**COOK TIME:** 45 minutes

**INGREDIENTS | SERVES 8**

½ pound smoked bacon, chopped

1 large onion, peeled and chopped

4 medium russet potatoes, peeled and cut into ½" cubes

2 (8-ounce) bottles clam juice

1 teaspoon salt

½ teaspoon freshly cracked black pepper

½ teaspoon seafood seasoning, such as Old Bay

4 tablespoons unsalted butter

¼ cup all-purpose flour

3 cups half and half

1 cup whole milk

3 (7-ounce) cans minced clams

½ cup heavy cream

½ teaspoon hot sauce

1. Heat a 6- or 8-quart Dutch oven over medium heat. Add bacon and cook until all the fat has rendered and bacon is crisp, about 10 minutes. Remove bacon to a paper towel–lined plate to drain. Set aside.

2. To the bacon drippings add onion and cook until tender and translucent, about 5 minutes. Add potatoes, clam juice, salt, pepper, and seafood seasoning, then cover with a lid and cook until potatoes are tender, about 15 minutes.

3. In a medium saucepan over medium heat add butter. Once it foams add flour and cook, stirring constantly, until flour is cooked through and smooth, about 3 minutes. Reduce heat to low and add half and half and milk, whisking constantly. Whisk flour mixture and clams with their juice into the soup, then increase heat to medium and allow soup to come to a boil and thicken, about 10 minutes.

4. Reduce heat to low, stir in heavy cream, hot sauce, and half the cooked bacon. Serve hot and garnish with the remaining bacon.

# Mulligatawny Soup

*This soup is traditionally served garnished with lots of freshly ground black pepper along with the chopped cilantro.*

**PREP TIME:** 10 minutes
**COOK TIME:** 1 hour 45 minutes

**INGREDIENTS | SERVES 8**

8 chicken thighs
1 stalk celery, cut in half
1 large carrot, peeled and cut in 4 pieces
1 small yellow onion, peeled and quartered
8 cups water, divided
1 tablespoon ghee
2 stalks celery, finely diced
4 large carrots, peeled and finely diced
1 medium yellow onion, peeled and diced
2 cloves garlic, peeled and minced
¼ teaspoon turmeric
½ teaspoon ground coriander
¼ teaspoon dried red pepper flakes
½ teaspoon dried cumin
½ teaspoon ground cardamom
½ teaspoon ground dried ginger
½ teaspoon salt
½ teaspoon freshly cracked black pepper
4 cups chicken broth
¼ cup chopped fresh cilantro

1. Add chicken thighs, celery halves, carrot pieces, quartered onion, and 4 cups water to a 6- or 8-quart Dutch oven. Bring to a simmer over medium heat; reduce heat, cover, and simmer 1 hour.

2. Strain broth into a bowl and set aside. Discard cooked vegetables. Once chicken has cooled enough to handle it, remove meat from the bones, discarding the skin and the bones; set aside.

3. Melt ghee in the Dutch oven over medium heat. Add diced celery and carrot and sauté 3–5 minutes, or until soft. Add diced onion and sauté until transparent, about 5 minutes. Add garlic and sauté an additional 30 seconds.

4. Stir turmeric, coriander, red pepper flakes, cumin, cardamom, ginger, salt, and pepper into sautéed vegetables. Stir in chicken broth and remaining 4 cups water. Bring to a boil; reduce heat, cover, and simmer 30 minutes.

5. Add cooked chicken; simmer uncovered, stirring occasionally, an additional 5 minutes to bring the meat to temperature. Taste for seasoning and add additional salt, if needed. Serve garnished with additional freshly cracked black pepper and chopped cilantro.

## Fat Adds Flavor—and Calories

Fat is tasty, but it adds extra calories to a dish. If you favor lean over flavor, you can either remove the skin before you cook the thighs or refrigerate the broth to make it easier to skim the fat off the top.

# Shrimp and Crab Bisque

*Adding carrots and potatoes to this dish turns it into a one-pot meal. It may be stretching it to continue to call it "bisque," but when you consider the cost of the ingredients, it still deserves an expensive-sounding name.*

**PREP TIME:** 15 minutes
**COOK TIME:** 35 minutes

**INGREDIENTS | SERVES 6–8**

2 tablespoons plus ½ cup unsalted butter, divided

4 stalks celery with leaves, finely chopped

1 (1-pound) bag baby carrots

1 large yellow onion, peeled and finely chopped

2 cloves garlic, peeled and minced

3 cups fish or shrimp stock, or chicken broth

4 large russet potatoes, peeled and diced

2 whole cloves

1 bay leaf

6 peppercorns

2 cups whole milk

½ cup all-purpose flour

1 pound raw shrimp, peeled and deveined

1 pound cooked crabmeat, broken apart

2 cups heavy cream

½ teaspoon salt

½ teaspoon white pepper

1 tablespoon dry sherry

2 green onions, green part only, chopped

1. Melt 2 tablespoons butter in a 6-quart Dutch oven over medium heat. Add celery and stir. Finely dice 6 baby carrots and stir into butter and celery; sauté 2 minutes. Add onion and sauté until transparent, about 5 minutes. Stir garlic into the sautéed mixture.

2. Chop remaining carrots into thirds and add to Dutch oven along with stock or broth and potatoes.

3. Wrap cloves, bay leaf, and peppercorns in cheesecloth or put them in a cheesecloth or muslin cooking bag; add to broth. Bring to a boil then lower the temperature, cover, and simmer 10 minutes.

4. Add milk. Bring to a boil over medium heat.

5. Mix ½ cup butter and flour together to form a paste and stir it into broth, 1 teaspoon at a time. Once all of the butter-flour mixture is added, boil 1 minute, then lower temperature and let simmer until mixture begins to thicken and the raw flour taste is cooked out of broth. Remove the cheesecloth or cooking bag.

6. Add shrimp and cook just until they begin to turn pink; do not overcook. Stir in crabmeat and cream and bring to a simmer. Season with salt, white pepper, and dry sherry. Remove from heat and serve immediately. Garnish with chopped green onion.

# Clam Chowder

*Canned clams are salty, so chances are you won't need to add any salt to the chowder. Also, be sure to read the label on the cans if anyone in your family has food sensitivities; some canned clams have monosodium glutamate.*

**PREP TIME:** 15 minutes
**COOK TIME:** 30 minutes

**INGREDIENTS | SERVES 8–10**

½ cup unsalted butter

2 cloves garlic, peeled and minced

1 stalk celery, finely chopped

2 baby carrots, grated

1 large yellow onion, peeled and diced

½ teaspoon white pepper

⅛ teaspoon dried thyme, crushed

½ cup all-purpose flour

3 cups chicken broth or water

3 cups whole milk

1 bay leaf

4 large russet or red potatoes, peeled or unpeeled, and diced

2 (6.5-ounce) cans chopped or minced clams

2 cups heavy cream

1. Melt butter in a 6-quart Dutch oven over medium heat. Add garlic, celery, and carrots and sauté 2 minutes. Add onion and sauté until transparent. Stir in pepper, thyme, and flour. Whisk until butter is absorbed into flour, about 2 minutes.

2. Slowly add broth or water, whisking continuously to blend it with butter-flour roux. Add milk, bay leaf, and potatoes.

3. Bring to a boil; reduce heat, cover, and simmer 10–15 minutes, or until potatoes are tender. Check and stir the chowder frequently to prevent it from burning.

4. Stir in clams and cream. Bring the mixture to a simmer, remove bay leaf, and serve immediately.

## Clam Salad

Chop leftover steamed clams and add them to a macaroni salad. For a complete quick and easy lunch, serve it over lettuce and garnish the clam-macaroni salad with chopped fresh parsley or dill.

# CHAPTER 6

# Pasta Dishes

# Baked Five-Cheese Macaroni and Cheese

*If you love cheese, this is the dish for you! Five different cheeses are combined to create the ultimate cheese lover's macaroni and cheese delight!*

**PREP TIME:** 10 minutes
**COOK TIME:** 1 hour 10 minutes
**INGREDIENTS | SERVES 8**

1 pound elbow pasta
3 tablespoons unsalted butter
3 tablespoons all-purpose flour
2 cups whole milk
1 cup half and half
½ teaspoon salt
½ teaspoon freshly cracked
black pepper
4 ounces cream cheese
4 ounces sharp Cheddar, shredded
4 ounces Gruyère, shredded
4 ounces smoked Gouda, shredded
2 tablespoons unsalted butter, melted
1 cup panko bread crumbs
½ cup grated Parmesan cheese

### Moist Baked Macaroni and Cheese

Baked macaroni and cheese can sometimes come out dry and gritty. Talk about disappointing! To make sure your baked macaroni and cheese stays moist you should keep a few things in mind. First, slightly undercook your pasta. As the pasta bakes it will absorb liquid, so only undercook it by a minute or two. Second, add a little extra milk or cream to your sauce. This extra liquid will cook the pasta, and keep the sauce creamy. Finally, don't overbake! Macaroni and cheese should be golden brown on top and bubbling around the edges. If the center is bubbling there is a good chance your macaroni and cheese will be dry.

1. Cook pasta in salted water according to the package directions, reducing the cooking time by 2 minutes. Drain and rinse with cool water to stop the cooking. Set aside.

2. Heat oven to 350°F.

3. Heat an 8-quart ovenproof Dutch oven over medium heat. Add butter and once it starts to foam add flour. Cook, stirring constantly, until flour is smooth and just turning golden brown, about 3 minutes.

4. Reduce heat to low and slowly whisk in milk and half and half. Increase heat to medium and cook, stirring constantly, until the sauce thickens and comes to a boil, about 8 minutes. Add salt and pepper and stir to combine.

5. Reduce heat to low and add cream cheese. Once that has melted add shredded cheeses a handful at a time, making sure each addition has completely melted before adding the next. Turn off heat and stir in pasta.

6. In a small bowl combine melted butter and bread crumbs. Toss until bread crumbs are evenly coated, then add Parmesan cheese and mix well.

7. Top macaroni and cheese with bread crumbs and bake 40–45 minutes or until the topping is golden brown and the macaroni and cheese is bubbling around the edges. Cool 10 minutes before serving.

# Quick Stovetop Mac and Cheese

*This version is as easy to make as boxed macaroni and cheese, but it tastes infinitely better!*
*You can use any combination of smooth melting cheeses here, so use your imagination!*

**PREP TIME:** 10 minutes
**COOK TIME:** 20 minutes

**INGREDIENTS | SERVES 8**

1 pound elbow pasta or small tube-shaped pasta

2 tablespoons unsalted butter

1⅓ cups evaporated milk

2 large eggs, beaten

1 teaspoon dry mustard powder

¼ teaspoon hot sauce

½ teaspoon salt

¼ teaspoon freshly cracked black pepper

2 cups shredded Cheddar cheese

1. In a 6-quart Dutch oven cook pasta in salted water according to the package directions, reducing the cooking time by 1 minute. Drain pasta and return to the Dutch oven.

2. Place Dutch oven over medium heat and add butter. Cook until butter has completely melted, about 1 minute.

3. In a small bowl combine remaining ingredients except cheese and add to buttered pasta. Reduce heat to medium-low and cook, stirring constantly, until sauce thickens, about 5 minutes.

4. Remove Dutch oven from heat then add cheese in four batches, making sure the first is melted completely before adding the next. Serve immediately.

# Crunchy Topped Taco Mac

*Kids will love this cheesy, meaty macaroni and cheese! If you prefer you can use ground chicken or turkey in place of the beef.*

**PREP TIME:** 10 minutes
**COOK TIME:** 1 hour 5 minutes
**INGREDIENTS | SERVES 8**

8 ounces elbow pasta

1 tablespoon unsalted butter

1 medium onion, peeled and chopped

1 pound ground beef

1 (10-ounce) can diced tomatoes and green chilies

1 (1.25 ounce) packet taco seasoning

½ teaspoon salt

1 cup evaporated milk

1 large egg

6 ounces sharp Cheddar cheese, shredded, divided

1 cup roughly crushed tortilla chips

## Homemade Taco Seasoning

Want to create your own taco seasoning blend at home? Combine 1 tablespoon chili powder, 1 teaspoon cumin, ½ teaspoon each coriander, freshly cracked black pepper, oregano, smoked paprika, and ¼ teaspoon each onion powder, garlic powder, cornstarch, cayenne pepper, and salt. Brown your ground beef, then add the seasoning and ½ cup of water and cook 10 minutes on medium heat.

1. In a 6-quart Dutch oven cook pasta in salted water according to the package directions, reducing the cooking time by 1 minute. Drain and set aside.

2. Heat oven to 350°F.

3. In a 6- or 8-quart ovenproof Dutch oven over medium heat melt butter until it foams. Add onion and cook until it begins to soften, about 3 minutes. Add ground beef and cook until thoroughly browned, about 10 minutes. Drain away any excess fat. Add diced tomatoes and green chilies, taco seasoning, and salt and cook, stirring occasionally, until thickened, about 5 minutes. Turn off heat and cool slightly.

4. In a medium bowl whisk evaporated milk and egg until well mixed. Pour egg mixture into the beef and stir well to combine. Add cooked pasta, ¾ of shredded cheese, and carefully stir to coat. Top with crushed tortilla chips and remaining cheese.

5. Bake 30 minutes, or until casserole is bubbling and top is melted and browned. Cool 5 minutes before serving.

# No-Boil Baked Ziti

*This no-boil take on the classic is easy for any night of the week, and impressive enough to serve guests!*

**PREP TIME:** 10 minutes
**COOK TIME:** 1 hour 10 minutes

**INGREDIENTS | SERVES 8**

1 (24-ounce) jar marinara or tomato sauce

1½ cups water

½ teaspoon ground fennel

½ teaspoon oregano

¼ teaspoon crushed red pepper flakes

8 ounces ziti, uncooked

1 (15-ounce) container ricotta cheese, divided

3 cups shredded mozzarella, divided

½ cup grated Parmesan

1. Heat oven to 350°F and lightly spray a 4-quart Dutch oven with nonstick cooking spray.

2. In a medium bowl combine marinara sauce, water, fennel, oregano, and red pepper flakes. Once well combined stir in pasta, half the ricotta cheese, and 2 cups mozzarella cheese.

3. Pour half the pasta mixture into the prepared Dutch oven. Dollop remaining ricotta cheese evenly onto mixture in the pot, then pour remaining pasta mixture over top. Cover with a lid and bake 50 minutes.

4. Remove lid and spread the remaining mozzarella and Parmesan cheese evenly over the top. Bake another 10 minutes, or until cheese is melted and bubbling. Cool 10 minutes before serving.

# Roasted Vegetable Lasagna

*This dish is the perfect way to use up leftover roasted vegetables from the grill.*

**PREP TIME:** 40 minutes
**COOK TIME:** 1 hour 45 minutes
**INGREDIENTS | SERVES 8**

2 tablespoons olive oil
2 medium zucchini, cut into ½" slices
2 medium yellow squash, cut into ½" slices
1 pint button mushrooms, quartered
½ teaspoon salt
½ teaspoon freshly cracked black pepper
2 tablespoons unsalted butter
1 (28-ounce) can diced fire-roasted tomatoes
2 cloves garlic
½ teaspoon ground fennel
½ teaspoon oregano
1 (15-ounce) container ricotta cheese
1 large egg
½ cup grated Parmesan cheese
2 cups shredded mozzarella cheese, divided
1 (9-ounce) package no-boil lasagna noodles

1. In a large zip-top bag add olive oil, zucchini, squash, mushrooms, salt, and pepper. Let stand at room temperature 30 minutes.

2. Heat oven to 425°F.

3. Spread vegetables out on a baking sheet in a single layer. Roast until vegetables are tender, about 10 minutes. Remove from oven and let cool.

4. In a 6- or 8-quart ovenproof Dutch oven over medium heat combine butter, tomatoes, garlic, fennel, and oregano. Cook, stirring often, until mixture comes to a boil and reduces slightly, about 20 minutes. Transfer sauce to a bowl to cool.

5. Wipe out the Dutch oven and spray lightly with nonstick cooking spray. Reduce heat of oven to 375°F.

6. In a medium bowl combine ricotta, egg, Parmesan cheese, and 1 cup mozzarella. Mix well.

7. To assemble, spread a few tablespoons of sauce on the bottom of the Dutch oven. Break pasta noodles in half and create a layer using ¼ of the noodles on the bottom of the pot. Spread ¼ of ricotta mixture over noodles, then layer ⅓ of roasted vegetables and ⅓ of tomato sauce. Repeat this process ending with pasta and ricotta on top. Sprinkle remaining mozzarella over lasagna.

8. Cover the Dutch oven with the lid and bake 50 minutes, then remove lid and bake 15–20 minutes more, or until cheese is brown and bubbling. Cool 10 minutes before serving.

# Turkey "Lasagna" Pie

*Cook the lasagna noodles in the same Dutch oven in which you'll eventually assemble the lasagna. Baking in a deep Dutch oven means you don't have to worry about the lasagna boiling over, and it cooks more evenly than it would in a rectangular pan.*

**PREP TIME:** 10 minutes
**COOK TIME:** 1 hour 20 minutes

**INGREDIENTS | SERVES 8**

12 dried whole-wheat or regular lasagna noodles

½ cup basil pesto

1 teaspoon grated lemon peel

1 large egg, beaten

1 (15-ounce) carton ricotta cheese

2 cups grated mozzarella cheese, divided

¼ teaspoon salt

¼ teaspoon freshly cracked black pepper

2 cups chopped fresh spinach

½ cup chopped walnuts, toasted if desired, divided

2 cups chopped cooked turkey, divided

1 (8-ounce) package fresh button or cremini mushrooms, cleaned and thinly sliced

1 (24-ounce) bottle marinara or pasta sauce, divided

½ cup dry red wine

Fresh Italian flat-leaf parsley leaves, optional

1. Heat oven to 375°F. Cook lasagna noodles according to the package directions until almost tender. Drain noodles and rinse in cold water. Drain and set aside.

2. In a small bowl, mix pesto and lemon peel; set aside.

3. In a medium bowl add egg, ricotta cheese, 1 cup mozzarella cheese, salt, and pepper and mix well.

4. Lightly coat 6- or 8-quart Dutch oven with nonstick cooking spray. Arrange 4 noodles in the bottom of the pan, trimming and overlapping them to fit.

5. Top with spinach. Sprinkle with half the walnuts. Spread half the ricotta cheese mixture evenly over walnuts. Spread half the pesto mixture evenly over ricotta, then sprinkle half the turkey over pesto. Pour half the pasta sauce evenly over turkey. Top with another layer of noodles. Top with mushrooms. Spread remaining ricotta cheese mixture over mushrooms. Spread remaining pesto mixture over ricotta. Sprinkle remaining turkey over pesto, and then pour the rest of the pasta sauce over turkey. Top with another layer of noodles.

6. Pour wine into the empty marinara sauce jar, screw on lid and shake. Pour over top layer of noodles.

7. Cover the Dutch oven and bake 45 minutes. Remove the cover. Sprinkle remaining mozzarella cheese over top. Bake 15–30 minutes, or until cheese is melted and bubbly. Let set 10 minutes and then garnish with parsley if desired. To serve, cut into pizza slice–style wedges.

# Spicy Sausage Lasagna

*Fresh hot Italian sausage links can be found in most grocery stores in the meat market, and taste better than the ready-cooked variety. If you prefer sweet Italian sausage feel free to use that here.*

**PREP TIME:** 10 minutes
**COOK TIME:** 1 hour 35 minutes

**INGREDIENTS | SERVES 8**

1 pound fresh hot Italian sausage links

1 (24-ounce) jar marinara sauce

1 cup water

½ teaspoon salt

½ teaspoon ground fennel

½ teaspoon oregano

½ teaspoon freshly cracked black pepper

1 (15-ounce) container ricotta cheese

1 large egg

½ cup grated Parmesan cheese

2 cups shredded mozzarella cheese, divided

1 (9-ounce) package no-boil lasagna noodles

1. In an ovenproof 6- or 8-quart Dutch oven over medium heat, combine Italian sausages, marinara sauce, water, salt, fennel, oregano, and pepper. Bring mixture to a boil and then reduce heat to medium-low and simmer 20 minutes, or until sausages are cooked through. Remove sausages to a cutting board to cool, then slice into ½" pieces. Pour sauce into a bowl to cool.

2. Heat oven to 425°F.

3. Wipe out the Dutch oven and spray lightly with nonstick cooking spray. Reduce the heat of the oven to 375°F.

4. In a medium bowl combine ricotta, egg, Parmesan cheese, and 1 cup mozzarella. Mix well.

5. To assemble, spread a few tablespoons of sauce on the bottom of the Dutch oven. Break the pasta noodles in half and create a layer using ¼ of the noodles on the bottom of the pot. Spread ¼ of ricotta mixture over the noodles, then layer ⅓ of sliced sausage and ⅓ of marinara sauce. Repeat this process ending with pasta and ricotta on top. Sprinkle remaining mozzarella over the lasagna.

6. Cover the Dutch oven with the lid and bake 50 minutes, then remove lid and bake 15–20 minutes more, or until the cheese is brown and bubbling. Cool 10 minutes before serving.

# Spinach Alfredo Shells

*This dish is creamy, rich, and perfect for entertaining. For a little kick try adding cooked crumbled hot Italian sausage to the cheese mixture.*

**PREP TIME:** 10 minutes
**COOK TIME:** 1 hour 5 minutes

**INGREDIENTS | SERVES 8**

1 (12-ounce) package jumbo pasta shells

1 (10-ounce) bag chopped frozen spinach, thawed and drained well

1 (15-ounce) container ricotta cheese

2 cups shredded mozzarella, divided

½ teaspoon oregano

¼ teaspoon crushed red pepper flakes

¼ teaspoon salt

1 teaspoon freshly cracked black pepper, divided

8 tablespoons (1 stick) unsalted butter

1 clove garlic, peeled and minced

2 cups heavy cream

1 cup grated Parmesan cheese

⅛ teaspoon grated nutmeg

## Alfredo Sauce

Alfredo sauce was created in Rome during the 1920s by Alfredo di Lello. The dish combines hot fettuccine noodles with a sauce made of butter, heavy cream, and Parmesan cheese. In this recipe black pepper and a bit of nutmeg are added to enhance the flavor. The sauce is so popular it can also be found in other dishes such as pizza or casseroles.

1. Cook pasta in salted water according to package directions. Drain and rinse with cool water. Set aside.

2. Heat oven to 350°F.

3. In a large bowl combine spinach, ricotta cheese, 1 cup mozzarella, oregano, red pepper flakes, salt, and ¼ teaspoon pepper. Mix until well combined, then spoon cheese mixture into cooked pasta shells. Set aside.

4. In an ovenproof 6-quart Dutch oven over medium heat add butter. Once butter has melted add garlic and cook 30 seconds. Do not let butter or garlic brown. Add heavy cream and let sauce come to a boil, then reduce heat to medium-low and reduce the sauce until it thickly coats the back of a spoon, about 5 minutes. Remove the Dutch oven from heat and stir in Parmesan cheese, remaining pepper, and nutmeg. Spoon out half of the sauce and reserve.

5. Arrange stuffed pasta shells open side up in the Dutch oven. Top with reserved sauce, and sprinkle remaining mozzarella cheese evenly over the shells.

6. Cover and bake 30 minutes, then remove lid and bake 10–15 minutes more, or until cheese is bubbling. Cool 5 minutes before serving.

# Baked Rigatoni with Mini Chicken Meatballs

*Kids will love the mini meatballs in this dish, and rolling the meatballs is a great job for the little ones!*

**PREP TIME:** 1 hour 15 minutes
**COOK TIME:** 1 hour 20 minutes

**INGREDIENTS | SERVES 8**

1 pound ground chicken

⅓ cup panko bread crumbs

2 large eggs, beaten

½ cup grated Parmesan cheese

½ medium onion, peeled and finely chopped

1 clove garlic, peeled and minced

1 teaspoon tomato paste

½ teaspoon ground fennel

½ teaspoon oregano

¼ teaspoon salt

¼ teaspoon freshly cracked black pepper

4 tablespoons olive oil, divided

1 (24-ounce) jar marinara sauce

1 cup water

1 (16-ounce) box rigatoni pasta

2 cups shredded mozzarella cheese, divided

1. In a large bowl combine chicken, bread crumbs, eggs, Parmesan cheese, onion, garlic, tomato paste, fennel, oregano, salt, and pepper. Mix until thoroughly combined, then shape into ½" balls. (It helps to moisten your hands with water to shape the balls.) Place the meatballs on a baking sheet and refrigerate, uncovered, 1 hour.

2. Heat oven to 350°F.

3. Heat an ovenproof 6- or 8-quart Dutch oven over medium heat. Add 1 tablespoon olive oil and brown ¼ of the meatballs on all sides. Removed from pan and repeat with remaining olive oil and meatballs. Set aside.

4. Add marinara sauce and water to the Dutch oven. Once well combined add meatballs back to the pot along with rigatoni pasta and 1 cup shredded mozzarella cheese. Cover with lid and bake 50 minutes.

5. Uncover and top with remaining cheese. Bake an additional 10–15 minutes, or until cheese is melted and bubbling. Cool 10 minutes before serving.

# Beef Stroganoff

*This dish comes from Russia and was made popular in the 1950s*
*by servicemen returning from Europe after WWII.*

**PREP TIME:** 15 minutes
**COOK TIME:** 1 hour 50 minutes

**INGREDIENTS | SERVES 4**

1 pound beef stew meat
1 tablespoon vegetable oil
¼ pound mushrooms, sliced
½ small onion, peeled and chopped
2 cloves garlic, peeled and minced
½ teaspoon dried oregano
¼ teaspoon salt
¼ teaspoon pepper
¼ teaspoon dried thyme
1 bay leaf
1½ cups beef broth
¼ cup sherry
½ cup sour cream
¼ cup all-purpose flour
2 tablespoons water
½–¾ cup cooked noodles per person

1. Heat oven to 325°F. Trim any excess fat from beef and cut meat into 1" cubes.

2. Place an ovenproof 6- or 8-quart Dutch oven over medium-high heat. Once warmed, add oil and beef. Let beef cook until each side is browned, about 5 minutes. Drain the fat.

3. Add mushrooms, onion, and garlic. Cook 5–7 minutes. Add oregano, salt, pepper, thyme, bay leaf, broth, and sherry, stirring to combine.

4. Cook, uncovered, in the middle of the oven for 1½ hours. Discard bay leaf. Remove beef from Dutch oven and cover to keep warm.

5. Place Dutch oven over low heat on the stovetop.

6. In a small bowl, combine sour cream, flour, and water. Slowly pour 1 cup of hot liquid from the Dutch oven into sour cream mixture. Once everything is combined, stir dairy mixture into the Dutch oven and whisk to combine. Stir in reserved meat and simmer an additional 3 minutes.

7. Pour stroganoff mixture over noodles and serve immediately.

# Chicken Tortellini and Broccoli Casserole

*To turn this into a southwestern casserole, substitute ground cumin and a pinch of cayenne pepper for the dried parsley and add a layer of crushed tortilla chips to the top of the casserole before you add the Colby cheese.*

**PREP TIME:** 10 minutes
**COOK TIME:** 1 hour

**INGREDIENTS | SERVES 8**

1 (9-ounce) package cheese tortellini

3 tablespoons extra-virgin olive oil

2 cups broccoli florets

1 medium yellow onion, peeled and diced

1 medium red bell pepper, seeded and diced

3 tablespoons all-purpose flour

¾ cup chicken broth

¾ cup milk

1 teaspoon dried parsley

4 cups diced cooked chicken

6 ounces Monterey jack cheese, grated

4 ounces Colby cheese, grated

## Grated Cheese

Each ounce of soft cheese like Cheddar or Colby equals ¼ cup of grated cheese. Keep this in mind when you go to the grocery store and pick up the bags of shredded cheese. They'll tell you the weight but not the measurement in cups, so it's up to you to remember that part.

1. Heat oven to 325°F.

2. In 6- or 8-quart Dutch oven, cook tortellini according to package directions; drain and keep warm.

3. Wipe out the Dutch oven. Add oil and bring it to temperature over medium-high heat. Add broccoli, onion, and bell pepper and stir-fry about 3 minutes, or until crisp-tender. Remove broccoli from Dutch oven and set it aside with cooked tortellini and keep warm.

4. Reduce heat to low and whisk flour into oil and remaining vegetables in the Dutch oven, stirring constantly, until smooth.

5. Stir in broth, milk, and parsley. Bring to a boil over medium heat, stirring constantly, then remove from heat.

6. Stir in chicken, Monterey jack cheese, tortellini, and broccoli. Bake uncovered 30 minutes, or until bubbly. Sprinkle Colby cheese over the top of casserole; return to oven and bake 10 minutes, or until cheese topping is melted.

# Beefy Ravioli Bake

*Fresh ravioli can be found in the deli section of most grocery stores, but if your store does not carry them you can use frozen ravioli instead.*

**PREP TIME:** 10 minutes
**COOK TIME:** 50 minutes

**INGREDIENTS | SERVES 8**

1 pound ground beef

1 medium onion, peeled and finely chopped

2 cloves garlic, peeled and minced

½ teaspoon ground fennel

½ teaspoon oregano

½ teaspoon salt

¼ teaspoon freshly cracked black pepper

1 (28-ounce) can diced tomatoes, undrained

2 pounds fresh cheese ravioli

1 cup shredded mozzarella cheese

1. Heat oven to 350°F.

2. Heat an ovenproof 6- or 8-quart Dutch oven over medium heat. Once it is hot add ground beef and cook until beef is thoroughly browned. Add onion and garlic and cook, stirring frequently, until onion has softened, about 5 minutes. Add fennel, oregano, salt, and pepper and stir to combine.

3. Add diced tomatoes with their juice and ravioli and stir to combine. Cover with the lid and bake 30 minutes, or until ravioli are tender.

4. Remove lid and top with shredded cheese. Bake 10–15 minutes or until cheese is melted and bubbling. Cool 5 minutes before serving.

# Hot Chicken Fajita Pasta Salad

*You can easily stretch this recipe to 8 servings by serving the pasta salad over lettuce or along with baked corn tortilla chips.*

**PREP TIME:** 15 minutes
**COOK TIME:** 30 minutes

**INGREDIENTS | SERVES 6**

1 (3-pound) rotisserie chicken

12 ounces dried egg noodles

2 tablespoons extra-virgin olive oil

1 medium yellow onion, peeled, halved, and thinly sliced

1 medium red sweet pepper, seeded and cut into thin strips

1 fresh Anaheim chili pepper, seeded and cut into thin strips

2 tablespoons chopped fresh cilantro

1 (8-ounce) carton sour cream

½ cup chipotle liquid meat marinade

2 tablespoons lime juice

1 teaspoon chili powder

1 teaspoon ground cumin

½ teaspoon dried red pepper flakes, crushed

1. Remove and discard the skin from chicken; remove meat from the bones and shred it. Set aside.

2. In a 6- or 8-quart Dutch oven, cook noodles according to the package directions; drain and keep warm. Wipe out the Dutch oven, add oil, and bring it to temperature over medium heat. Add onion, sweet pepper, Anaheim pepper, and cilantro. Sauté 5 minutes, or until crisp-tender.

3. Add sour cream, marinade, lime juice, chili powder, cumin, and crushed red pepper to a medium bowl; stir to mix.

4. Add the cooked noodles, chicken, and sour cream mixture to the sautéed vegetables; toss to coat. Leave on the heat long enough to reheat the noodles and warm the chicken if necessary. Serve warm.

## Heat Hints

The dried red pepper flakes and Anaheim chili pepper will add heat to Hot Chicken Fajita Pasta Salad, which will be somewhat tempered by the cooked noodles and sour cream. If you prefer a milder taste, reduce the amount you add at first, taste the salad, and then add more if needed.

# Chicken Tetrazzini

*This is an easy one-dish meal, and the leftovers are great reheated the next day for lunch!*

**PREP TIME:** 15 minutes
**COOK TIME:** 45 minutes

**INGREDIENTS | SERVES 8**

1 (3-pound) roasted chicken

8 ounces dried spaghetti or linguine, broken in half

12 ounces fresh asparagus, trimmed and cut into 1" pieces

2 tablespoons unsalted butter

8 ounces small whole fresh button or cremini mushrooms, cleaned and sliced

1 large red sweet pepper, seeded and cut into 1" pieces

1 large yellow sweet pepper, seeded and cut into 1" pieces

¼ cup all-purpose flour

⅛ teaspoon freshly cracked black pepper

1 (14-ounce) can chicken broth

¾ cup milk

2 ounces Swiss cheese, grated

1 tablespoon finely shredded lemon peel, divided

1½ cups bread cubes

1 tablespoon extra-virgin olive oil

2 tablespoons snipped fresh parsley, optional

1. Heat oven to 350°F.

2. Remove and discard the skin from chicken; remove meat from the bones and shred it. Set aside.

3. In 6- or 8-quart Dutch oven, cook spaghetti according to package directions. Add asparagus during the last minute of the cooking. Drain; set aside and keep warm.

4. Wipe out the Dutch oven; add butter and melt it over medium heat. Add mushrooms and peppers and sauté 8 minutes, or until mushrooms are tender. Stir in flour and black pepper until well combined. Whisk in broth and milk; cook, stirring frequently, until thickened and bubbly, about 5 minutes.

5. Add cooked spaghetti, asparagus, chicken, Swiss cheese, and half the lemon peel; toss gently to coat.

6. In a medium-sized bowl, toss together bread cubes, olive oil, and remaining lemon peel; spread on top of spaghetti mixture. Bake uncovered 15 minutes, or until bread cubes are golden brown. Let stand 5 minutes before serving. Garnish with parsley before serving, if desired.

## Bread Cubes Wisdom

One thick-cut slice of bread will make about ¾ cup of bread cubes. Keep in mind that the cubes will only be as good as the bread you use to make them. Sourdough bread works well in this Chicken Tetrazzini recipe.

# Creamy Chicken Noodle Bake

*This creamy noodle dish is perfect for cold days, and makes a satisfying dinner with some sautéed green beans and a hunk of Crusty No-Knead Bread (Chapter 3).*

**PREP TIME:** 10 minutes
**COOK TIME:** 1 hour 10 minutes

**INGREDIENTS | SERVES 8**

4 boneless, skinless chicken breasts, about 1 pound total

2 cups chicken broth

2 cups water

1 (12-ounce) package wide egg noodles

6 tablespoons unsalted butter, divided

1 medium onion, peeled and chopped

1 stalk celery, chopped

1 medium carrot, peeled and chopped

1 clove garlic, peeled and minced

¼ teaspoon thyme

¼ teaspoon crushed red pepper flakes

¼ teaspoon salt

¼ teaspoon freshly cracked black pepper

¼ cup all-purpose flour

2 cups half and half

1 cup panko bread crumbs

1. In an ovenproof 6- or 8-quart Dutch oven add chicken breasts, chicken broth, and water. Bring mixture to a boil over high heat and cook 10 minutes, or until chicken is cooked through. Remove chicken breasts from liquid and set aside to cool. Once cool enough to handle shred chicken.

2. Add egg noodles to the boiling broth and cook according to the package directions, reducing the cooking time by 1 minute. Drain noodles, reserving the cooking liquid.

3. Heat oven to 350°F.

4. Return the Dutch oven to the heat and add 4 tablespoons butter. Once it foams add onion, celery, and carrot and cook, stirring frequently, until vegetables are tender, about 5 minutes. Add garlic, thyme, red pepper flakes, salt, and pepper and cook until garlic is fragrant, about 30 seconds.

5. Sprinkle flour over vegetables and cook until flour is moistened and is starting to turn golden brown, about 3 minutes.

6. Whisk in 1½ cups of reserved cooking liquid, making sure to whisk out any lumps, then whisk in half and half. Stir in shredded chicken and egg noodles. Remove the Dutch oven from the heat.

7. Melt remaining butter in the microwave and combine with bread crumbs. Top chicken mixture with bread crumbs, then bake 30–40 minutes, or until bread crumbs are browned and casserole is bubbling around the edges. Cool 10 minutes before serving.

# Turkey and Noodle Casserole

*This easy recipe leaves you all evening to enjoy this satisfying comfort food.*

**PREP TIME:** 10 minutes
**COOK TIME:** 1 hour

**INGREDIENTS | SERVES 8**

1 pound (16 ounces) dried extra-wide egg noodles

1 tablespoon extra-virgin olive oil

6 slices bacon, chopped

2½ pounds ground turkey

1 pound white mushrooms, cleaned and sliced

1 large yellow onion, peeled and diced

½ teaspoon salt

½ teaspoon freshly cracked black pepper

1 tablespoon dried thyme

1 cup dry white wine

2 cups chicken broth

1 cup heavy cream

¼ teaspoon freshly grated nutmeg

8 ounces Gruyère cheese, grated

1 cup plain bread crumbs

2 tablespoons unsalted butter, melted

1. Cook noodles in a 6- or 8-quart Dutch oven according to package directions. Drain, set aside, and keep warm.

2. Heat oven to 350°F.

3. Wipe out the Dutch oven. Add oil and bring it to temperature over medium-high heat. Add bacon and cook 3 minutes until bacon begins to brown at the edges and renders its fat.

4. Add ground turkey and cook until brown, crumbling it apart, about 8 minutes. Add mushrooms and onions and cook until tender, about 5 minutes. Sprinkle with salt, pepper, and thyme.

5. Stir in wine, deglazing the Dutch oven by scraping up any food stuck to the bottom of the pan. Stir in broth and bring to a boil; boil 2 minutes, stirring occasionally. Lower heat to a simmer and whisk in cream.

6. Stir in nutmeg and cheese. Stir in noodles. Top with bread crumbs; drizzle melted butter over bread crumbs. Bake 30 minutes, or until bread crumbs are browned.

# Seafood Pasta

*Herbs can add a distinctive touch to your cooking. Try a variety of fresh herbs in this recipe to create a wide range of different flavors.*

**PREP TIME:** 10 minutes
**COOK TIME:** 35 minutes

**INGREDIENTS | SERVES 4–6**

1 pound dried linguine

2 tablespoons extra-virgin olive oil

2 celery stalks, diced

1 small yellow onion, peeled and diced

4 cloves garlic, peeled and minced

½ teaspoon dried basil

¼ teaspoon dried dill

¼ teaspoon dried fennel

½ teaspoon salt

½ teaspoon freshly cracked black pepper

Pinch dried red pepper flakes

1 (16-ounce) can diced tomatoes, undrained

½ cup white wine or chicken broth

4 tablespoons unsalted butter

1 pound grouper, salmon, or snapper, cut into bite-sized pieces

1 (10-ounce) can boiled baby clams or (6.5-ounce) can of whole shelled mussels

½ pound shrimp, peeled and deveined

¼ cup chopped fresh parsley

1. In a 6- or 8-quart Dutch oven cook the pasta to al dente according to package directions. Drain, set aside, and keep warm.

2. Wipe out the Dutch oven. Add oil over medium heat. Once the oil is hot and starts to simmer add the celery and cook 3–5 minutes, or until soft. Add onion and sauté until transparent. Add garlic and cook for an additional 30 seconds.

3. Stir in dried herbs, salt, pepper, crushed red pepper, and tomatoes. Add wine or broth; bring to a simmer and then add butter, fish, and clams or mussels. Cover and simmer about 5 minutes.

4. Add the shrimp; simmer until shrimp are firm and pink in color, about 2–3 minutes. Serve over pasta, topped with chopped parsley.

# Baked Crab and Orzo Pasta

*Orzo is small rice-shaped pasta that is often used in salads and soups. Here it is baked with sweet lump crabmeat and a little Parmesan cheese in a dish sure to delight crab lovers!*

**PREP TIME:** 10 minutes
**COOK TIME:** 1 hour 10 minutes
**INGREDIENTS | SERVES 8**

1 (12-ounce) package orzo
6 tablespoons unsalted butter, divided
1 medium onion, peeled and chopped
1 medium red bell pepper, seeded and chopped
1 stalk celery, chopped
1 clove garlic, peeled and minced
1 teaspoon seafood seasoning, such as Old Bay
¼ teaspoon thyme
¼ teaspoon crushed red pepper flakes
¼ teaspoon salt
¼ teaspoon freshly cracked black pepper
¼ cup all-purpose flour
1½ cups seafood stock or vegetable stock
2 cups half and half
1 pound fresh lump crabmeat
1 cup panko bread crumbs

## Seafood Stock

Seafood stock is usually made of seafood shells (shrimp, crab, and lobster are common), along with vegetables, a little tomato paste, and fresh herbs. One pound of shells are covered with water and simmered 1 hour. They should not come to a boil. Any scum from the shells is skimmed off during this time. Next, 1 onion, 1 carrot, 1 rib of celery, a bay leaf, a few sprigs of thyme, and 1 teaspoon of tomato paste are added and the stock is simmered 30 minutes more. It is strained well and cooled.

1. Cook orzo according to the package directions, reducing the cooking time by 1 minute. Drain the pasta and set aside.

2. Heat oven to 350°F.

3. Heat an ovenproof 6- or 8-quart Dutch oven over medium heat and add 4 tablespoons butter. Once it foams add onion, bell pepper, and celery and cook, stirring frequently, until vegetables are tender, about 5 minutes.

4. Add garlic, seafood seasoning, thyme, red pepper flakes, salt, and pepper and cook until garlic is fragrant, about 30 seconds. Sprinkle flour over vegetables and cook until flour is moistened and starting to turn golden brown, about 3 minutes.

5. Whisk in seafood stock or vegetable stock, making sure to whisk out any lumps, then whisk in half and half. Fold in lump crabmeat and orzo. Remove the Dutch oven from the heat.

6. Melt remaining butter in the microwave and combine with bread crumbs. Top chicken mixture with bread crumbs, then bake 30–40 minutes, or until bread crumbs are browned and casserole is bubbling around the edges. Cool 10 minutes before serving.

# Orzo Pilaf

*Orzo makes a nice change of pace from traditional rice pilaf, and toasting it before cooking in the liquid gives this pilaf a luscious, nutty flavor.*

**PREP TIME:** 10 minutes
**COOK TIME:** 30 minutes

**INGREDIENTS | SERVES 8**

2 tablespoons unsalted butter

1 tablespoon olive oil

2 shallots, minced

4 cloves garlic, peeled and minced

1 (16-ounce) box orzo pasta

4 cups vegetable broth

1 medium red bell pepper, seeded and chopped

1 cup frozen baby peas

½ cup heavy cream

½ cup grated Havarti cheese

½ cup grated Parmesan cheese

1. In 6- or 8-quart Dutch oven melt butter with olive oil over medium heat. Once melted add shallots and garlic and cook until tender, about 4 minutes.

2. Add orzo and cook until it begins to turn light brown around the edges, about 3 minutes. Remove from heat and add vegetable broth.

3. Return to heat and bring to a simmer. Cover and simmer 7 minutes. Uncover and add bell pepper and peas, then cover and cook 4–5 minutes longer, or until pasta is tender and vegetables are hot.

4. Add cream and cheeses, and cook until cheeses melt. Serve immediately.

## Keep It Safe

This orzo dish is quite portable, but it does include perishable ingredients, so you have to use the two-hour rule. Cover the pan with its lid, then wrap several times in heavy-duty foil. Wrap this in a blanket or place in an insulated carrier to take to the party.

# Savory Sides

# Scalloped Potatoes

*These creamy potatoes are wonderful served with grilled steak, roasted chicken, or cedar plank salmon. Once the potatoes are sliced, do not rinse them. You need the natural starch to thicken the sauce.*

**PREP TIME:** 15 minutes
**COOK TIME:** 1 hour 10 minutes
**INGREDIENTS | SERVES 8**

2 cups heavy cream

2 cups whole milk

1 clove garlic, peeled and smashed

2 tablespoons unsalted butter

½ teaspoon salt

¼ teaspoon freshly cracked black pepper

⅛ teaspoon grated nutmeg

6 large russet potatoes, peeled and thinly sliced

1 cup shredded Gruyère cheese

## Picking Potatoes

Certain types of potatoes are better than others in certain dishes. For soups, stews, and casseroles go with starchy potatoes like russets. For salads, roasting, and steaming go with a waxy potato like red or fingerling. No matter what kind of potato you are shopping for they should be smooth, firm, and have no soft spots or growths on the outside for the best flavor and texture.

1. In an ovenproof 6- or 8-quart Dutch oven add cream, 2 cups milk, garlic, butter, salt, pepper, and nutmeg. Heat mixture over medium heat, stirring constantly, until it comes to a boil. Add sliced potatoes, reduce heat to low, and simmer 10 minutes.

2. Heat oven to 350°F.

3. After 10 minutes, carefully remove potatoes with a slotted spoon to a bowl and set aside. Increase heat to medium, bring milk mixture to a boil and, stirring constantly, let mixture reduce by half, about 8 minutes.

4. Turn off heat, return potatoes to the Dutch oven, shaking it gently to evenly distribute potato slices, and top with shredded cheese. Bake 25–30 minutes, or until potatoes are bubbling around the edges and cheese has browned. Cool 10 minutes before serving.

# Potatoes Au Gratin

*Cooking this dish in a Dutch oven should give you crunchier edges and crust. Use an enameled Dutch oven, or a well-seasoned cast-iron Dutch oven, when making this dish to prevent sticking.*

**PREP TIME:** 20 minutes
**COOK TIME:** 1 hour 15 minutes
**INGREDIENTS | SERVES 6**

2 tablespoons olive oil
1 tablespoon unsalted butter
1 small onion, peeled and finely chopped
1 large clove garlic, peeled and minced
1 tablespoon all-purpose flour
1¼ cups milk
1½ cups heavy cream
1 cup shredded Gruyère cheese
¼ teaspoon salt
¼ teaspoon freshly cracked black pepper
2½ pounds potatoes, peeled and sliced ⅛" thick
¼ cup shredded Parmesan cheese

## Melty Cheese Substitutes

Gruyère and Emmenthaler are great cheeses to use in dishes like this when you want a subtly complex flavor and smooth melting. But if you can't find Gruyère cheese, or are looking for a more economical substitute, you can substitute Monterey jack for a milder flavor or a mixture of provolone and Cheddar cheese for a stronger flavor.

1. Heat oven to 350°F and place a rack in the center of oven.

2. Place an ovenproof 6-quart Dutch oven over medium heat. Once it is heated add olive oil, butter, and onion. Cook 3–5 minutes until translucent but not brown. Add garlic and cook 1 minute.

3. Add flour to the Dutch oven and stir 1 minute. Slowly add milk, stirring continually to prevent lumps. Slowly add cream, stirring continually until it just comes to a simmer. Reduce heat to low and simmer until slightly thickened, about 5 minutes.

4. Add Gruyère cheese and stir until it melts. Turn off the heat.

5. Sprinkle salt and pepper on potatoes. Slowly add them to the pan, a few at a time. Use a spoon to push potatoes to the bottom of the Dutch oven and make even layers.

6. Once all of potatoes have been added, sprinkle Parmesan cheese on top and bake 45 minutes. Let it rest 10 minutes before serving.

# Sweet Potato Casserole with Praline Topping

*This dish is the perfect sweet foil to a savory meal. It is creamy, crunchy, and sweet enough to complement things like salty ham, roast beef, and roasted turkey.*

**PREP TIME:** 20 minutes
**COOK TIME:** 1 hour 20 minutes

**INGREDIENTS | SERVES 12**

10 small sweet potatoes, peeled and cut into 1" cubes

2 sticks unsalted butter, divided

1½ teaspoons salt, divided

1 teaspoon grated nutmeg, divided

½ cup sugar

⅓ cup honey

1¼ cups packed light brown sugar, divided

3 large eggs, beaten

3 cups half and half or whole milk, warmed

1 teaspoon vanilla

1 cup all-purpose flour

½ teaspoon cinnamon

1. In an ovenproof 8-quart Dutch oven add the cubed sweet potatoes and enough water to cover. Bring the mixture to a boil over high heat and cook until the sweet potatoes are fork tender, about 10 minutes. Drain well and transfer the sweet potatoes to the work bowl of a stand mixer, or a large bowl with a hand mixer.

2. Heat oven to 375°F and lightly spray the Dutch oven with nonstick cooking spray.

3. To the hot sweet potatoes add 1 stick butter, 1¼ teaspoons salt, ½ teaspoon nutmeg, sugar, honey, and ¼ cup brown sugar. Mix until the potatoes are smooth, about 3 minutes.

4. Add the eggs and warmed half and half and mix on low speed until thoroughly combined, about 3 minutes. Stir in the vanilla.

5. Pour the sweet potato mixture into the prepared Dutch oven and gently shake to remove any air bubbles. Set aside while you prepare the topping.

6. Dice the remaining butter and combine it in a medium bowl along with remaining salt, nutmeg, brown sugar, flour, and cinnamon. With your fingers rub the butter into the dry ingredients until the mixture is well mixed and crumbly. Spread the topping evenly over the sweet potato mixture.

7. Bake 35–45 minutes, or until the casserole has puffed all over and the topping is golden brown. Cool 10 minutes before serving.

# Roasted Root Vegetables

*If you want to add a touch of sweetness to this dish you can toss in ½ cup dried golden raisins or dried cranberries during the last 10 minutes of cooking time.*

**PREP TIME:** 10 minutes
**COOK TIME:** 50 minutes

**INGREDIENTS | SERVES 8**

2 tablespoons olive oil

2 small sweet potatoes, peeled and cut into 1½" chunks

1 cup baby carrots

1 cup pearl onions, peeled, or 1 large onion, peeled and cut into 6 wedges

1 pound baby potatoes, red, yellow, blue, or a mix of all three

½ teaspoon chopped fresh rosemary

½ teaspoon sea salt

½ teaspoon freshly ground black pepper

1. Heat oven to 400°F.

2. In an ovenproof 6- or 8-quart Dutch oven combine all ingredients and toss well to coat. Bake 40–50 minutes, stirring after 20 minutes, or until potatoes and carrots are fork tender. Serve hot.

# Down-Home Classic Green Beans

*This dish is great hot or warm and it can be made ahead of time and warmed later when ready to serve.*

**PREP TIME:** 10 minutes
**COOK TIME:** 15 minutes

**INGREDIENTS | SERVES 4–6**

3 slices bacon, diced

1 small onion, peeled and diced

1 pound fresh green beans, trimmed

1 russet potato, peeled and diced

½ cup chicken broth

1 clove garlic, peeled and minced

1 teaspoon salt

¼ teaspoon pepper

1. Place a 6-quart Dutch oven over medium heat. Once the Dutch oven is warmed, add bacon and onion and cook until bacon is brown but not crispy, about 5 minutes.

2. Add green beans, potato, chicken broth, garlic, salt, and pepper and cook 3–4 minutes.

3. Reduce heat to medium-low and cover. Cook 5 minutes. The potatoes should be almost soft and green beans should be bright green. Remove the lid and increase the heat to medium-high. Let the broth evaporate. Serve immediately.

# Creamed Mushrooms

*These mushrooms are a delicious side dish with roast beef, but can also be used as the filling for a mushroom omelet, or spooned over buttered egg noodles for a yummy vegetarian meal.*

**PREP TIME:** 10 minutes
**COOK TIME:** 35 minutes

**INGREDIENTS | SERVES 8**

4 tablespoons unsalted butter

3 pounds sliced fresh button or cremini mushrooms

2 tablespoons all-purpose flour

½ teaspoon salt

½ teaspoon freshly cracked black pepper

¼ teaspoon thyme

⅛ teaspoon crushed red pepper flakes

⅛ teaspoon grated nutmeg

¼ cup sherry

2 cups half and half

¼ cup chopped fresh parsley

1. Heat a 4-quart Dutch oven over medium heat. Once hot add butter and, once it has melted and starts to foam, add mushrooms and cook, stirring frequently, until mushrooms are tender, about 6–8 minutes.

2. Add flour, salt, pepper, thyme, red pepper, and nutmeg. Cook until flour mixture is just turning golden brown, about 3 minutes. Add sherry and half and half and stir well to combine.

3. Bring mixture to a boil, then reduce heat to medium-low and simmer until mushroom mixture is thick, about 8 minutes. Remove from the heat and stir in fresh parsley. Serve immediately.

## Mushrooms

Mushrooms are, technically speaking, the spore-bearing fruit body of a fungus. While that doesn't sound delicious, mushrooms add "umami" or savory flavor to soups, stews, casseroles, and other dishes. Offering a lot of nutrition, mushrooms are a good source of B vitamins, selenium, and potassium, among other nutrients. With improved cultivation techniques, it is now easy to find a wide variety of fresh mushrooms at most grocery stores. You can use other varieties of mushrooms such as cremini, maitake, and shiitake mushrooms in your favorite recipes.

# Green Beans with Bacon Dressing

*Blanching the green beans and shocking in ice water will help them retain their bright green color after roasting.*

**PREP TIME:** 15 minutes
**COOK TIME:** 35 minutes

**INGREDIENTS | SERVES 8**

12 cups water

1 teaspoon salt

2 pounds fresh green beans, trimmed

½ pound bacon, chopped

2 tablespoons unsalted butter

1 clove garlic, peeled and minced

1 teaspoon packed light brown sugar

½ teaspoon dry mustard powder

¼ teaspoon smoked paprika

¼ teaspoon freshly cracked black pepper

## Steam-in-the-Bag Green Beans

If you prefer, you can use fresh steam-in-the-bag green beans for this recipe. Just steam according to the package directions, then place the steamed beans in a bowl of ice water to shock the beans and stop the cooking. Be sure to check the beans after they have cooled and remove any rogue stems.

1. Bring water to a boil in an ovenproof 6- or 8-quart Dutch oven. Add salt and then green beans. Cook 3 minutes, then drain well and plunge immediately into a large bowl of ice water. Once cool drain well and pat dry with paper towels.

2. Heat oven to 375°F.

3. Return the Dutch oven to medium heat and add chopped bacon. Cook, stirring frequently, until the fat has rendered and bacon is crisp. Remove bacon with a slotted spoon to a paper towel–lined plate to drain. Pour off all but 2 tablespoons of bacon drippings.

4. Return the Dutch oven to the heat and add butter. Once butter has melted add garlic, brown sugar, dry mustard, paprika, and pepper. Cook until sugar has melted and garlic is fragrant, about 30 seconds. Add green beans and crisp bacon to the Dutch oven and toss to coat.

5. Roast in the oven uncovered 20 minutes or until the beans are tender. Serve hot.

# Cornbread Dressing

*This dressing is very wet before going into the oven, and that is exactly what you want because then the dressing will be very moist after baking. A little grated tart apple keeps this dressing from being too heavy.*

**PREP TIME:** 30 minutes
**COOK TIME:** 1 hour 20 minutes

**INGREDIENTS | SERVES 12**

2 (8.5-ounce) boxes cornbread mix, prepared per box directions

10 slices oven-dried white bread, cut into small pieces

½ cup unsalted butter

2 stalks celery, finely chopped

1 large onion, peeled and finely chopped

1 medium Granny Smith apple, peeled, cored, and grated

2 teaspoons poultry seasoning

1 teaspoon salt

½ teaspoon freshly cracked black pepper

6 cups chicken stock

5 large eggs, beaten

## Stuffing versus Dressing

Dressing and stuffing are the same basic thing, except stuffing is literally stuffed inside the cavity of the turkey. Stuffing a turkey is generally frowned upon as it is difficult to keep the turkey moist while you wait for the stuffing to reach a safe temperature to prevent foodborne illness. To mimic the flavor of stuffing add ½ cup of turkey drippings to your dressing before baking. It will add the rich turkey flavor without any of the danger of food poisoning.

1. Crumble cornbread in a large bowl along with the bread. Set aside.

2. In an ovenproof 8-quart Dutch oven over medium heat add butter. Once butter has melted and foamed add celery and onion. Cook until vegetables are tender, about 5 minutes, then add apple, poultry seasoning, salt, and pepper. Cook until the apple softens, about 3 minutes. Remove the Dutch oven from the heat.

3. Heat oven to 350°F.

4. Pour cornbread mixture into the Dutch oven and toss to combine bread and vegetables.

5. In a medium bowl combine stock and eggs and whisk to combine. Pour stock mixture over cornbread mixture then stir to evenly moisten all the bread. The mixture will be very wet.

6. Bake 50–60 minutes or until the dressing is golden brown all over, firm around the edges and just slightly jiggly in the center, and a knife inserted near the center of the dressing comes out clean. Cool 10 minutes before serving.

# Cornbread Soufflé

*This dish is not a true soufflé, but it will come out of the oven slightly puffed. If you want you can add a can of drained tomatoes with green chilies for extra flavor.*

**PREP TIME:** 15 minutes
**COOK TIME:** 55 minutes

**INGREDIENTS | SERVES 8**

8 ounces sour cream

4 tablespoons unsalted butter, melted and cooled

2 (10-ounce) bags frozen whole kernel corn, thawed and drained

1 (15-ounce) can cream-style corn

2 large eggs, beaten

1 (8.5-ounce) box cornbread mix

1 cup shredded jack or queso quesadilla cheese

1. Heat oven to 350°F and lightly spray an ovenproof 4-quart Dutch oven with nonstick cooking spray.

2. In a large bowl combine sour cream, butter, thawed corn, cream corn, and eggs and mix until well combined. Add cornbread mix and mix until the dry ingredients are just moistened. Add shredded cheese and fold until well mixed with no large lumps of dry mix remaining.

3. Pour mixture into the prepared Dutch oven and bake 45–50 minutes, or until a knife inserted into the center comes out clean. Cool 10 minutes before serving.

# Tex-Mex Pinto Beans

*Canned beans are used here to save time, but if you want to use dried beans soak them overnight, then cook them in simmering water until tender, about 1–1½ hours.*

**PREP TIME:** 10 minutes
**COOK TIME:** 20 minutes

**INGREDIENTS | SERVES 8**

2 tablespoons vegetable oil

1 medium onion, peeled and finely chopped

2 cloves garlic, peeled and minced

1 teaspoon cumin

1 (28-ounce) can pinto beans, drained and rinsed

1 (10-ounce) can tomatoes and green chilies, drained

½ (10-ounce) package frozen cut corn, thawed and drained

¼ cup roughly chopped cilantro

1 cup chicken or vegetable broth

1. Heat a 4-quart Dutch oven over medium heat. Once hot, add oil. When oil shimmers add onion and cook until tender, about 3 minutes. Add garlic and cumin and cook until garlic is fragrant, about 30 seconds.

2. Add remaining ingredients and bring to a boil. Reduce heat to medium-low and let beans simmer 15 minutes, or until most of the liquid has evaporated away and beans are hot. Serve hot.

# Corn Pudding

*When you stir this pudding halfway through cooking, the browned bits get mixed into the casserole, adding lots of flavor.*

**PREP TIME:** 10 minutes
**COOK TIME:** 1 hour 20 minutes

**INGREDIENTS | SERVES 8**

2 tablespoons unsalted butter

1 medium onion, peeled and chopped

2 cloves garlic, peeled and minced

1 medium green bell pepper, seeded and chopped

2 tablespoons all-purpose flour

½ teaspoon salt

⅛ teaspoon pepper

1 teaspoon dried thyme leaves

1 cup milk

1 (15-ounce) can cream-style corn

1½ cups frozen corn, thawed and drained

2 large eggs, beaten

1 cup shredded Gouda cheese

1. Heat oven to 375°F.

2. In an ovenproof 6- or 8-quart Dutch oven melt butter over medium heat. Add onion, garlic, and bell pepper and cook until tender, about 5 minutes. Add flour, salt, pepper, and thyme and cook until bubbly, about 3 minutes.

3. Add the milk and whisk until thickened and bubbling, about 5 minutes. Remove from heat and stir in cream-style corn, thawed corn, eggs, and cheese.

4. Bake 30 minutes, then stir mixture, pulling the browned sides into the center. Return to oven and bake 20–30 minutes longer until set and browned.

# Chinese Vegetables in Brown Sauce

*Brown sauce is a savory sauce that can be used with vegetables, beef, or chicken.
To make this vegetarian use vegetable broth and vegetarian oyster sauce.*

**PREP TIME:** 10 minutes
**COOK TIME:** 10 minutes

**INGREDIENTS | SERVES 4–6**

2 tablespoons vegetable oil

1 teaspoon fresh grated ginger

1 clove garlic, peeled and minced

1 carrot, peeled and cut into ⅛" slices

1 medium onion, peeled and thinly sliced

2 pints fresh shiitake mushrooms, stems removed

2 baby bok choy, sliced in half lengthwise

1 cup beef broth

2 tablespoons oyster sauce

1 tablespoon Shaoxing wine or sherry

1 teaspoon dark soy sauce

1 teaspoon sweet soy sauce, or
1 teaspoon light brown sugar

1 tablespoon cornstarch

1. Heat a 4-quart Dutch oven over high heat. Once hot add oil. When oil shimmers and starts to smoke lightly, add ginger and garlic. Cook until fragrant, about 10 seconds, then add carrots and onion and cook, stirring constantly, until just tender, about 2 minutes.

2. Add mushrooms and bok choy and cook until bok choy is bright green and mushrooms are starting to soften, about 2 minutes.

3. In a small bowl combine remaining ingredients and whisk to incorporate cornstarch. Pour into vegetables, then lower heat to medium-low and cook until sauce is thick and coats the vegetables, about 2–3 minutes. Serve immediately.

## Dutch Oven Stir-Fry

Most people think to make a good stir-fry you need a wok, but if you do not stir-fry often and do not want to invest in a wok you can use a Dutch oven in its place. Because Dutch ovens conduct and hold heat well they can be used for stir-fry dishes that cook quickly, or dishes that are first stir-fried then simmered in sauce. Be sure the Dutch oven is thoroughly heated before adding your oil, and that you stir your ingredients constantly to prevent burning.

# Puerto Rican Rice and Pigeon Peas

*If you want to serve this as a main dish, increase the amount of ham called for in the recipe. Otherwise, the recipe serves 8 as a side dish.*

**PREP TIME:** 1 hour 10 minutes
**COOK TIME:** 1 hour

**INGREDIENTS | SERVES 8**

½ pound dried gandules (pigeon peas)

3 cups water

1 tablespoon extra-virgin olive oil

1 ounce salt pork or bacon, chopped

2 ounces cooked ham, chopped

2 cloves garlic, peeled and minced

1 medium red bell pepper, seeded and diced

1 medium green pepper, seeded and diced

1 large yellow onion, peeled and diced

1 medium tomato, finely chopped

1 tablespoon Annatto Oil (see sidebar)

2 cups chicken broth or water

1 cup instant white rice

½ teaspoon salt

½ teaspoon freshly cracked black pepper

1. Add gandules and water to a 6-quart Dutch oven; bring to a boil over medium heat. Cover and turn off the heat; allow to sit 1 hour. Drain, reserving 1½ cups water.

2. Add oil, salt pork or bacon, and ham to the Dutch oven and sauté over medium heat 3 minutes. Add garlic, red pepper, green pepper, and onion; sauté until onion is transparent, about 5 minutes.

3. Add tomato, drained gandules, and reserved water. Bring to a boil; cover, lower heat, and simmer 15 minutes or until gandules are almost tender and have absorbed most of the liquid.

4. Stir in annatto oil and broth or water. Bring to a boil over medium heat. Add rice, cover, turn off the burner, and let set 30 minutes, or until the liquid is absorbed and rice is tender. Stir to fluff rice. Season with salt and pepper.

## Annatto Oil

Put ½ cup of peanut, sesame, or vegetable oil in a small heavy saucepan and heat until the oil smokes, or reaches about 350°F. Remove the pan from the heat and stir ¼ cup of annatto seeds into the oil. Cool and strain the seeds from the oil. Store in a covered jar in the refrigerator.

# Refried Beans

*Lard is the best fat to use for making authentic refried beans, but if you prefer not to use lard you can use bacon drippings, vegetable oil, or peanut oil instead.*

**PREP TIME:** 8–12 hours
**COOK TIME:** 2 hours 30 minutes

**INGREDIENTS | SERVES 12**

1 pound dried pinto beans

2 quarts water

½ bunch cilantro, tied with twine

¼ cup lard

1 medium onion, peeled and finely chopped

2 cloves garlic, peeled and minced

1 teaspoon cumin

1 teaspoon coriander

½ teaspoon salt

1. Rinse and sort dried beans in a colander, then transfer to a large bowl. Cover beans with 3" cold water, and let beans soak overnight in the refrigerator. Once soaked, drain the beans well.

2. Add soaked beans to a 6- or 8-quart Dutch oven along with 2 quarts water and bundle of cilantro and bring the mixture to a boil. Once beans come to a boil reduce the heat to low, cover, and let beans simmer 2 hours, stirring occasionally, until beans are tender. Once tender, reserve 1 cup cooking liquid, discard cilantro bundle, and drain beans. Set aside.

3. Return the Dutch oven to medium heat and add lard. Once lard has melted add onion and cook until tender, about 5 minutes. Add garlic, cumin, coriander, and salt and cook until garlic is fragrant, about 30 seconds.

4. Add cooked beans to the pot and, with a potato masher, roughly mash beans. Cook until beans are thick and hot, adding splashes of the reserved cooking liquid if beans are too thick. Serve hot.

# Boston Baked Beans

*The molasses in this recipe has made this dish a Boston specialty since the colonial days, when the city was part of the rum trade—molasses being a key ingredient in the making of rum.*

**PREP TIME:** 8–12 hours
**COOK TIME:** 4 hours 50 minutes

**INGREDIENTS | SERVES 6–8**

1 pound small white or pink beans

4 ounces salt pork, rind removed and cut into ½" cubes

3 slices bacon, cut into matchsticks

1 medium onion, peeled and finely chopped

½ cup molasses

2 tablespoons stone-ground or brown mustard

1 tablespoon apple cider vinegar

Pinch salt

Pinch pepper

1. Rinse beans and remove any bad beans or debris. Cover beans with 3" water and soak overnight. Place salt pork in water in the refrigerator overnight.

2. Heat oven to 300°F. Place salt pork and bacon in an ovenproof 6- or 8-quart Dutch oven over medium-high heat. Cook 7–9 minutes until bacon is crispy. Drain off almost all pork fat. Add onion and cook 7–8 minutes, or until the onion is tender.

3. Stir in molasses, mustard, drained beans, and 9 cups water. Turn heat to high and bring to a boil, then stir, cover with the lid, and transfer the Dutch oven to the oven and bake for 3 hours.

4. Remove the lid and stir. Cook another 1–1½ hours uncovered. The liquid should thicken to a syrup consistency. Stir in vinegar, salt, and pepper. Serve hot or warm.

Crusty No-Knead Bread (Chapter 3)

Vegetable Barley Soup (Chapter 5)

Cheesy Corn Dip (Chapter 4)

Salted Caramel Apple Crumble (Chapter 15)

Ham and Cheese Biscuit Spirals (Chapter 3)

Spinach Alfredo Shells (Chapter 6)

BBQ Pulled Pork (Chapter 10)

Golden Fried Chicken Tenders (Chapter 9)

Sweet Cornbread (Chapter 3)

Quick Stove-Top Mac and Cheese (Chapter 6)

Quinoa Porridge (Chapter 2) with jam
and slivered almonds

Cheeseburger Pie (Chapter 13)

Old-Fashioned Chicken and Dumplings (Chapter 5)

Sweet and Spicy Cocktail Sausages (Chapter 4)

Pearl Couscous with Corn, Black Beans, and Tomatoes (Chapter 12)

Meat Lovers Deep Dish Pizza (Chapter 13)

Braciole (Chapter 8)

Baked Shrimp Scampi (Chapter 11)

Devil's Food Cake Doughnuts and Apple Fritters (both recipes in Chapter 2)

Paneer Masala (Chapter 12)

Cornbread Soufflé (Chapter 7)

Broiled S'mores Casserole (Chapter 15)

Broccoli Rice Casserole (Chapter 7)

Beer-Battered Fish Planks (Chapter 11)

# Cuban Black Beans

*As with almost any bean dish, you can add chopped celery and carrots if you like.*

**PREP TIME:** 1 hour
**COOK TIME:** 2 hours
**INGREDIENTS | SERVES 4–6**

1 pound dried black beans

4 cups water, or more, as needed

3 cloves garlic, peeled and minced

1 medium green pepper, seeded and chopped

1 large yellow onion, peeled and chopped

½ pound salt pork or bacon, chopped

1 pound smoked ham hocks

2 teaspoons paprika

1 tablespoon ground cumin

2 bay leaves

4 cups chicken broth

¼ teaspoon chili powder

1 tablespoon red wine vinegar

½ teaspoon salt

½ teaspoon freshly cracked black pepper

1. Rinse beans and put them in a 6-quart Dutch oven with 4 cups water. Bring to a boil over medium-high heat; cover and boil 2 minutes. Turn off heat and let set 1 hour.

2. Add garlic, green pepper, onion, salt pork or bacon, ham hocks, paprika, cumin, bay leaves, chicken broth, and chili powder. Add enough additional water so that the beans are completely covered. Cover and simmer 2 hours over low heat, or until beans are tender.

3. Remove ham hocks and take meat off bones; return meat to the Dutch oven. Remove and discard bay leaves. Add vinegar, salt, and pepper, and stir to mix.

## Using Leftovers

It's easy to turn Cuban Black Beans into a satisfying soup. Once the beans are tender, simply add more chicken broth and bring to a simmer. After you've added the vinegar, salt, and pepper, taste for seasoning and adjust by adding more vinegar and other seasonings if needed.

# Cheesy Spaghetti Squash

*Turn this dish into a casserole by topping the spaghetti squash with buttered bread crumbs and baking 20 minutes at 350°F.*

**PREP TIME:** 15 minutes
**COOK TIME:** 25 minutes

**INGREDIENTS | SERVES 8**

4 tablespoons (½ stick) unsalted butter

1 medium onion, peeled and finely chopped

1 pint sliced button mushrooms

1 clove garlic, peeled and minced

½ teaspoon salt

¼ teaspoon freshly cracked black pepper

¼ teaspoon oregano

1 large spaghetti squash, cooked and shredded

3 tablespoons all-purpose flour

2 cups half and half

1 cup shredded Cheddar cheese, divided

1 cup shredded Gruyère cheese, divided

1. Heat a 4-quart Dutch oven over medium heat. Once hot add butter. Once butter melts and starts to foam add onion and mushrooms and cook until they begin to soften, about 5 minutes. Add garlic, salt, pepper, and oregano and cook until the garlic is fragrant, about 30 seconds. Add the cooked spaghetti squash and cook until hot, about 1 minute.

2. Add flour and cook until flour is moistened and cooked, about 3 minutes. Reduce the heat to low and slowly stir in half and half, making sure to stir out any lumps. Once all half and half is added increase heat to medium and let sauce come to a boil and thicken, about 8–10 minutes, stirring constantly.

3. Reduce heat to low and add cheese in four additions, making sure each addition is melted before the next is added. Serve hot.

## Cooking a Spaghetti Squash

Pierce your spaghetti squash a few times with a sharp knife and microwave for 2 minutes to soften the skin. Carefully remove from the microwave and cut the squash in half lengthwise and remove the seeds. Place the squash cut side down in a baking dish with ¼ cup of water. Tightly cover with foil and bake at 350°F for 40 minutes, or until fork tender. You can also place the squash and water in a microwave-safe dish, cover with plastic, and microwave 10–12 minutes, or until fork tender.

# Quinoa Pilaf

*Quiona comes in a variety of colors—red, black, and white—so feel free to use any color you like best, or use a mix of colors for a festive touch!*

**PREP TIME:** 10 minutes
**COOK TIME:** 30 minutes

**INGREDIENTS | SERVES 2**

1 tablespoon olive oil
½ small onion, peeled and chopped
¼ teaspoon ground cinnamon
½ teaspoon ground coriander
½ teaspoon ground turmeric
⅛ teaspoon red chili flakes
1 cup vegetable broth
1 small clove garlic, peeled and minced
½ cup quinoa
½ of a (15-ounce) can red kidney beans, rinsed and drained
1 roma tomato, chopped
6 black olives, chopped
2 tablespoons dried currants or cranberries
¼ teaspoon salt
¼ teaspoon freshly cracked black pepper

1. Place a 6- or 8-quart Dutch oven over medium heat and when warm add olive oil and onion. Cook 5–7 minutes, stirring occasionally. The onion should be soft and just starting to turn golden. Add the cinnamon, coriander, turmeric, and chili flakes. Stir continually for 1 minute and then add the vegetable broth.

2. Use a spatula to loosen any spices or onion that may have stuck to the bottom of the Dutch oven. Add garlic, quinoa, and beans. Reduce heat to low, cover, and simmer 15 minutes. The liquid should be mostly absorbed.

3. Add the tomato, olives, dried fruit, salt, and pepper. Stir and cook 5 more minutes, or until the liquid is evaporated. Fluff with a fork and serve immediately.

## Quinoa: Superfood

Quinoa is a grain-like crop from the Andes mountains in South America. Cultivated by the Incas, it was called the "mother of all grains," and is very high in protein and fiber. Quinoa grows with an outer coating, but most quinoa sold in America has this coating removed and is ready to use.

# Almond Barley Casserole

*Barley is very good for you and it's delicious too. The nutty flavor is accented by two kinds of almonds, onions, and garlic.*

**PREP TIME:** 10 minutes
**COOK TIME:** 1 hour 10 minutes

**INGREDIENTS | SERVES 6–8**

2 tablespoons unsalted butter
1 tablespoon olive oil
½ cup slivered almonds
1 large onion, peeled and chopped
3 cloves garlic, peeled and minced
1 (8-ounce) package sliced mushrooms
1½ cups medium pearl barley
3 cups vegetable broth
½ cup sliced almonds

1. Heat oven to 350°F.

2. In an ovenproof 6- or 8-quart Dutch oven melt butter with olive oil over medium heat. Once butter melts add slivered almonds and cook, stirring constantly, until toasted. Remove with a slotted spoon.

3. Add onion, garlic, and mushrooms to the Dutch oven and cook until just softened, about 6–8 minutes. Add the barley and stir until coated.

4. Add broth and toasted almonds to the Dutch oven and bring to a simmer, then remove from heat and top with sliced almonds. Bake 65–75 minutes or until barley is tender and broth is absorbed.

# Hopped-Up Hoppin' John

*Hoppin' John is a Southern dish traditionally eaten on New Year's Day. This version is hopped up by adding carrots to make it a one-dish meal.*

**PREP TIME:** 10 minutes
**COOK TIME:** 40 minutes

**INGREDIENTS | SERVES 6–8**

½ pound thick-cut bacon, diced
1 stalk celery, minced
1 (1-pound) bag baby carrots
1 large yellow onion, peeled and diced
2 (15-ounce) cans black-eyed peas, rinsed and drained
3 cups cooked long-grain rice
4 cups chicken broth
½ teaspoon salt
½ teaspoon freshly cracked black pepper

1. Add the bacon to a 6- or 8-quart Dutch oven and cook over medium heat until fat begins to render out of bacon, about 8–10 minutes. Add celery and sauté 2 minutes.

2. Shred 4 baby carrots and add them to the pan with celery; sauté 1 minute. Add onion and sauté 5 minutes, or until transparent.

3. Dice remaining baby carrots. Stir into vegetables along with black-eyed peas, rice, and chicken broth. Bring to a simmer; cover, reduce heat, and simmer 10 minutes or until warmed through.

4. Turn off heat and let set, covered, 10 minutes. Add salt and pepper before serving.

# Basic Sautéed Swiss Chard

*Swiss chard is a hardy green with large leaves and a thick stem. It has a much milder and less-bitter taste than mustard or collard greens. Avoid leaves that are wilted, yellow, or that have holes in the spines.*

**PREP TIME:** 10 minutes
**COOK TIME:** 20 minutes

**INGREDIENTS | SERVES 2–3**

1 pound Swiss chard
1 tablespoon olive oil
½ small onion, peeled and chopped
1 clove garlic, peeled and minced
Pinch crushed red pepper flakes
1 tablespoon cider or balsamic vinegar
Pinch nutmeg
½ cup chicken stock
¼ teaspoon salt
¼ teaspoon freshly cracked black pepper

1. Run chard under cold water to remove any leftover dirt. Cut the thick part of the stem out of the leaves and set aside. Tear leaves into several pieces and place on a towel. Chop stems into ½" pieces.

2. Place a 6- or 8-quart Dutch oven over medium heat. Once hot, add oil, stem pieces, and onion. Cook 5–7 minutes, or until the onion is translucent and just starting to brown.

3. Add garlic, pepper flakes, vinegar, nutmeg, and stock. Stir to combine and bring to a boil.

4. Add leaves and stir, cooking 2–3 minutes before covering. They should be starting to wilt. Cook 4–5 minutes, or until leaves are cooked through and limp.

5. Remove the lid and stir frequently as the liquid evaporates. Season with the salt and pepper. Serve immediately.

# Kale with Bacon and Tomatoes

*If you can't find kale, substitute spinach or Swiss chard and reduce the cooking time from 15 minutes to 5. You can also keep more of the bacon fat and omit the olive oil to get a truly flavorful dish. Be sure to taste the dish before adding more salt.*

**PREP TIME:** 10 minutes
**COOK TIME:** 30 minutes

**INGREDIENTS | SERVES 6–8**

2 pounds kale

4 slices bacon

1 tablespoon olive oil

1 small onion, peeled and chopped

2 cloves garlic, peeled and minced

¼ teaspoon salt

¼ teaspoon freshly cracked black pepper

2 roma tomatoes, seeded and chopped

2 tablespoons balsamic vinegar

## All Hail Kale

Kale has been cooked in so many parts of the world, and for so long, that food historians don't know where it originated. Because it grows easily in all climates, it has migrated with travelers throughout most of the world. It's incredibly high in vitamins and minerals and has helped sustain people during rough times.

1. Strip all the stems from the kale leaves and discard. Wash the leaves thoroughly and shake or drain until fairly dry. Chop or tear the leaves into large pieces and set aside.

2. Place a 6- or 8-quart Dutch oven over medium-high heat and when heated, add bacon. Cook until crisp, remove from the Dutch oven, and let cool. Pour off all but 1 tablespoon of bacon fat.

3. Add olive oil and chopped onion to the Dutch oven. Cook 5–7 minutes, or until the onion is soft and starting to brown. Stir in minced garlic clove and cook until fragrant, about 30 seconds.

4. Add a large bunch of kale to the Dutch oven and add the salt and pepper. Cover with a lid 1 minute to wilt the kale. Use a spoon to move wilted kale to the edges of the pot. Repeat until all of the kale has been added. Stir frequently and cook 15–20 minutes until tender.

5. Crumble cooked bacon and sprinkle on top with tomato. Sprinkle balsamic vinegar over kale and toss to combine. Remove to a bowl and serve immediately.

# Spicy Mustard Greens

*Mustard greens are less bitter than kale or collard greens, and have a much more peppery flavor, similar to arugula. A splash of spicy vinegar will help combat any remaining bitter flavor.*

**PREP TIME:** 10 minutes
**COOK TIME:** 55 minutes

**INGREDIENTS | SERVES 6**

2 large bunches mustard greens
3 tablespoons olive oil
2 medium onions, peeled and chopped
6 cloves garlic, peeled and minced
1 teaspoon ground cumin
1 teaspoon dried crushed red pepper flakes
1 cup chicken or vegetable broth
¼ teaspoon salt
¼ teaspoon freshly cracked black pepper

1. Remove veins from mustard green leaves and rinse them thoroughly in cold water. Shake dry and tear into large pieces.

2. Place a 6- or 8-quart Dutch oven over medium-high heat and once heated, add oil and onions. Stir frequently until onions are soft and starting to turn brown, about 10 minutes.

3. Stir in garlic, cumin, and crushed red pepper and cook 3 minutes.

4. Add one batch of the greens and cover 1–2 minutes until the greens wilt. Repeat with the other batches until all greens have been added and have wilted.

5. Add broth, cover, and reduce the heat to low. Let greens cook 30–45 minutes. They should be very tender. Season with the salt and pepper. Serve hot.

# Onion Rings

*To get truly tasty onion rings, use large sweet onions. Look for the brand name Vidalia or for Spanish onions. If you don't have beer, substitute with water mixed with 1 tablespoon apple cider vinegar. Serve these with ketchup or other dipping sauces.*

**PREP TIME:** 4 hours
**COOK TIME:** 15 minutes

**INGREDIENTS | SERVES 6**

1 cup all-purpose flour
1 large egg
1 tablespoon unsalted butter, melted
1 teaspoon salt
½ cup beer
1 large Spanish or Vidalia onion, peeled
1 quart vegetable oil

1. To make batter, process flour, egg, butter, salt, and beer in a blender until smooth. Cover and refrigerate at least 4 hours.

2. Heat oven to 200°F. Place a wire rack over a baking tray. Remove the batter from the refrigerator to warm up slightly.

3. Slice onion into ¾" slices. Separate the rings. Place a 6- or 8-quart Dutch oven over medium heat. Add 3" oil, making sure there is a 3" air gap at the top of the pot.

4. Once oil reaches 350°F, dip a few rings into the batter, then lower into hot oil. Cook 5–6 minutes, turning halfway through, or until golden on each side.

5. Remove from oil and place on the rack in the oven. Repeat with remaining rings.

# French Fries

*Frying the potatoes twice seems like a lot of work, but they'll be crispier
on the outside and puffier on the inside if you do.*

**PREP TIME:** 1 hour 10 minutes
**COOK TIME:** 25 minutes

**INGREDIENTS | SERVES 4–6**

4 large russet potatoes, peeled
Water, as needed
1 quart peanut oil
¼ teaspoon salt
¼ teaspoon freshly cracked
black pepper

1. Cut potatoes into ¼" slices. Cut those slices into ¼"
   strips. To remove the starch, rinse potatoes in cold
   water until water runs clear. Put potatoes in a bowl and
   cover with ice water. Refrigerate 1 hour. Drain and
   pat dry.

2. Place a 6- or 8-quart Dutch oven over medium to
   medium-high heat and add 3" oil making sure there is
   a 3" air gap at the top of the pot. Heat oil to 360°F.

3. Add a handful of potatoes to oil, being careful not to
   splash your hand. Use a skimmer or a slotted spoon to
   keep the potatoes from sticking to each other. Cook
   until they're a very light blond, about 3 minutes.
   Remove from the oil and drain on paper towels.
   Repeat with the rest of the potatoes. When all potatoes
   are cooked, let rest 10 minutes. While the potatoes rest
   adjust the heat of oil to 350°F.

4. Heat the oven to 275°F.

5. Return potatoes in batches to the oil and cook
   1 minute, or until they're golden brown and
   slightly puffed.

6. Place on a wire rack over a cookie sheet in the middle
   of the oven to stay warm and crisp. They will darken
   slightly as they cool. Season with salt and pepper.
   Serve warm.

# Dirty Rice

*This dish gets its name from the appearance the chopped chicken livers add to the rice. If you prefer a milder liver taste, use ½ pound chicken livers and ½ pound chicken gizzards instead of all livers.*

**PREP TIME:** 10 minutes
**COOK TIME:** 1 hour 15 minutes

**INGREDIENTS | SERVES 4**

2 tablespoons bacon fat or peanut oil
1 small green bell pepper, seeded and diced
2 stalks celery, chopped
1 medium yellow onion, peeled and diced
1 clove garlic, peeled and minced
½ pound lean ground pork
½ pound Italian sausage
3 cups chicken broth
1 pound chicken livers
½ tablespoon Worcestershire sauce
½ teaspoon salt
½ teaspoon freshly ground black pepper
¼ teaspoon cayenne pepper
1 tablespoon dried parsley
1 cup uncooked long-grain rice
Water, if needed
2 green onions, chopped

1. Add bacon fat or oil to a 6- or 8-quart Dutch oven and heat over medium heat. Add green pepper and celery and sauté 3 minutes. Add yellow onion and sauté 5 minutes, or until onions are transparent and vegetables are tender. Add garlic and sauté 30 seconds.

2. Stir in ground pork and sausage; fry until meat is lightly browned. Drain off and discard any excess fat.

3. Stir in chicken broth and bring to a boil. Add chicken livers, cover, and lightly boil 30 minutes. Use a slotted spoon to remove the chicken livers; set them aside to cool.

4. Stir in Worcestershire sauce, salt, pepper, cayenne, parsley, and rice; bring to a boil. Reduce heat to medium-low, cover, and cook 15 minutes.

5. Chop chicken livers. Stir into rice-sausage mixture. Cover and simmer 20 minutes; stir occasionally to keep rice from sticking. Add water if additional moisture is needed. Stir in green onion.

# Broccoli Rice Casserole

*Traditionally this casserole is made with condensed soup and processed cheese sauce. This recipe is completely from scratch, but just as easy to make!*

**PREP TIME:** 10 minutes
**COOK TIME:** 1 hour

**INGREDIENTS | SERVES 8**

2 (10-ounce) bags frozen chopped broccoli

1 tablespoon water

4 tablespoons (½ stick) unsalted butter

1 medium onion, peeled and chopped

2 stalks celery, chopped

1 pint sliced button mushrooms

2 cloves garlic, peeled and minced

½ teaspoon salt

½ teaspoon freshly cracked black pepper

¼ cup all-purpose flour

2 cups half and half

2 cups sharp Cheddar cheese, divided

3 cups cooked white rice

1. Heat oven to 350°F.

2. Place broccoli in a microwave-safe bowl, add 1 tablespoon water, cover with plastic, and microwave 6–8 minutes. Carefully remove the plastic, avoiding the steam, and drain. Set aside.

3. In an ovenproof 6-quart Dutch oven over medium heat add butter. Once butter has melted and starts to foam add onion and celery and cook until tender, about 5 minutes. Add mushrooms and cook until mushrooms are softened, about 5 minutes. Add garlic, salt, and pepper and cook until garlic is fragrant, about 30 seconds.

4. Add flour and cook until flour is moistened, about 3 minutes, then slowly add half and half, making sure to stir out any lumps. Bring mixture to a boil, then reduce heat to medium-low and cook until sauce thickens, about 8 minutes.

5. Turn the heat to low and add 1½ cups Cheddar cheese in three batches, making sure the first batch is melted before adding the next. Add cooked broccoli and rice and fold to combine. Top with remaining cheese.

6. Bake 30–35 minutes, or until the casserole is bubbling around the edges and the cheese has browned. Cool 5 minutes before serving.

# Spanish Rice

*Spanish rice is an excellent well-flavored pilaf. It can be served as an accompaniment to grilled meats, or as the centerpiece of a vegetarian meal.*

**PREP TIME:** 10 minutes
**COOK TIME:** 40 minutes

**INGREDIENTS | SERVES 6**

3 tablespoons olive oil, divided
1¼ cups long-grain white rice
1 medium onion, peeled and chopped
3 cloves garlic, peeled and minced
2 jalapeño peppers, seeded and minced
1 medium green bell pepper, seeded and chopped
1 (14-ounce) can diced tomatoes, undrained
1½ cups vegetable broth
1½ teaspoons paprika
1 teaspoon dried thyme leaves
1 cup frozen baby peas, thawed
⅓ cup chopped flat-leaf parsley

1. In a 6- or 8-quart Dutch oven heat 1 tablespoon olive oil. Add rice and cook until browned, about 7–9 minutes. Watch rice closely as it can easily go from browned to burned. Remove from the Dutch oven and set aside.

2. In the Dutch oven heat remaining 2 tablespoons olive oil over medium heat. Add onion, garlic, and jalapeño peppers and cook until tender, about 5 minutes.

3. Add rice to onion mixture. Add remaining ingredients except peas and parsley; bring to a simmer. Cover and simmer 20–30 minutes until rice is tender. Add peas; cook 3 minutes longer.

4. Remove from the heat, stir in parsley, let stand for 5 minutes, fluff with fork, and serve.

## Rice Pilaf for a Party

When hosting a party buffet it is nice to offer several different flavors of rice pilaf, especially when you serve any dish with a sauce. The pilaf can be simple or more complicated depending on the party theme. Think about adding sautéed bell peppers, roasted garlic, toasted nuts, dried fruits, or bold spices like curry powder or spicy chilies. In fact, with some grilled chicken or pork chops and cheese sauce, you can offer a mix-and-match pilaf buffet.

CHAPTER 8

# Beef

# Braciole

*This Italian stuffed steak is simmered in red wine and tomato sauce until very tender. Butcher's twine, a thick cotton string, is used to hold the braciole's shape while cooking and can be found in most grocery stores in the meat market. If you want to save time feel free to use your favorite jarred tomato sauce.*

**PREP TIME:** 15 minutes
**COOK TIME:** 2 hours

**INGREDIENTS | SERVES 4**

4 tablespoons salted butter

1 medium onion, peeled and chopped

1 clove garlic, peeled and minced

1 (28-ounce) can diced tomatoes, undrained

1 teaspoon fennel

½ teaspoon oregano

¼ teaspoon thyme

½ cup Italian bread crumbs

⅓ cup grated Parmesan

⅓ cup shredded mozzarella

¼ cup shredded smoked provolone

3 tablespoons olive oil, divided

1 (1½-pound) flank steak

½ teaspoon salt

¼ teaspoon freshly cracked black pepper

1 cup red wine

2 tablespoons chopped parsley, for garnish

## Cooking with Wine

The old adage about only cooking with wine you would drink is actually true. The flavors of the wine will reduce and concentrate, so a bottle of poor wine won't improve with cooking. That does not mean you have to spend a fortune. You can get a good bottle of wine for under $20, often for less than $10, in most markets.

1. In an ovenproof 6- or 8-quart Dutch oven over medium heat add butter. Once butter has melted and starts to foam add onion and cook until just tender, about 3 minutes. Add garlic, tomatoes, fennel, oregano, and thyme and bring to a boil. Cook, stirring often, until sauce thickens slightly, about 10 minutes. Transfer sauce to a bowl and set aside. Wipe out the Dutch oven.

2. Heat oven to 350°F.

3. In a small bowl combine bread crumbs, cheeses, and 2 tablespoons olive oil. Mix until bread crumbs are all moistened by oil. Lay flank steak out on work surface. Season both sides with salt and pepper, then spread the bread crumb mixture evenly on one side of the steak. Roll the short side of steak to enclose the filling and tie with butcher's twine.

4. Heat the Dutch oven over medium-high heat and add remaining oil. Brown steak on all sides then add red wine and, with a wooden spoon or heatproof spatula, release any browned bits from the bottom of the pan. Add tomato sauce and stir to combine, rolling steak to coat.

5. Cover the Dutch oven with the lid and bake, basting with sauce every 15 minutes, until steak is tender, about 1 hour. Remove the lid and let steak bake an additional 30 minutes, or until sauce is reduced and the steak is very tender.

6. Let braciole rest in sauce 10 minutes before carefully removing to a cutting board. Remove butcher's twine and cut into ½"-thick slices. Serve the slices topped with sauce and parsley for garnish.

# Beef Short Ribs and Onion Gravy

*The braising liquid for these ribs will eventually become the gravy. Serve these tender short ribs with mashed potatoes or fresh cooked rice.*

**PREP TIME:** 10 minutes
**COOK TIME:** 3 hours 30 minutes

**INGREDIENTS | SERVES 6**

6 bone-in beef short ribs, about 5 pounds
½ teaspoon salt
½ teaspoon freshly cracked black pepper
2 tablespoons olive oil, divided
2 cups beef stock
1 medium onion, peeled and sliced
1 stalk celery, cut in half
2 cloves garlic, peeled and minced
1 bay leaf
Water, to cover the ribs
1 tablespoon cornstarch
2 tablespoons water

1. Heat oven to 350°F.

2. Season all sides of short ribs with salt and pepper. Heat an ovenproof 6- or 8-quart Dutch oven over medium heat. Add 1 tablespoon oil and brown half of ribs on all sides. Let the ribs get very brown and crusty, about 2 minutes per side. Transfer to a plate to rest while you repeat with remaining oil and ribs.

3. Add beef stock to the Dutch oven and, with a wooden spoon or heatproof spatula, scrape off any browned bits from the bottom of the pot. Return ribs to the pot along with onion, celery, garlic, bay leaf, and enough water so that the ribs are just covered. Cover the Dutch oven with the lid and bake 2½–3 hours, or until ribs are fork tender. Remove the lid and cook 30 additional minutes so the braising liquid can reduce.

4. Remove ribs from braising liquid and set on a plate to rest. Tent the plate with foil to keep ribs warm. Remove bay leaf and celery and discard.

5. Place the Dutch oven over medium heat and bring remaining braising liquid to a boil. Mix cornstarch with 2 tablespoons water and add half of this slurry to braising liquid. Add additional slurry until liquid has thickened to coat the back of a spoon thickly. Reduce heat to low and put ribs into gravy and turn to coat. Serve hot.

# Hungarian Goulash

*Goulash is a thick soup, or thin stew depending on whom you ask, that is flavored with Hungarian paprika. Serve goulash over rice or egg noodles with extra sour cream.*

**PREP TIME:** 15 minutes
**COOK TIME:** 2 hours 30 minutes

**INGREDIENTS | SERVES 8**

¼ cup all-purpose flour
¼ teaspoon salt
3 pounds chuck roast, cut into 2" cubes
¼ cup vegetable oil, divided
2 large onions, peeled and sliced
2 cloves garlic, peeled and minced
¼ cup Hungarian sweet paprika
4 tablespoons tomato paste
2 cups beef broth
Water, to cover beef
½ cup sour cream, for garnish

## Paprika

Paprika is best when it is fresh, so if you are not sure how old your paprika is, or if it is older than 1 year, it is time to replace it. Old paprika will have a weak flavor and a rusty color. Fresh paprika has an earthy flavor and a bold red color. This same rule applies to any dried spices and herbs; they are best when they are fresh. Check the bottles. If they do not have a date, just a code, they are probably old and need to be replaced.

1. In a large zip-top bag combine flour and salt. Add cubed beef and toss to coat.

2. Heat a 6- or 8-quart Dutch oven over medium heat and add 1 tablespoon oil. Brown beef on all sides in two batches, adding more oil between batches, and making sure not to crowd the pan, about 5–8 minutes per batch. Transfer browned beef to a plate and set aside.

3. Add remaining 2 tablespoons of oil to the pan along with onion. Cook until onion is soft, about 5 minutes, then add garlic, paprika, and tomato paste. Cook until spices and tomato paste have browned slightly, about 5 minutes. Return beef to the pan and coat beef with the onions and paprika.

4. Add beef broth to the pan and, with a wooden spoon or heatproof spatula, scrape any browned bits off the bottom of the Dutch oven. Add enough water to just cover beef and bring mixture to a boil. Once it reaches a boil reduce heat to low, cover with the lid, and simmer 2 hours or until the meat is fork tender. Serve the goulash with dollops of sour cream.

# Slow-Roasted Beef Ribs

*These ribs are fall-apart tender and are sure to please a crowd!*

**PREP TIME:** 15 minutes
**COOK TIME:** 2 hours 50 minutes

**INGREDIENTS | SERVES 6**

3 pounds beef back ribs, cut into
1-rib portions

½ teaspoon salt

½ teaspoon freshly cracked
black pepper

2 tablespoons vegetable oil

1 medium onion, peeled and sliced

2 cloves garlic, peeled and minced

1 (12-ounce) can beer, stout or lager

2 cups beef stock

1 cup barbecue sauce

¼ cup bourbon

## Finished on the Grill

Want to give your braised ribs a char-grilled finish? Just remove them from the braising liquid about 20 minutes before the end of the directed cooking time and allow the ribs to cool about 30 minutes, or refrigerate overnight. When your grill is hot simply grill them for a few minutes per side. You can also glaze your ribs with the sauce at this stage so they are sticky and a little messy!

1. Heat oven to 350°F. Season ribs with salt and pepper. Set aside.

2. Heat an ovenproof 8-quart Dutch oven over medium heat. Add oil and once it shimmers add onions. Cook, stirring often, until tender, about 5 minutes. Add garlic and cook until fragrant, about 30 seconds. Add the beer and beef stock, and stir to combine.

3. Add ribs to the pot and add water if needed to cover the ribs. Cover with the lid and bake 2 hours or until meat is tender and falls away from the bone easily.

4. In a small saucepan combine barbecue sauce and bourbon. Bring to a simmer over medium-low heat and cook until the sauce thickens, about 15 minutes. Set aside.

5. Remove ribs from braising liquid and place meat-side up on a roasting pan. Discard the liquid. Baste with prepared sauce and bake 30 minutes, basting with the sauce every 10 minutes. Serve hot.

# Osso Bucco

*Veal shanks should be tied with butcher's twine to keep them from falling apart in the pot. Do it yourself or ask your butcher to do it for you. Serve this dish with freshly cooked rice.*

**PREP TIME:** 10 minutes
**COOK TIME:** 1 hour 45 minutes

**INGREDIENTS | SERVES 6–8**

4 (1-pound) veal shanks
1 teaspoon salt
½ teaspoon freshly cracked black pepper
¼ cup all-purpose flour
⅓ cup olive oil
1 medium onion, peeled and diced
1 large carrot, diced
1 large stalk celery, diced
2 tablespoons tomato paste
1 cup white wine
2 sprigs fresh thyme
2 bay leaves
2 cloves garlic, peeled and pressed
3 cups veal or chicken broth
⅓ cup minced parsley
Zest of 1 large lemon

1. Sprinkle veal shanks with salt and pepper, then dust them with flour.

2. In a 6- or 8-quart Dutch oven over medium-high heat add olive oil and once it shimmers add veal shanks. Brown on all sides, about 5 minutes per side, then remove from pan.

3. Add onion, carrot, and celery to oil and cook, stirring constantly, until just tender, about 3 minutes.

4. Add tomato paste and cook 1 minute, then add wine, thyme, bay leaves, and garlic. Bring to a boil, then reduce heat to medium-low and simmer 3 minutes.

5. Return veal shanks to pan along with broth. Cover with the lid and simmer 1½ hours. Check veal often, basting and keeping the lower ⅔ of the shank height covered with liquid.

6. When shanks are almost falling apart, carefully remove to a serving dish. Ladle sauce and vegetables around shanks, then sprinkle parsley and lemon zest over all.

# Classic Pot Roast

*For some, nothing says comfort better than a simple pot roast. This dish is a meal in itself, but a few slices of crusty bread with salted butter would be welcome on the side.*

**PREP TIME:** 15 minutes
**COOK TIME:** 2 hours

**INGREDIENTS | SERVES 8**

1 (3-pound) chuck roast
½ teaspoon salt
½ teaspoon freshly cracked black pepper
2 tablespoons vegetable oil
1 cup red wine
2 medium onions, peeled and quartered
2 large carrots, cut into 1" pieces
2 large russet potatoes, scrubbed and cut into 1" pieces
2 cloves garlic, peeled and minced
½ teaspoon thyme
1 bay leaf
2 cups low-sodium beef broth

1. Heat oven to 350°F. Season roast with salt and pepper on all sides. Set aside.

2. In an ovenproof 6- or 8-quart Dutch oven over medium heat add oil. Once oil is hot and starts to shimmer add roast and brown well on all sides. Remove roast to a plate to rest.

3. Add red wine to the Dutch oven and, with a wooden spoon or heatproof spatula, scrape any brown bits off the bottom of the Dutch oven.

4. Add roast back to the Dutch oven along with the remaining ingredients, cover with the lid, and bake 1½–2 hours or until meat is fork tender. Remove bay leaf before serving.

## Perfect Pot Roast

Pot roast is a slow-braised dish that cooks a tough cut of meat until the connective tissues break down and the meat is fall-apart tender. Meats with little fat are best for pot roast; cuts of meat traditionally used include chuck roast or round roast. In a pinch you can also use a beef brisket. Be sure to brown the meat very well on all sides to add flavor and to make the roast pretty.

# Italian Beef for Sandwiches

*Use top sirloin for the best flavor and tenderness. If that is not available you can use top round or bottom round.*

**PREP TIME:** 10 minutes
**COOK TIME:** 2 hours 30 minutes

**INGREDIENTS | SERVES 10**

1 (3-pound) top sirloin, trimmed
2 teaspoons freshly cracked black pepper
1 teaspoon salt
2 tablespoons olive oil
3 cups beef broth
2 cups water
1 large onion, peeled and quartered
4 cloves garlic, peeled and smashed
1 teaspoon oregano
1 teaspoon dry basil
½ teaspoon crushed red pepper flakes

## Italian Beef Sandwiches

To make Italian beef sandwiches split fluffy Italian rolls lengthwise ¾ of the way through the roll. If you like a wet sandwich spoon some of the juice onto the roll. Layer the sandwich with beef, giardiniera (pickled vegetables), and mozzarella or provolone cheese if desired. If you want the cheese hot, stick the sandwiches under the broiler until the cheese melts. Serve it with a cup of hot juice for dipping.

1. Heat oven to 325°F. Season sirloin on all sides with pepper and salt. Set aside.

2. In an ovenproof 6- or 8-quart Dutch oven over medium heat add oil. Once oil is hot and starts to shimmer add roast and brown well on all sides.

3. Add remaining ingredients to the Dutch oven, cover with the lid and bake 2 hours or until meat is tender but not falling apart. It needs to be firm enough to slice. Remove meat from the Dutch oven to a cutting board, tent meat with foil, and let rest 20 minutes.

4. While meat rests, strain braising liquid through a fine strainer. Keep the juice warm in a covered saucepan on the stove.

5. Once meat has rested, thinly slice it. Dunk slices into the hot juice before assembling your sandwiches.

# Corned Beef and Cabbage

*This recipe isn't just for St. Patrick's Day. It makes a satisfying meal any time of year.*

**PREP TIME:** 15 minutes
**COOK TIME:** 2 hours 40 minutes

**INGREDIENTS | SERVES 6**

1 (2–2½-pound) corned beef brisket
Water as needed
1 teaspoon whole black peppercorns
2 bay leaves
3 medium carrots, peeled and quartered
2 medium parsnips, peeled and cut into chunks
2 medium red onions, peeled and cut into wedges
6 medium red potatoes, cleaned and quartered
1 small cabbage, cut into 6 wedges

1. Trim any excess fat from meat. Place brisket in a 4- to 6-quart Dutch oven along with juices and spices from the package that came with corned beef. Add enough water to cover the brisket. Add peppercorns and bay leaves.

2. Bring to a boil over medium-high heat; reduce heat and simmer, covered, 2 hours. At this point, the meat should be almost tender.

3. Add carrots, parsnips, and onions to meat. Return to a simmer; cover and cook 10 minutes. Add potatoes and cabbage. Cover and cook 20 minutes, or until the vegetables and meat are tender.

4. Remove bay leaves and discard. Remove pot from the heat, cover, and let meat rest in broth for 10 minutes.

5. Transfer meat to a platter and thinly slice it across the grain. Spoon vegetables around meat on the platter and ladle some of broth from the pan over meat. Strain some of the broth and transfer to a gravy boat to have at the table.

# Beer-Braised Beef Brisket

*This tender indoor brisket is perfect for a Sunday supper, or served on rolls for the big game!*

**PREP TIME:** 10 minutes
**COOK TIME:** 2 hours

**INGREDIENTS | SERVES 8**

3 pounds beef brisket
½ teaspoon salt
½ teaspoon freshly cracked
black pepper
1 tablespoon vegetable oil
2 medium onions, peeled and sliced
2 cloves garlic, peeled and minced
2 tablespoons tomato paste
1 (12-ounce) can beer, stout or lager
2 cups beef broth

1. Heat oven to 375°F. Season brisket with salt and pepper. Set aside.

2. Heat an ovenproof 8-quart Dutch oven over medium heat. Add oil and once it shimmers add onions. Cook, stirring often, until tender, about 5 minutes. Add garlic and tomato paste and cook until fragrant, about 30 seconds. Add the beer and stir to combine.

3. Add brisket to the Dutch oven and add enough beef broth to come halfway up the side of the brisket. Cover with the lid and bake 1½–2 hours, or until meat is fork tender.

4. Carefully remove brisket from the Dutch oven and rest, tented with foil, 20 minutes. Cut thick slices of brisket across the grain and arrange on a platter. Spoon some of braising liquid over brisket. Serve hot.

# Beef Bourguignon

*Serve Beef Bourguignon over buttered noodles or mashed potatoes,
along with a salad and a steamed vegetable.*

**PREP TIME:** 10 minutes
**COOK TIME:** 2 hours 45 minutes

**INGREDIENTS | SERVES 8**

8 slices bacon, diced

1 (3-pound) boneless English or chuck roast

1 large yellow onion, peeled and diced

4 cups Burgundy wine

2 cups beef broth or water

2 tablespoons tomato paste

3 cloves garlic, peeled and minced

½ teaspoon thyme

1 bay leaf

½ teaspoon salt

½ teaspoon freshly cracked black pepper

1 large yellow onion, peeled and thinly sliced

½ cup plus 2 tablespoons unsalted butter, divided

16 ounces fresh button or cremini mushrooms, cleaned and sliced

½ cup all-purpose flour

1. Add bacon to a 6- or 8-quart Dutch oven and fry it over medium heat until it renders its fat, about 8–10 minutes. Use a slotted spoon to remove bacon and reserve it for another use.

2. Trim roast of any fat and cut it into bite-sized pieces; add beef pieces to the Dutch oven and stir-fry 5 minutes. Add diced onion and sauté 3 minutes, or until transparent.

3. Add Burgundy, broth or water, tomato paste, garlic, thyme, bay leaf, salt, and pepper; stir to combine. Bring the contents of the pan to a boil; reduce the heat to medium-low, cover, and simmer 2 hours or until meat is tender.

4. Add sliced onion to a microwave-safe bowl along with 2 tablespoons of the butter; cover and microwave on high 2 minutes. Add mushrooms; cover and microwave on high 1 minute. Stir, cover, and microwave on high in 30-second increments until mushrooms are sautéed and onion is transparent.

5. Stir mushroom-onion mixture into the Dutch oven; cover and simmer 20 minutes.

6. In a small bowl or measuring cup, mix the remaining ½ cup butter together with flour to form a paste; whisk in some of the pan liquid a little at a time to thin the paste. Strain out any lumps. Increase heat to medium-high and bring contents of the Dutch oven to a boil.

7. Whisk butter-flour mixture into the meat and juices in the pan; boil 1 minute. Reduce heat and simmer uncovered, stirring occasionally, until the pan juices have been reduced to make a gravy.

# Beef Burgundy

*Beef Burgundy is a classic recipe that everyone will love. It's a good choice for serving a crowd. Serve this dish over hot cooked rice.*

**PREP TIME:** 4–6 hours
**COOK TIME:** 1 hour 15 minutes

**INGREDIENTS | SERVES 8**

1¼ cups Burgundy wine

¼ cup olive oil

3 tablespoons low-sodium soy sauce

3 tablespoons oyster sauce

4 cloves garlic, peeled and minced

1 teaspoon dried marjoram leaves

2 pounds sirloin strip steak, cut into 1" cubes

3 tablespoons unsalted butter

2 medium onions, peeled and chopped

1 (8-ounce) package sliced mushrooms

2 tablespoons all-purpose flour

⅛ teaspoon freshly ground black pepper

1½ cups beef broth

### Keep It Healthy

Wine, in moderation, is very good for you. Most, but not all, of the alcohol will burn off in the high heat of the stovetop. Keep this in mind if you have any recovering alcoholics on the guest list. And use a Burgundy wine that you would drink. The flavor is concentrated during cooking, and you want the best flavor in your recipes.

1. In a large bowl, combine wine, olive oil, soy sauce, oyster sauce, garlic, and marjoram leaves; mix well. Add steak, cover, and refrigerate 4–6 hours.

2. When ready to cook, drain meat, reserving marinade. Melt butter in a 6- or 8-quart Dutch oven over medium heat, then add beef. Cook until browned on all sides, about 5–6 minutes. Remove meat from the Dutch oven.

3. Add onions and mushrooms to the Dutch oven and cook, stirring frequently to scrape up browned bits, about 10 minutes. Sprinkle with flour and pepper, and bring to a simmer.

4. Add beef broth, reserved marinade, and steak to Dutch oven and cook, stirring frequently, until mixture returns to a simmer. Reduce heat to low, cover with the lid, and simmer for 1 hour, stirring occasionally.

# Braised Beef Shank with Potatoes, Carrots, and Cauliflower

*Beef shanks are horizontal cuts from the front leg of the cow. They have a lot of connective tissue, which dissolves into a gelatinous broth. This cut of beef is often inexpensive and very flavorful.*

**PREP TIME:** 10 minutes
**COOK TIME:** 4 hours 30 minutes
**INGREDIENTS | SERVES 3–4**

2 (6-ounce) beef shanks, 2" thick
2 tablespoons unsalted butter
4 tablespoons vegetable oil
1 tablespoon dry peppercorns
1 large onion, peeled and chopped
1 (5-ounce) can tomato paste
2 quarts water
1 cup balsamic vinegar
2 tablespoons fresh thyme
2 bay leaves
4 cloves garlic, peeled and minced
4 carrots, peeled and cut into ½" pieces
3 medium potatoes, peeled and cut into ½" pieces
½ head cauliflower, cut into ½" pieces
½ teaspoon salt
¼ teaspoon freshly cracked black pepper

1. Bring meat to room temperature. Place an 8-quart Dutch oven over medium-high heat. Add butter and oil. Once butter has melted add meat and sear on each side for 4 minutes, then remove to a plate to rest. Add peppercorns to Dutch oven and cook 2 minutes. Add onion to the pan and place the meat on top of the onion.

2. In a small bowl, stir tomato paste into water. Add mixture to Dutch oven along with balsamic vinegar. Bring to a boil then reduce heat to low. Once it reduces to a simmer, skim off the foam and discard.

3. Add thyme and bay leaves. Cover the pan and cook 3½–4 hours. Remove the meat and keep warm.

4. Strain the stock and return it to pot. Add garlic, carrots, potatoes, and cauliflower to pot. Place it over medium heat and cook 30 minutes, uncovered. Continue to skim off any foam as it cooks. Add salt and pepper.

5. Separate beef into pieces and pour sauce over meat. Serve with vegetables on the side.

### Cauliflower, the Cabbage Flower

Cauliflower is actually a member of the cabbage family and is also related to mustard. It is most commonly found as a white vegetable but can also be purple or orange. To choose the best head of cauliflower, look for produce that doesn't have brown markings or curds that seem loose. A tightly packed head is freshest.

# Ropa Vieja

*Ropa Vieja is Spanish for "old clothes." This Cuban dish is served with cooked white or yellow rice, Cuban Black Beans (Chapter 7), and tortillas.*

**PREP TIME:** 10 minutes
**COOK TIME:** 2 hours 45 minutes

**INGREDIENTS | SERVES 4**

1 teaspoon cumin

1 teaspoon paprika

1 teaspoon mild chili powder

1 teaspoon ground coriander

1 teaspoon dried oregano

1 pound flank steak

2 teaspoons olive oil

1 large carrot, sliced

1 medium onion, peeled and sliced

1 large celery stalk, sliced

1 medium poblano pepper, sliced

1 large red bell pepper, seeded and sliced

2 cloves garlic, peeled and minced

2 tablespoons tomato paste

4 large tomatoes, roughly chopped

¼ cup sherry vinegar

2 cups beef broth

½ teaspoon salt

¼ teaspoon freshly cracked black pepper

1. Combine cumin, paprika, chili powder, coriander, and oregano in a small bowl. Trim the excess fat from the steak, and press spices into the meat.

2. Place Dutch oven over high heat and add oil. When oil is hot sear meat 2 minutes on each side. Reduce heat to medium, remove meat, place in a bowl, and cover.

3. Sprinkle carrot, onion, celery, peppers, and garlic into the pan, stirring continuously 7–10 minutes.

4. Add tomato paste, tomatoes, and vinegar; stir. Return meat to pan and add enough beef broth so half of the pan is full, but don't cover meat.

5. Turn heat to high and as soon as the liquid starts to simmer, turn heat to medium-low, cover with a lid, and cook on a low simmer 1½–2 hours. Take meat out of the pan and rest in a bowl.

6. Turn off heat and let the pan sit 10 minutes. Use a large spoon to skim the fat off the surface. Turn heat up to high and boil until it is reduced to a third of its original volume, about 15 minutes.

7. Shred the meat, then add it back to the pan. Cook 3–5 minutes. Season with the salt and pepper. Serve hot.

# Beef Mornay

*This rich dish is served over toasted English muffins but can also be served over baked puff pastry shells or hot cooked rice.*

**PREP TIME:** 20 minutes
**COOK TIME:** 25 minutes

**INGREDIENTS | SERVES 6–8**

1 pound beef round steak, sliced into ¼" × 4" strips

2 tablespoons lemon juice

¼ cup all-purpose flour

½ teaspoon salt

⅛ teaspoon freshly ground black pepper

4 tablespoons unsalted butter

1 large onion, peeled and chopped

2 cloves garlic, peeled and minced

1 (8-ounce) package sliced mushrooms

1 medium red bell pepper, seeded and sliced

1 (12-ounce) can evaporated milk

½ cup light cream

1½ cups beef broth

1½ cups grated Gruyère cheese

⅓ cup grated Parmesan cheese

8 English muffins, split and toasted

1. In a large bowl, toss beef with lemon juice, then let stand 10 minutes. Drain, sprinkle with flour, salt, and pepper and set aside.

2. In 6- or 8-quart Dutch oven over medium heat add butter. Once it melts add beef strips and cook and stir until browned, about 5–6 minutes. Remove beef from the Dutch oven and add onions and garlic. Cook until tender, about 5 minutes.

3. Add mushrooms and bell pepper, and cook until tender, about 4 minutes. Add evaporated milk, cream, and beef broth and return beef to the Dutch oven.

4. Simmer 4–5 minutes until sauce has thickened. Stir in cheeses until melted. Serve over toasted English muffins.

## Party Fun

Choose a few skillet dishes and offer a variety of foods to serve them over. Baked puff pastry squares, puff pastry shells, toasted English muffins, hot cooked wild rice, mashed potatoes, or pasta tossed with a little olive oil can all be offered as a comfort food buffet. Keep everything warm in slow cookers and on warming trays.

# Beef Cholent

*The secret to this whole meal in a pot is long, slow cooking.*
*Resist the urge to stir things up while it is baking.*

**PREP TIME:** 20 minutes
**COOK TIME:** 10–15 hours

**INGREDIENTS | SERVES 8**

⅓ cup vegetable oil

2 pounds boneless chuck roast, cut into 4" pieces

2 pounds flank steak, cut into 4" pieces

2 large onions, peeled and sliced

2 cloves garlic, peeled and minced

1 cup dried kidney beans

1 cup dried lima beans

6 cups beef broth

⅓ cup ketchup

1 cup pearl barley

6 white potatoes, peeled and cut in large chunks

½ teaspoon salt

¼ teaspoon freshly cracked black pepper

1. Heat oven to 200°F.

2. Heat oil in an ovenproof 6- or 8-quart Dutch oven. Brown beef pieces well on all sides, about 3 minutes per side, and set aside. Add onions and cook until they start to soften, about 3 minutes.

3. Add garlic and beans and cook until the beans are heated through, about 3 minutes. Stir in beef, beef broth, ketchup, barley, potatoes, salt, and pepper. Add water to cover beef, if needed. Bring mixture to a boil then remove from heat and cover with the lid.

4. Place the Dutch oven in the oven and roast for 10–15 hours. Check occasionally to make sure broth hasn't been absorbed or evaporated. Serve in bowls.

## Savoring the Sabbath

Cholent is a traditional Saturday noon meal for many Jewish families. The dish originated from the desire to have a hot entrée on the Sabbath, without breaking religious laws that forbid lighting a fire between sundown Friday and sundown Saturday. All the preparation for the dish, including turning on the oven, can be done Friday afternoon and the cholent can be left to cook until the family is ready to eat on Saturday. Those who are squeamish about leaving an oven on all night can use a slow cooker instead.

# Chicken-Fried Steak

*While the exact origins of chicken-fried steak are unclear, many credit German and Austrian immigrants in Texas with creating this dish as it is similar to schnitzel.*

**PREP TIME:** 15 minutes
**COOK TIME:** 10 minutes

**INGREDIENTS | SERVES 4**

1 cup all-purpose flour
1 teaspoon salt
½ teaspoon freshly cracked black pepper
2 large eggs, lightly beaten
4 (¼-pound) cube steaks, or round steaks tenderized by your butcher
Oil, for frying

## Cream Gravy

Cream gravy with plenty of black pepper is the traditional topping for chicken-fried steak. To make it add 4 tablespoons of the oil used to fry the steaks to a saucepan over medium heat. Add 4 tablespoons of all-purpose flour and cook until the flour is golden brown, about 3 minutes. Reduce the heat to low and whisk in 2 cups milk and 1 cup half and half. Increase the heat to medium and cook, whisking constantly, until the gravy comes to a boil and thickens. Season with salt and plenty of freshly cracked black pepper.

1. In a large zip-top bag add flour, salt, and pepper. Close the bag and shake well to combine.

2. Place beaten egg into a shallow dish or pie plate.

3. Place steaks, one at a time, into seasoned flour. Shake well to coat, and knock off any excess flour. Place steaks into egg mixture and turn to coat, allowing any excess egg to drip off. Return steak to flour and toss to coat. Place coated steaks on a wire rack while you heat the oil.

4. Heat 2" oil in a deep Dutch oven, leaving a 3" air gap at the top of the pot, to 350°F. Fry steaks one or two at a time until they are golden brown on both sides, about 2 minutes per side.

5. Transfer cooked steaks to a warm oven while you prepare the remaining steaks. Serve hot with gravy (see sidebar), if desired.

# Unstuffed Green Peppers Casserole

*You can use a can of whole tomatoes instead of diced, if you prefer. Just crush or cut up the tomatoes when you add them (and their juices) to the casserole.*

**PREP TIME:** 10 minutes
**COOK TIME:** 40 minutes

**INGREDIENTS | SERVES 4–6**

1 pound ground beef

1 medium yellow onion, peeled and chopped

1 (14.5-ounce) can chopped tomatoes

1 (8-ounce) can whole kernel corn, drained

2½ cups herb-seasoned bread crumbs, divided

2 large green bell peppers, seeded and cut into large dice

1 tablespoon unsalted butter, melted

1. Heat oven to 400°F.

2. Add beef and onion to an ovenproof 4-quart ovenproof Dutch oven; brown the hamburger over medium-high heat. Pour off any excess fat. Add tomatoes, corn, 2 cups bread crumbs, and green pepper pieces. Mix well. Cover and bake 25 minutes, or until the green peppers are tender.

3. In a small bowl, mix the remaining bread crumbs with the melted butter. Remove the cover from the casserole and sprinkle the bread crumbs over the top. Bake an additional 5 minutes, or until the bread crumbs are golden brown.

# Corn Chip and Chili Casserole

*Corn chips are salty, so consider using a reduced- or low-sodium chili in this recipe.*

**PREP TIME:** 10 minutes
**COOK TIME:** 20 minutes

**INGREDIENTS | SERVES 4–8**

3 cups corn chips, divided

1 large yellow onion, peeled and chopped

1 cup grated American cheese, divided

4 cups Texas Red Chili (Chapter 5) or 1 (19-ounce) can beef chili

1. Heat oven to 350°F.

2. Lightly spray a 6- or 8-quart Dutch oven with nonstick cooking spray. Spread 2 cups corn chips over the bottom of the pan. Distribute onion and ½ cup cheese over the top of corn chips, and then top with chili.

3. Add remaining corn chips and cheese over the top of chili.

4. Bake 15–20 minutes, or until casserole is heated through and cheese is melted.

# Cottage Pie

*While most people would call this dish shepherd's pie, it isn't. A true shepherd's pie is made with lamb, while the same dish made with beef is called cottage pie.*

**PREP TIME:** 10 minutes
**COOK TIME:** 1 hour 30 minutes

**INGREDIENTS | SERVES 8**

2 medium russet potatoes, peeled and cut into ½" pieces

1 tablespoon unsalted butter, softened

½ cup milk or half and half, at room temperature, divided

1 cup shredded sharp Cheddar cheese, divided

1½ teaspoons salt, divided

2 tablespoons vegetable oil

2 pounds ground beef

2 large onions, peeled and chopped

2 large carrots, peeled and chopped

2 stalks celery, chopped

3 cloves garlic, peeled and minced

½ teaspoon thyme

3 tablespoons all-purpose flour

1 cup red wine

2 cups beef stock

1. In an ovenproof 6-quart Dutch oven over high heat boil potatoes in salted water until they are fork tender, about 10 minutes. Drain potatoes and transfer to a bowl. With a masher or hand mixer, mash potatoes until smooth. Add butter and half the milk. Mix, adding additional milk as needed, until potatoes are smooth and creamy. Stir in ½ cup cheese and ¼ teaspoon of the salt. Set aside to cool.

2. Heat oven to 350°F.

3. Return the Dutch oven to medium heat and add oil. Once it shimmers add ground beef and cook until well browned. Add the remaining salt, onion, carrot, celery, garlic, and thyme and cook until vegetables are tender, about 10 minutes.

4. Add flour and, stirring constantly, cook 3 minutes, then add red wine and beef stock and stir well to work out any lumps. Bring mixture to a boil and, stirring occasionally, let the sauce thicken, about 5 minutes.

5. Spread potatoes over the top of beef mixture, using a fork to create lines in potato topping. Sprinkle reserved cheese evenly over the top and bake 35–40 minutes, or until potatoes and cheese are golden brown. Cool 10 minutes before serving.

# Unstuffed Cabbage Rolls

*Use Italian-seasoned tomatoes and cooked orzo pasta instead of the rice to give this dish a Tuscan flair. If you prefer German flavors, add 1 teaspoon of caraway seeds and 2 teaspoons of brown sugar with the rice.*

**PREP TIME:** 10 minutes
**COOK TIME:** 1 hour 10 minutes

**INGREDIENTS | SERVES 8**

2 tablespoons extra-virgin olive oil
6 stalks celery, diced
6 large carrots, peeled and diced
1 pound lean ground beef
1 large yellow onion, peeled and diced
2 cloves garlic, peeled and minced
1 teaspoon salt
¾ teaspoon freshly cracked black pepper
1 teaspoon granulated sugar
2 (15-ounce) cans diced tomatoes
2 cups cooked rice
4 cups coleslaw mix
1½ cups chicken broth
1 cup dry white wine

1. Heat oven to 350°F.

2. Heat oil over medium heat in a 6- or 8-quart Dutch oven. Add celery and carrots; sauté 5 minutes. Add ground beef and onion; stir-fry until beef is browned and broken apart and onion is transparent. Drain off and discard any excess fat.

3. Add remaining ingredients; stir into the beef mixture. Use the back of a spoon to press the mixture down evenly in the pan.

4. Cover and bake 45 minutes. Uncover and bake an additional 15 minutes, or until most of the liquid has evaporated.

# Potato Caraway Meatballs

*Potatoes add moisture, texture, and great flavor to these simple meatballs. Serve the meatballs over hot mashed potatoes.*

**PREP TIME:** 2–3 hours
**COOK TIME:** 50 minutes

**INGREDIENTS | SERVES 6**

1 cup frozen hash brown potatoes, thawed

½ teaspoon salt

⅛ teaspoon freshly ground black pepper

½ teaspoon lemon zest

1 teaspoon caraway seeds, divided

1 large egg

½ cup minced onion

2 cloves garlic, peeled and minced

1 pound ground beef

2 tablespoons olive oil

1 medium onion, peeled and chopped

3 cups beef broth, divided

¼ cup tomato paste

2 tablespoons cornstarch

¼ cup tomato juice

1. Drain potatoes and cut into finer pieces. In large bowl add potatoes along with salt, pepper, lemon zest, ½ teaspoon caraway seeds, egg, minced onion, and garlic. Mix well. Add ground beef and combine. Form into 2" meatballs and chill 2–3 hours.

2. When ready to eat, heat a 6- or 8-quart Dutch oven over medium-high heat. Add olive oil and once it shimmers add chopped onion. Cook, stirring constantly, until tender, about 5 minutes. Add meatballs and brown 5 minutes, turning frequently. You may need to work in batches to avoid crowding the Dutch oven.

3. In a small bowl, combine 1 cup beef broth with tomato paste and whisk until blended. Add to the Dutch oven along with remaining broth. Cover with the lid and simmer 25–30 minutes, or until the meatballs are tender.

4. In a small bowl, combine cornstarch and tomato juice. Stir into the Dutch oven along with the remaining ½ teaspoon caraway seeds and simmer 5–10 minutes, or until the sauce thickens.

# Meatball Curry

*Frozen, ready-to-heat meatballs make this dish a quick fix. To make it child friendly, substitute sweet bell pepper for the jalapeños. Serve this dish with basmati rice.*

**PREP TIME:** 10 minutes
**COOK TIME:** 20 minutes

**INGREDIENTS | SERVES 4**

2 tablespoons unsalted butter
1 large onion, peeled and sliced
2 jalapeño peppers, seeded and chopped
2 cloves garlic, peeled and minced
2 teaspoons curry powder
2 (15-ounce) cans diced tomatoes
½ cup coconut milk
24 frozen beef meatballs, thawed
¼ cup chopped fresh cilantro
Lime wedges, for garnish

1. In a 6- or 8-quart Dutch oven heat butter over medium-high heat. Once melted add onion, peppers, and garlic. Cook until tender, about 5 minutes.

2. Sprinkle curry powder over onion mixture and cook until fragrant, about 1 minute.

3. Add tomatoes, coconut milk, meatballs, and cilantro. Bring to a boil, then reduce the heat to medium and simmer 15 minutes, or until meatballs are heated through. Garnish with lime wedges.

## A World of Curries

Curry is both a dish—a stew—and a spice mix. Just as curry recipes differ from country to country, so do the recipes for curry spice blends. The curry powders available in most supermarkets reflect ingredients common to Indian curries, such as turmeric, cumin, cardamom, fenugreek, coriander, and peppers. Caribbean curry powders usually contain an extra shot of pepper as well as cloves, cinnamon, and nutmeg. Thai and Chinese curry seasonings are often sold in paste form and reflect the blend of aromatic roots, herbs, and peppers common to dishes in those countries.

# Chicken, Duck, and Turkey

# Chicken Cacciatore

*Cacciatore means hunter-style in Italian cooking, which means the meal is prepared with herbs, fresh vegetables like bell peppers and onions, and wine. You can use white or red wine in this dish, so use what is handy!*

**PREP TIME:** 15 minutes
**COOK TIME:** 1 hour

**INGREDIENTS | SERVES 4–6**

½ cup all-purpose flour

1 teaspoon salt, divided

1 teaspoon freshly cracked black pepper, divided

2–3 pounds bone-in, skin-on chicken breasts and thighs, breasts cut in half

½ cup olive oil

1 large onion, peeled and chopped

2 medium red bell peppers, seeded and chopped

2 cloves garlic, peeled and minced

1 cup dry white wine

1 (28-ounce) can diced tomatoes, undrained

1 cup low-sodium chicken broth

1 teaspoon oregano

1 bay leaf

½ teaspoon crushed red pepper flakes

¼ cup roughly chopped fresh basil leaves

## Selecting a Chicken

Your typical grocery store will have a wide variety of chicken available, but which one should you choose? When buying chicken look for birds that are organic, antibiotic and hormone free, and free range or, if you can source it, pasture raised. Pasture-raised chickens have the best flavor as they have been allowed to live free of cages, meaning the muscles have been worked more, and they have been allowed to peck for worms and bugs. These birds may not be as big as the traditional cage-raised birds and may cost a bit more, but they are much more flavorful!

1. In a zip-top bag add flour, ½ teaspoon salt, and ½ teaspoon pepper. Shake to combine, then add chicken pieces and shake to coat. Remove chicken to a wire rack while you heat the oil.

2. In a 6- or 8-quart Dutch oven over medium-high heat add olive oil. Once oil shimmers add chicken pieces to the pan making sure there is about ½" of space between pieces. You may need to fry in batches. Brown chicken well on both sides, about 5 minutes per side. Remove chicken to a plate to rest.

3. Reduce heat to medium and add onion and bell peppers. Sauté 3 minutes, or until just tender, then add garlic and cook until fragrant, about 30 seconds.

4. Pour in wine and, with a wooden spoon or heatproof spatula, scrape up any browned bits on the bottom of the Dutch oven. Once wine has reduced by half add remaining ingredients except basil and stir to combine.

5. Add chicken pieces to the pan and simmer until the chicken is cooked through, about 30–45 minutes.

6. Remove chicken to a platter and tent with foil to keep warm. Increase heat to medium-high and bring the sauce to a boil. Cook, stirring often, until the sauce reduces and thickens, about 6–8 minutes.

7. Return chicken to the Dutch oven, turn to evenly coat, and serve hot with basil as a garnish.

# Chicken Stew a la Bonne Femme

*This recipe can be made with 3 pounds of bone-in chicken breast halves or pieces of your choice.*

**PREP TIME:** 15 minutes
**COOK TIME:** 3 hours

**INGREDIENTS | SERVES 4–6**

1 pound bacon
1 (3-pound) chicken, cut into pieces
3 pounds white potatoes, peeled and cut in chunks
2 large onions, peeled and chopped
1 large green bell pepper, seeded and chopped
2 stalks celery, sliced
3 cloves garlic, peeled and minced
2 green onions, sliced
¼ cup minced parsley
½ teaspoon salt
½ teaspoon freshly cracked black pepper
¼ teaspoon cayenne pepper
3 cups chicken broth

1. In an ovenproof 6- or 8-quart Dutch oven over medium heat fry bacon until crisp and the fat has rendered, about 8–10 minutes. Remove bacon to a paper towel–lined plate to drain.

2. Add chicken to bacon drippings remaining in pot and brown well on both sides, about 3 minutes per side. Remove to a plate to rest. Add potato chunks to pot; brown on all sides, about 5 minutes, and remove to rest with the chicken.

3. In a medium bowl, combine onions, bell pepper, celery, garlic, green onions, and parsley; mix well. In a small bowl combine salt, pepper, and cayenne.

4. Heat oven to 350°F.

5. Carefully remove all but 1 or 2 tablespoons of the bacon drippings from pot. Layer the ingredients in Dutch oven in following order: ½ each of chicken, potatoes, bacon, vegetable mixture, and seasonings; remaining potatoes, bacon, chicken, vegetable mixture, and seasonings.

6. Carefully pour broth into the Dutch oven, cover with the lid, and roast for 2½ hours. Let stand 10 minutes before serving.

# Chicken Fricassee

*Chicken fricassee tops many folks' comfort food lists. This version smells heavenly while cooking. Serve this dish over rice.*

**PREP TIME:** 10 minutes
**COOK TIME:** 1 hour 45 minutes
**INGREDIENTS | SERVES 4–6**

1 teaspoon salt
½ teaspoon freshly ground black pepper
½ teaspoon cayenne pepper
½ teaspoon garlic powder
1 (4-pound) chicken, cut into 8 pieces
½ cup vegetable oil
⅔ cup all-purpose flour
1 large onion, peeled and diced, divided
6 cups chicken broth
1 large green bell pepper, seeded and diced
Pinch thyme
3 green onions, minced

## Dumplings Anyone?

Chicken-and-dumpling lovers will find this stew a perfect foil for white clouds of dough. At end of cooking time, remove the chicken pieces from the sauce and keep warm. Bring the sauce to a boil. Add a little more broth if it seems too thick. Prepare your favorite dumpling recipe (biscuit mix packages often have easy recipes printed on the back) and drop dumplings into the boiling broth. Reduce heat to medium, cover the pot, and simmer dumplings 12–15 minutes. Return chicken to the pot and serve.

1. Combine salt, pepper, cayenne, and garlic powder in a small bowl. Sprinkle the seasonings over the chicken.

2. Heat a 6- or 8-quart Dutch oven over medium-high heat. Add oil and once it shimmers add chicken and brown well on both sides, about 5 minutes per side. Remove chicken to a plate to rest.

3. Add flour into hot oil and cook, stirring constantly, until flour turns dark brown, about 8–10 minutes. Add ½ of onion and cook until fragrant, about 1 minute.

4. Carefully add the broth, stirring constantly, until flour mixture is dissolved in broth. Return chicken to pot along with remaining onion, bell pepper, and thyme.

5. Reduce heat to medium and cook, stirring occasionally, for 1½ hours, or until chicken is tender and sauce is thick. Stir in green onions.

# Chicken Divan

*This is a versatile casserole. You can stretch it to 8 servings by adding 1–2 cups of cooked diced potatoes. You can also substitute American, Cheddar, or Swiss cheese for the Parmigiano-Reggiano.*

**PREP TIME:** 10 minutes
**COOK TIME:** 45 minutes

**INGREDIENTS | SERVES 6**

¼ cup unsalted butter

¼ cup all-purpose flour

1 cup chicken broth

1 cup milk

½ teaspoon salt

½ teaspoon freshly cracked black pepper

⅛ teaspoon ground nutmeg

½ cup freshly grated Parmigiano-Reggiano, divided

3 tablespoons dry sherry

3 cups cooked chicken, cut into bite-sized pieces

1 (1-pound) bag broccoli florets, thawed

1 cup slivered almonds, divided

½ cup heavy cream

1. Heat oven to 350°F.

2. Melt butter over medium heat in an ovenproof 2-quart or larger Dutch oven. Add flour and cook, stirring constantly, 1 minute.

3. Gradually whisk in broth and milk; cook 3 minutes, or until it begins to thicken. Stir in salt, pepper, nutmeg, ¼ cup cheese, and sherry; cook until cheese melts.

4. Remove from heat and stir in the chicken, broccoli, half of almonds, and cream. Sprinkle remaining almonds and cheese over the top. Bake uncovered 35 minutes, or until bubbly and golden brown.

## Different Chicken Divan

For a lighter sauce, whip the cream until it reaches soft peaks and then fold it into the other Chicken Divan ingredients before you top the casserole with the remaining almonds and cheese. If you don't have heavy cream on hand, you can substitute sour cream or melt 4 ounces of cream cheese into the sauce before you add the chicken.

# Golden Fried Chicken Tenders

*Chicken tenders are easier and faster to prepare than bone-in fried chicken, and can be an appetizer with dipping sauces for a party, a main dish with mashed potatoes for dinner, or added to green salads for a speedy lunch!*

**PREP TIME:** 15 minutes
**COOK TIME:** 15 minutes

**INGREDIENTS | SERVES 4–6**

1 cup all-purpose flour
1 teaspoon salt
1 teaspoon freshly cracked black pepper
2 large eggs, beaten
1 cup buttermilk
1 teaspoon hot sauce, optional
2 pounds chicken tenders
Oil, for frying

1. In a large zip-top bag add flour, salt, and pepper. Shake well to coat.

2. In a shallow dish or pie pan add eggs and buttermilk. Whisk to combine, then add hot sauce, if desired, and whisk to incorporate.

3. Add a few tenders at a time to flour, toss to coat, then remove from the bag, shaking off any excess flour. Dip tenders into buttermilk mixture, allowing any excess to drip off, then return tenders to flour and toss again to coat. Transfer coated tenders to a wire rack to dry while you prepare remaining tenders.

4. In a 6- or 8-quart deep Dutch oven heat 3" oil over medium-high heat to 350°F, making sure there is a 3" air gap at the top of the pot. Once oil is hot add 3–4 tenders at a time and fry until golden brown and floating, about 3 minutes per side. Transfer to a clean wire rack over a sheet pan to drain. You may store cooked tenders in a warm oven while you fry the rest.

# Crispy Fried Chicken

*The double-dredge in this recipe is what makes the chicken so crispy.*
*The trick is to make the first flour coating very thin.*

**PREP TIME:** 4–12 hours
**COOK TIME:** 20 minutes

**INGREDIENTS | SERVES 4–6**

1 quart buttermilk
½ head garlic, peeled and minced
3 bay leaves
1 tablespoon chili powder
¼ cup sugar
¼ cup salt
2 tablespoons freshly ground black pepper
3½–4 pounds chicken pieces
4 cups all-purpose flour
1 large egg
1 teaspoon baking powder
½ teaspoon baking soda
1 cup whole milk
3 cups peanut or corn oil for frying

### Avoiding Dough Hands

If you keep one hand reserved for the flour and vow to not get it wet, and keep the other hand reserved for the batter and vow to not let it touch flour, you should be able to coat the chicken without letting the dough coat your fingers. Letting the chicken rest to drip off excess batter and flour will result in a thinner and crispier coat with less waste floating in the oil.

1. In a gallon-sized, zip-top plastic bag combine buttermilk, garlic, bay leaves, chili powder, sugar, salt, and pepper. Trim off any extra pieces of fat or skin from chicken. Pat the pieces dry and nestle them into the bag. Squeeze out any excess air, seal bag, and refrigerate overnight or at least 3 hours.

2. Place a wire rack over a baking sheet and place chicken pieces on the rack. Drain 30 minutes. Put flour in a shallow bowl. In a second bowl, whisk egg, baking powder, and baking soda. Once combined, add milk.

3. Place chicken pieces, one at a time, in flour and turn to coat. Shake off any excess and roll the pieces in egg mixture with your other hand. Drain to remove any excess and place back in flour. Turn to coat. Place pieces on the rack.

4. Heat 2" oil in a 6- or 8-quart Dutch oven over medium-high heat to 360°F making sure there is a 3" air gap at the top of the pot. Add a piece of chicken to the pan, skin side down. Add in two more pieces of chicken, waiting 1 minute between each. Cover and cook 4 minutes, or until the bottom of the first piece is a deep golden brown. Turn over. Turn over other pieces after waiting for intervals of 1 minute. Cook second side of each for 6–7 minutes.

5. Remove cooked chicken from pot and place on a paper towel–lined plate. Wait 4–5 minutes, or until oil has come back up to 375°F, before repeating Step 4 with the next batch of chicken. Serve warm or cold.

# Whole Roast Chicken with Fresh Herbs

*This chicken makes an impressive Sunday supper, and leftovers can be chopped up for chicken salad, or shredded and added to soups and stews, such as Old-Fashioned Chicken and Dumplings (Chapter 5).*

**PREP TIME:** 15 minutes
**COOK TIME:** 1 hour 15 minutes

**INGREDIENTS | SERVES 4–6**

1 (2–3 pound) whole chicken
2 teaspoons kosher salt
1 teaspoon freshly cracked black pepper
1 small bundle fresh thyme
1 small bundle fresh sage
2 sprigs fresh rosemary
1 medium lemon, cut into 4 wedges

### Make It a Whole Meal

If you want to make your chicken a complete meal just add 2 or 3 red potatoes, scrubbed and cut into quarters, 1 cup baby carrots, and 1 medium onion, cut into 1" pieces, to the bottom of the heated Dutch oven. Coat with 1 tablespoon olive oil and a pinch of salt and pepper and toss to coat. Place the chicken on the bed of vegetables and roast as directed. The fat from the chicken will run into the vegetables and give them a lot of flavor!

1. Heat oven to 450°F. Place an ovenproof 6- or 8-quart Dutch oven into oven to heat.

2. Pat chicken dry inside and out with paper towels, then coat the outside of chicken with salt and pepper, making sure to rub the spices into the skin evenly.

3. Stuff the cavity of the bird with fresh herbs and lemon wedges. Truss the bird by tying the legs together with butcher's twine, then wrapping twine around the base of the bird so the wings are held close to the body.

4. Carefully transfer chicken to the heated Dutch oven. Roast 50–60 minutes or until the juices from the thigh run clear and the internal temperature of the breast and thigh reach 160°F.

5. Allow chicken to rest 15 minutes. Remove and discard the twine and herbs and lemon from the chicken cavity and serve.

# Buttermilk Roasted Chicken Legs

*These chicken legs are tender, moist, and very juicy. They can be served hot or cold, so you can make these the night before for a picnic or potluck meal where you need a cold dish.*

**PREP TIME:** 4–12 hours
**COOK TIME:** 45 minutes

**INGREDIENTS | SERVES 4**

2 cups buttermilk
1 tablespoon maple syrup
1 teaspoon smoked paprika
½ teaspoon salt
½ teaspoon freshly cracked black pepper
½ teaspoon poultry seasoning
½ teaspoon hot sauce
8 chicken drumsticks, about 1½ pounds

1. In a large zip-top bag add all of ingredients except chicken. Close the bag and shake to combine then add chicken, seal the bag, and refrigerate 4 hours or overnight.

2. Remove chicken from the buttermilk and place in a colander 30 minutes to drain.

3. Heat oven to 400°F. Place an ovenproof 8- or 10-quart Dutch into oven to heat.

4. Once heated, lightly spray the Dutch oven with nonstick cooking spray. Arrange drumsticks in the bottom of the pan in a single layer. Roast 35–45 minutes, turning the legs halfway through, or until chicken legs reach an internal temperature of 160°F and the juices run clear.

# Wine-Braised Chicken Thighs

*The secret to braised chicken thighs with crisp skin is to get the chicken skin very crisp and browned, and to be sure the braising liquid only reaches halfway up the chicken.*

**PREP TIME:** 2–12 hours
**COOK TIME:** 1 hour

**INGREDIENTS | SERVES 4**

1–1½ pounds bone-in, skin-on chicken thighs
½ teaspoon salt
½ teaspoon freshly ground black pepper
¼ cup vegetable oil
1 medium onion, peeled and finely chopped
1 pint sliced button mushrooms
1 clove garlic, peeled and minced
¼ teaspoon thyme
¼ teaspoon crushed red pepper flakes
½ cup red wine
½ cup chicken broth
1 tablespoon unsalted butter

1. Season chicken thighs on all sides with salt and pepper. Place on a plate and refrigerate, uncovered, 2 hours or overnight, to dry out skin slightly.

2. In an ovenproof 6- or 8-quart Dutch oven over medium-high heat add oil. Once oil shimmers add chicken thighs skin side down, leaving ½" between each thigh. You may need to cook in batches. Cook until skin is very brown and crisp, about 6–8 minutes. Remove thighs to a plate and rest skin side up. Repeat with any remaining thighs.

3. Heat oven to 400°F.

4. Reduce Dutch oven heat to medium and add onions and mushrooms. Sauté until vegetables are tender, about 5 minutes, then add garlic, thyme, and red pepper flakes; cook until garlic is fragrant, about 30 seconds more.

5. Add red wine to the pan and, with a wooden spoon or heatproof spatula, scrape any browned bits off the bottom of the pan. Once wine has reduced by ¼, about 5–8 minutes, add chicken thighs back to the pot skin side up. Carefully pour in chicken broth until liquid reaches about halfway up the sides of the thighs. If you need more liquid use a little water.

6. Bake chicken uncovered 30–40 minutes, or until it is cooked through and reaches an internal temperature of 160°F. Remove thighs from the Dutch oven and return pan to medium heat.

7. Bring liquid to a boil and reduce by half, about 8 minutes, then reduce heat to medium-low and whisk in butter. Spoon sauce over thighs just before serving to preserve the crisp skin.

# Coq Au Vin

*This classic French dish, like so many others, was created to get the most out of the ingredients a farm kitchen was likely to have on hand. The long, slow cooking time was a great way to get a tasty dish out of what was probably an old rooster.*

**PREP TIME:** 10 minutes
**COOK TIME:** 2 hours 30 minutes

**INGREDIENTS | SERVES 4–5**

4 slices bacon

1 cup plus 2 tablespoons all-purpose flour, divided

1 teaspoon salt

¼ teaspoon ground pepper

1 fryer chicken cut into 8 pieces, or 3–4 pounds of chicken thighs

1 cup chicken broth

2 cups dry red wine

2 tablespoons Dijon mustard

2 cloves garlic, peeled and minced

3–4 sprigs fresh thyme

3 bay leaves

2 medium celery stalks, diced

2 large carrots, diced

1 medium onion, peeled and diced

1. Heat oven to 325°F.

2. Place an ovenproof 6- or 8-quart Dutch oven over medium heat. Cut bacon into 1" pieces and add to the pot. Cook until they start to turn crispy, then remove and reserve for another use. Drain all but 1 tablespoon of the drippings.

3. Combine 1 cup flour, salt, and pepper in a wide, shallow bowl. Dredge chicken pieces through flour and place them skin side down in the Dutch oven. Cook 3–4 minutes on each side, or until they're lightly honey-colored. Cook in batches if necessary.

4. Remove chicken once it's cooked. Add broth, wine, mustard, and garlic to pot, turn off heat, and place chicken back in Dutch oven. Tuck thyme and bay leaves amongst the chicken pieces. Sprinkle celery, carrots, and onion on top of the chicken. Cover and put in the oven. Cook 2–2½ hours.

5. Remove chicken and vegetables to a large bowl and cover to keep warm. Discard thyme and bay leaves. Place the Dutch oven over medium-high heat and let most of the liquid evaporate. Whisk in the remaining 2 tablespoons reserved flour quickly to keep from getting lumps. Once you have thick gravy, about 3 minutes, pour it over chicken pieces in bowl and serve warm.

# Smothered Chicken

*This chicken dish is truly a one-pot meal, and easy enough for a weeknight. All you need to make this perfect are some fluffy buttermilk biscuits!*

**PREP TIME:** 10 minutes
**COOK TIME:** 55 minutes

**INGREDIENTS | SERVES 8**

1 (4-pound) chicken, cut into 8 pieces

1 teaspoon salt, divided

½ teaspoon freshly ground black pepper, divided

¾ cup all-purpose flour, divided

4 tablespoons unsalted butter

2 medium carrots, peeled and chopped

1 medium onion, peeled and chopped

1 stalk celery, chopped

2 cloves garlic, peeled and minced

2 cups chicken broth

1. Pat chicken pieces dry with a paper towel and season all sides with ½ teaspoon salt mixed with ¼ teaspoon pepper. Place ½ cup flour in a large zip-top bag and add chicken. Shake the bag to coat chicken. Set aside.

2. In a 6- or 8-quart Dutch oven over medium-high heat, add butter. Once butter has melted and starts to foam add half the chicken pieces, browning well on all sides, about 3–5 minutes per side. Remove the browned chicken to a plate to rest while you brown remaining chicken. Add the second batch of chicken to the first and set aside.

3. To the Dutch oven add carrots, onion, and celery. Cook until vegetables are tender, about 5 minutes, then add garlic and cook until fragrant, about 30 seconds.

4. Add remaining salt, pepper, and flour to the Dutch oven, cook until flour starts to turn lightly golden, about 3 minutes, then slowly whisk in chicken broth, making sure to work out any lumps.

5. Add chicken back to the Dutch oven, reduce heat to medium-low, cover, and simmer for 30–40 minutes, or until chicken is cooked through and reaches an internal temperature of 160°F.

6. Remove the lid and let gravy thicken, about 10 minutes. Serve hot.

# Puerto Rican Chicken and Beans

*Puerto Rican cooking has Spanish, African, Taíno (pre-Columbian inhabitants of the Bahamas), and American influences.*

**PREP TIME:** 15 minutes
**COOK TIME:** 2 hours

**INGREDIENTS | SERVES 8**

¼ pound salt pork or bacon, diced
1 large carrot, peeled and shredded
1 celery stalk, finely diced
1 large yellow onion, peeled and diced
3 cloves garlic, peeled and minced
½ pound Spanish or Mexican chorizo sausage, diced or thinly sliced
½ pound ham, chopped
2 pounds chicken thighs
4 cups water, or more, as needed
2 teaspoons Worcestershire sauce
½ teaspoon hot sauce
4 large russet potatoes, peeled and diced
1 small head cabbage, cored and thinly sliced
2 cups kale, tough stems removed, and thinly sliced
4 turnips, diced
1 (15-ounce) can white beans, rinsed and drained
½ teaspoon salt
½ teaspoon freshly cracked black pepper

## Or, If You Prefer . . .

If you or someone at your table insists on eating the chicken skin, you can skip Step 5. Proceed straight to Step 6, and add the thighs to the top of the stew after you've stirred in the beans.

1. Add salt pork or bacon to a 6- or 8-quart Dutch oven; cook over medium heat until the fat is rendered from bacon, about 8–10 minutes. Add carrot and celery; sauté 3–5 minutes, or until soft. Add onion and sauté until transparent, about 5 minutes. Add garlic and sauté an additional 30 seconds.

2. Stir in sausage; continue to stir as it fries, 2–3 minutes, then stir in ham. Add chicken to the pan, skin side down, pushing other ingredients to the side so that as much of the chicken as possible touches the pan bottom. Cover and cook 10 minutes.

3. Add water, Worcestershire sauce, and hot sauce; bring to a simmer. Reduce heat, cover, and simmer 35–45 minutes or until chicken is cooked through. Remove chicken from pan and set aside.

4. Add potatoes, cabbage, kale, and turnips to the pan. Stir to combine with other ingredients. Cover and simmer 30 minutes.

5. Shred chicken, discarding skin and bones. Stir shredded chicken into the pan.

6. Stir beans into the pan. Add additional water if needed to prevent the pan from boiling dry. Cover and simmer 10 minutes. Season with salt and pepper.

# Barley and Mushroom Casserole

*This is a delicious way to use leftover chicken. Most other seasonings go well with the basil and parsley, but you can adjust the seasoning in this recipe according to how the chicken was cooked, if necessary.*

**PREP TIME:** 10 minutes
**COOK TIME:** 1 hour 15 minutes

**INGREDIENTS | SERVES 8**

6 tablespoons unsalted butter

1 large carrot, peeled and shredded

1 stalk celery, finely diced

2 medium yellow onions, peeled and diced

2 cloves garlic, peeled and minced

1 pound button or cremini mushrooms, cleaned and sliced

1 cup pearl barley

½ tablespoon dried basil

½ tablespoon dried parsley

3 cups chicken broth

2 cups cooked chicken, shredded or diced

½ teaspoon salt

½ teaspoon freshly cracked black pepper

1. Heat oven to 375°F.

2. Melt butter in an ovenproof 4-quart Dutch oven over medium heat. Add carrot and celery; sauté 3–5 minutes, or until soft. Add onion and sauté until transparent, about 5 minutes. Add garlic and sauté an additional 30 seconds.

3. Add mushroom slices and sauté 5 minutes or until they begin to brown.

4. Stir in barley, basil, parsley, broth, chicken, salt, and pepper; bring to a boil.

5. Remove from heat, cover, and bake 50 minutes, or until the barley is tender. Serve hot.

# Chicken Étouffée

*Étouffée comes from the French étouffer, which means "to smother," and is basically a meat smothered in sauce and then served over rice.*

**PREP TIME:** 10 minutes
**COOK TIME:** 1 hour 10 minutes
**INGREDIENTS | SERVES 6–8**

1½ pounds bone-in chicken thighs
Pinch salt
Pinch pepper
½ cup all-purpose flour, divided
½ cup vegetable oil
2 medium onions, peeled and chopped
2 medium bell peppers, seeded and chopped
2 jalapeño peppers, seeded, stemmed, and minced
3 cloves garlic, peeled and minced
2 teaspoons dried thyme
2 teaspoons dried sage
3 cups chicken broth
½ cup cooked white rice per serving
Hot sauce for serving

## Substitution Options

Making this dish with 1 pound of crawfish meat is most common in Louisiana, but since they're hard to get outside of the area, you can substitute 1 pound peeled shrimp or 1 pound of lump crabmeat. If you like you can make this with a combinations of crawfish, crab, and shrimp.

1. Season chicken with salt and pepper and coat with 2 tablespoons of flour. Heat a 6- or 8-quart Dutch oven over medium-high heat. Add oil. Once oil is heated add chicken and cook 7 minutes on the first side. Flip chicken and cook 6–7 minutes more. Don't crowd chicken; cook it in batches. Place cooked chicken on a plate and keep it warm.

2. Slowly add remaining flour to oil in Dutch oven, whisking constantly. Once all of flour is added, stir continuously up to 25 minutes, or until the mixture turns golden in color. Use the whisk to scrape the edges of the Dutch oven to prevent the roux from browning. This roux should be light. Add onions, peppers, and garlic.

3. Reduce heat to low and stir in thyme and sage. Add broth, slowly whisking flour mixture to prevent lumps. Once you have a smooth sauce, return chicken to the pot and bring to a boil.

4. Reduce heat to low, cover, and cook 20 minutes. The chicken should be very tender. Stir and flip occasionally.

5. Skim off any fat that may come to the top. Serve it over bowls of hot rice with hot sauce to taste.

# Chicken Asapao

*This chicken stew is fairly typical of a classic Puerto Rican dish. Serve this dish over rice with a sprinkle of freshly chopped cilantro and hot sauce if desired.*

**PREP TIME:** 10 minutes
**COOK TIME:** 1 hour 30 minutes

**INGREDIENTS | SERVES 4**

1 pound boneless, skinless chicken breasts

3 cups chicken broth

2 medium potatoes, peeled and cut into ½" cubes

1 (8-ounce) can tomato sauce

¼ cup Sofrito (see sidebar)

1 teaspoon salt

2 bay leaves

¼ cup small green olives

Juice from 1 medium lime

1. Place a 6- or 8-quart Dutch oven over medium heat. Once it is heated add chicken breasts and broth. Add water if necessary so breasts are covered. Cook 30 minutes. Remove breasts from the pan and cut into ¼" cubes.

2. Return chicken cubes to the pot with all remaining ingredients except the lime juice. Stir to combine. Reduce heat to low; cover. Simmer 45–60 minutes or until chicken is soft.

3. Remove bay leaves and stir lime juice into the pan.

## Sofrito

Peel 1 large onion; cut into quarters. Put into food processor with 3 cubanelle peppers, stems and seeds removed; 3 cloves garlic, peeled; half a bunch of cilantro; 3 tomatoes, stems removed; and 1 medium green bell pepper, stem and seeds removed. Pulse until well blended. Leftovers can be frozen.

# Alsatian Chicken

*This would be a great dish to serve with Scalloped Potatoes (Chapter 7) or Quick Stovetop Mac and Cheese (Chapter 6).*

**PREP TIME:** 10 minutes
**COOK TIME:** 1 hour 45 minutes

**INGREDIENTS | SERVES 4**

4 tablespoons unsalted butter, divided

1 pound chicken thighs, about 4 pieces

1 medium onion, peeled and sliced

8 ounces mushrooms, sliced

2 tablespoons brandy

1 cup Riesling wine

1 tablespoon dry mustard powder

¼ teaspoon salt

¼ teaspoon freshly cracked black pepper

¼ cup whole milk

## Taste Alsace

Cast-iron cookware is common in Alsace, France, a region near Germany. This dish, like many other dishes of the region, combines elements of classic French and German cooking to create a very flavorful one-pot meal. You could also add a few chopped potatoes and carrots before Step 5.

1. Heat oven to 350°F.

2. Place an ovenproof 6- or 8-quart Dutch oven over high heat. Once it is warmed, add 3 tablespoons butter. When it's melted, add chicken thighs, skin side down. Cook 6–7 minutes, or until the skin is golden brown. Turn chicken over and cook an additional 5 minutes.

3. Place chicken on a plate and keep it warm. Reduce heat to medium, add onion, and cook 5 minutes. Sprinkle mushrooms into pan and cook 5 minutes.

4. Add brandy, wine, and dry mustard to the Dutch oven and increase the heat slightly. Stir to scrape up any stuck-on bits. Once the liquid starts to simmer, turn off the burner and place chicken back in the Dutch oven.

5. Cover with the lid and place the Dutch oven in the middle of the oven and cook 1 hour and 15 minutes. Remove chicken to a clean plate and keep it warm. Place the Dutch oven over a medium-high burner and let the liquid reduce until 1 cup is left, about 10 minutes, then season with salt and pepper.

6. Stir milk and 1 tablespoon butter into the sauce. Melt butter and quickly whisk the sauce before pouring it over the chicken to serve.

# Chicken à la King

*Several venues claim to be the point of origin for Chicken à la King. There are two things we know: It is an American dish, and it first shows up in cookbooks in 1898.*

**PREP TIME:** 10 minutes
**COOK TIME:** 20 minutes

**INGREDIENTS | SERVES 4**

2 tablespoons unsalted butter

1 green onion, chopped

4 ounces mushrooms, quartered

1 small red bell pepper, seeded and diced

2 tablespoons all-purpose flour

1½ cups chicken broth

1 cup light cream

2 cups diced cooked chicken

¼ teaspoon salt

¼ teaspoon freshly cracked black pepper

4 puff pastry shells or 4 slices toast

1. In a 6- or 8-quart Dutch oven melt butter over medium-high heat. Add green onion, mushrooms, and bell pepper, and cook until tender, about 5 minutes.

2. Add flour and stir to coat. Add broth and stir until flour dissolves. Bring mixture to boil; cook, stirring often, 10 minutes or until the liquid is reduced by ⅓.

3. Reduce heat to medium-low. Stir in cream, chicken, salt, and pepper. Simmer 5 minutes, then remove from heat. Serve in puff pastry shells or over toast.

# Chicken Paprikash Medley

*The chopped red bell pepper usually found in broccoli stir-fry mix gives this dish an unexpected flavor. However, if you don't like the crunch added by the water chestnuts in the mix, you can substitute a 1-pound bag of broccoli florets or broccoli and cauliflower mix.*

**PREP TIME:** 15 minutes
**COOK TIME:** 25 minutes

**INGREDIENTS | SERVES 8**

1 tablespoon unsalted butter

1 tablespoon extra-virgin olive oil

1 large yellow onion, peeled and diced

1½ pounds boneless, skinless chicken breasts, cut into bite-sized pieces

4 cloves garlic, peeled and minced

½ teaspoon salt

½ teaspoon freshly cracked black pepper

4 tablespoons Hungarian paprika, divided

4 cups chicken broth, divided

2 tablespoons all-purpose flour

1 (1-pound) bag frozen broccoli stir-fry mix, thawed

16 ounces sour cream

4 cups cooked egg noodles or spaetzle

1. In a 6- to 8-quart Dutch oven add butter and oil over medium-high heat. Once the butter melts and starts to foam add onion and sauté 3 minutes. Add chicken to Dutch oven and stir-fry 5 minutes.

2. Stir in garlic, salt, pepper, 3 tablespoons of the paprika, and 3½ cups chicken broth; cover pan. Bring to a boil.

3. In a small bowl mix remaining ½ cup chicken broth with flour. Strain out any lumps then whisk broth mixture into the boiling broth. Boil 3 minutes.

4. Stir in broccoli stir-fry mix; lower the temperature, cover, and simmer 5 minutes.

5. Remove pan from the burner and stir in sour cream. Pour chicken and vegetable mixture over cooked noodles or spaetzle. Sprinkle remaining paprika over top. Serve immediately.

## Thickening or Thinning

The temperature at which you simmer the paprikash will affect how thick or thin the sauce gets. The sour cream added at the end of the cooking time will also thicken the sauce. If the sauce is too thin, add more sour cream. If it's too thick, slowly whisk in some additional chicken broth, milk, or water.

# Braised and Pan-Seared Duck Legs

*This dish is more commonly known as duck confit, but only if you plan on keeping the meat in the jar with the fat in your refrigerator.*

**PREP TIME:** 12 hours
**COOK TIME:** 3 hours 15 minutes

**INGREDIENTS | SERVES 2**

2 duck legs with skin on, about 1 pound
¼ teaspoon salt
¼ teaspoon freshly cracked black pepper
2 bay leaves, crumbled
Thumb-sized bundle fresh thyme
Skin from remainder of duck

## The Glory of Duck Fat

Duck fat rivals bacon fat for flavor, but its higher smoke point makes it perfect for frying. Duck fat can be substituted in any vegetable recipe that requires 1–3 tablespoons oil. French fries cooked in duck fat are the most flavorful you'll come across. They're perfect when served with garlicky mayonnaise for dipping.

1. Sprinkle duck legs with salt and pepper. Place in an airtight container with bay leaves and thyme and refrigerate 12–24 hours.

2. Place an ovenproof 4- or 6-quart Dutch oven over medium-low heat. Once it is heated, add duck skin to the Dutch oven and cook 1 hour, stirring occasionally to keep the fat from sticking. Cool 15 minutes then remove the skin and discard.

3. Heat oven to 300°F.

4. Carefully place duck legs in the Dutch oven with bay leaves and thyme. Place in the middle of the oven and cook 2 hours, or until the bone moves independently of the meat. The skin should be crispy.

5. Remove pan from the oven and set it aside to cool. Let oil cool and pour off the fat. Remove the duck legs. Duck meat can be eaten now, or shredded and used in another recipe.

6. Duck fat will keep up to 2 months in an airtight container in the refrigerator.

# Turkey, Spinach, and Artichoke Casserole

*This is an adaptation of traditional hot spinach and artichoke dip. If you want to serve it as a dip or for a light lunch, simply mix all ingredients together in a food processor and bake it according to the recipe instructions.*

**PREP TIME:** 10 minutes
**COOK TIME:** 40 minutes

**INGREDIENTS | SERVES 10–12**

1 (14-ounce) jar artichoke hearts, drained and chopped

3 (10-ounce) packages frozen chopped spinach, thawed and well drained

2 cups finely chopped cooked turkey

2 (8-ounce) packages cream cheese, cut into cubes

2 tablespoons mayonnaise

¼ cup unsalted butter or extra-virgin olive oil

6 tablespoons heavy cream or milk

½ teaspoon freshly cracked black pepper

½ cup freshly grated Parmigiano-Reggiano or Romano cheese

1. Heat oven to 375°F.

2. Evenly spread artichoke hearts across the bottom of an ovenproof 8-quart Dutch oven. Top with spinach and turkey.

3. Add cream cheese, mayonnaise, butter or oil, and cream or milk to a food processor; process until smooth. Spread over top of turkey. Sprinkle with pepper, and then cheese.

4. Bake uncovered 40 minutes, or until the cheese is bubbly and the casserole is lightly browned on top. This dish can be assembled the night before and refrigerated; allow extra baking time if you move the casserole directly from the refrigerator to the oven.

## Turkey, Spinach, and Artichoke Fondue

Add all ingredients to a food processor and process until smooth. Put into an electric fondue pot set at medium-high heat. Bring mixture to temperature, stirring frequently. Once it's heated through, reduce the setting to warm to hold the fondue. Serve with bread, crackers, or crudités.

# Turkey Mole

*Most true mole sauces are cooked for hours and require a lot of work. But this lazy mole gives a lot of the same flavor without as much effort. Serve this mole with rice and beans.*

**PREP TIME:** 10 minutes
**COOK TIME:** 2 hours 45 minutes

**INGREDIENTS | SERVES 6–8**

1 tablespoon vegetable oil

1 (3–5-pound) turkey breast

8 dried New Mexico chilies, stemmed and seeded

1 medium onion, peeled and chopped

4 cloves garlic, peeled and smashed

½ cup chopped peanuts

1 teaspoon dried oregano

2 tablespoons cumin

1 teaspoon salt

½ teaspoon freshly ground black pepper

¼ cup cocoa powder

Water, as needed

## The Legend of Mole

No one really knows how mole came about. Some say nuns witnessed an angelic vision revealing how to stretch their meager rations into a feast for a visiting archbishop. It's also rumored that Montezuma served the dish to the conquistadors, whom he thought were gods.

1. Heat oven to 275°F.

2. Place a 6- or 8-quart Dutch oven over medium heat. Once it is heated, add oil and turkey. Cook on each side 3–4 minutes, or until lightly browned. Remove from the pan; set aside.

3. Place chilies in a layer on bottom of pan. Sprinkle onion, garlic, peanuts, oregano, cumin, salt, pepper, and cocoa on top. Place turkey breast on top of the seasonings. Add just enough water so meat is covered.

4. Place Dutch oven in the center of oven, cover, and cook 2½ hours. Remove breast from pan and cover it to keep warm. Strain cooking liquid over a large bowl. Place all chilies, onions, garlic, and peanuts into a blender. Add 2 cups cooking liquid from bowl. Purée until smooth. Discard the rest of the cooking liquid.

5. Return puréed broth to the Dutch oven over medium-low heat. Slice turkey breast on an angle into thin slices. Return turkey to pan and heat until warm.

# Turkey Pilaf

*Adjust the amount of turkey you add to this recipe according to the number of people you need to serve or the amount of protein you prefer in a meal. Choose the vegetables according to your family's tastes.*

**PREP TIME:** 10 minutes
**COOK TIME:** 30 minutes

**INGREDIENTS | SERVES 4–6**

2 tablespoons unsalted butter

1 small yellow onion, peeled and chopped

1 cup uncooked long-grain rice

2 cloves garlic, peeled and minced

1½ cups chicken broth

½ cup dry white wine

½ teaspoon salt

1 (12-ounce) steam-in-the-bag frozen mixed vegetables

1–2 cups chopped cooked turkey

Freshly grated Parmigiano-Reggiano cheese, for garnish

### Veggies Fresh from the Garden Pilaf

This recipe variation will require a second pot, but you can cut up a pound of fresh vegetables—zucchini, yellow summer squash, and/or sweet peppers—and sauté them in 2 tablespoons of butter until tender. Substitute them for the microwave-steamed vegetables in Step 3.

1. Add the butter to a 6- or 8-quart Dutch oven and melt over medium heat. Add the onion and sauté 2 minutes. Add rice and brown it in butter, about 6–8 minutes. Watch carefully as the rice can burn easily. Add garlic and sauté 30 seconds.

2. Pour in broth and wine. Bring to a boil and then add salt. Cover; simmer 20 minutes, or until rice is tender.

3. While the rice cooks, microwave vegetables in the bag 4–5 minutes.

4. Uncover the rice and add turkey and microwave-steamed vegetables. Stir to combine. Cover and cook on low 2 minutes. Remove the cover and stir. Cover and continue to cook until the turkey is warmed through, if necessary.

5. Serve warm topped with cheese.

# Turkey and Biscuits

*You can punch up the flavor of this dish by adding ½ teaspoon dried sage and 1–2 teaspoons dried parsley when you add the pepper. The style of biscuits you use is up to you; just keep in mind that the bigger the biscuits, the longer they'll take to bake.*

**PREP TIME:** 10 minutes
**COOK TIME:** 40 minutes

**INGREDIENTS | SERVES 4**

1 tablespoon extra-virgin olive oil

1 tablespoon unsalted butter

1 medium yellow onion, peeled and chopped

1 stalk celery, chopped

½ teaspoon salt

3 tablespoons all-purpose flour

1 cup chicken broth

1½ cups milk

1 (12-ounce) package frozen peas and carrots

2 cups cubed cooked turkey

½ teaspoon freshly cracked black pepper

1 recipe Biscuit Topping for Savory Stews (Chapter 3)

1. Heat oven to 425°F.

2. Add oil and butter to a 6- or 8-quart Dutch oven over medium heat. Once the butter melts and starts to foam add onion, celery, and salt and sauté 5 minutes, or until onion is transparent. Sprinkle flour over cooked vegetables and stir-fry 2 minutes to cook flour.

3. Slowly add chicken broth to the pan, whisking to prevent lumps from forming. Stir milk into broth. Increase the temperature to medium-high and bring to a boil. Reduce heat and simmer 5 minutes, or until mixture begins to thicken. Add peas and carrots, turkey, and pepper. Mix well.

4. Scoop biscuit dough over the top of turkey mixture. Bake 20–25 minutes, or until biscuits are golden brown.

## Ground Turkey and Biscuits

You can substitute a pound of ground turkey for the cooked turkey in this recipe. Simply add it when you sauté the onion and celery. Fry it until the turkey is cooked through, using a spatula to break up the turkey as it cooks. You may need to drain off a little excess oil before you add the flour, but otherwise you simply follow the recipe.

# Oven-Roasted Turkey Breast with Asparagus

*The internal temperature of a baked turkey breast cutlet should be 170°F.
The size and thickness of the cutlet can alter the baking time.*

**PREP TIME:** 20 minutes
**COOK TIME:** 25 minutes

**INGREDIENTS | SERVES 4**

4 medium baking potatoes

2 tablespoons unsalted butter, softened

1 teaspoon Dijon mustard

1 (7-ounce) jar roasted red sweet peppers, drained and chopped

4 teaspoons peeled, finely chopped red onion or shallot

¼ teaspoon dried tarragon, crushed

½ teaspoon dried parsley, crushed

⅛ teaspoon salt

⅛ teaspoon freshly cracked black pepper

1 pound asparagus spears

2 tablespoons extra-virgin olive oil

4 (4-ounce) boneless turkey breast cutlets

## Pampering Picky Eaters

If you have someone in your family who doesn't want one food to touch another, you can bake this recipe in three separate baking dishes. Treat the dishes with non-stick spray and put the turkey cutlets in one, the potatoes in another, and the asparagus in the third. It defeats the one-pot concept of Dutch oven cooking, but it will probably keep your life simpler.

1. Heat oven to 325°F.

2. Clean and pierce potatoes. Place on a microwave-safe plate and microwave on high 6–10 minutes, or until they can be pierced easily with a knife.

3. In a small bowl, combine butter, mustard, peppers, onion or shallot, tarragon, parsley, salt, and black pepper; set aside.

4. Clean asparagus and snap off and discard the woody bases. Carefully cut potatoes into quarters. Add potatoes, asparagus, and olive oil to a large zip-top plastic bag. Close the bag and shake to coat vegetables. Pour potatoes and asparagus out of the bag into an ovenproof 8-quart Dutch oven.

5. Evenly spread butter mixture over the top of turkey cutlets. Place cutlets on top of potatoes and asparagus. Bake 15–20 minutes, or until turkey is baked through and asparagus is tender.

# Turkey Pipperade

*Buy ready-to-cook thin-sliced turkey cutlets at your supermarket meat counter. For a splurge, veal cutlets can be used in this recipe as well. Serve this dish over rice.*

**PREP TIME:** 10 minutes
**COOK TIME:** 15 minutes

**INGREDIENTS | SERVES 4**

1 pound turkey breast cutlets

⅓ cup all-purpose flour

1 teaspoon seasoned salt

2 tablespoons unsalted butter

1 medium onion, peeled and thinly sliced

1 small red bell pepper, seeded and thinly sliced

1 small green bell pepper, seeded and thinly sliced

1 cup turkey or chicken broth

1 cup white wine

¼ teaspoon salt

¼ teaspoon freshly cracked black pepper

1. Lightly pound turkey cutlets with a meat mallet. Combine flour and seasoned salt in a shallow dish, then dredge turkey in the mixture.

2. Heat butter in a 6- or 8-quart Dutch oven over medium-high heat. Place cutlets in butter and brown, about 3 minutes per side. Spread onions and peppers evenly over top of cutlets. Carefully add broth and wine to the Dutch oven.

3. Cover with the lid and cook until turkey is cooked through and vegetables are crisp-tender, about 10 minutes. Season with salt and pepper.

# CHAPTER 10

# Pork

# Braised Pork Shoulder

*Pork shoulder takes a long time to become tender, so if you need this to cook more quickly cut the pork shoulder into smaller pieces to speed things up.*

**PREP TIME:** 10 minutes
**COOK TIME:** 3 hours

**INGREDIENTS | SERVES 8**

1 (3-pound) pork shoulder
½ teaspoon cumin
½ teaspoon coriander
½ teaspoon salt
½ teaspoon freshly cracked black pepper
2 tablespoons vegetable oil
1 large onion, peeled and sliced
1 fennel bulb, sliced
2 cloves garlic, peeled and minced
¼ teaspoon crushed red pepper flakes
2 cups white wine
2 bay leaves
Water, to cover

1. Pat pork shoulder dry with paper towels. In a small bowl combine cumin, coriander, salt, and pepper. Rub spices on all sides of pork shoulder. Set aside.

2. In an ovenproof 6- or 8-quart Dutch oven over medium heat add oil. Add pork and brown well on all sides, about 5 minutes per side. Remove to a plate to rest.

3. Heat oven to 350°F.

4. To the Dutch oven add onion and fennel. Cook until vegetables are tender, about 5 minutes. Add garlic and crushed red pepper flakes and cook until fragrant, about 30 seconds.

5. Add wine to the pot and, with a wooden spoon or heatproof spatula, scrape any browned bits off the bottom of the Dutch oven. Add pork shoulder back to the Dutch oven along with bay leaves and enough water to come halfway up the side of the roast. Cover and bake 1 hour, then turn pork over and cook another hour.

6. Turn pork roast back over, uncover, and roast another 30–45 minutes, or until pork is fork tender and braising liquid has reduced. Remove pork from the liquid and allow to rest on a cutting board tented with foil 10 minutes.

7. Once rested slice pork and arrange on a platter. Skim any excess fat from the braising liquid, remove bay leaves, and pour liquid over pork slices. Serve hot.

# Pork Tenderloin in Roasted Root Vegetable Stew

*Serve this hearty, colorful dish in the fall just as the leaves are beginning to turn. For best results, vegetables should be diced 1" or smaller.*

**PREP TIME:** 15 minutes
**COOK TIME:** 1 hour 10 minutes

**INGREDIENTS | SERVES 6**

¼ cup plus 1 tablespoon olive oil, divided
1 tablespoon balsamic vinegar
1 medium onion, peeled and diced
8 large cloves garlic, peeled, divided
1 cup diced parsnips
1 cup diced rutabaga
1 cup diced turnips
1 cup diced beets
1 cup diced carrots
1 cup diced potatoes
1 cup diced sweet potatoes
½ teaspoon salt
½ teaspoon freshly cracked black pepper
2 tablespoons fresh rosemary leaves
1½ pounds pork tenderloin
1 tablespoon soy sauce
2 tablespoons orange zest
½ cup orange juice

1. Heat oven to 350°F.

2. In a small bowl, whisk together ¼ cup olive oil and balsamic vinegar.

3. In an ovenproof 6- or 8-quart Dutch oven combine onion, 6 cloves garlic, and all diced vegetables. Toss with oil and vinegar mixture to coat. Add salt, pepper, and rosemary, then bake 45 minutes, stirring occasionally.

4. Coat pork with the remaining olive oil and sprinkle with soy sauce. Put remaining garlic cloves through a press and spread evenly over pork along with orange zest. Place pork over the vegetables and bake 15–20 minutes. Add orange juice in last 5 minutes of cooking to deglaze the pan.

5. Remove pork to a serving platter and allow to rest 5 minutes. Slice thickly and ladle pan drippings and vegetables over the slices.

# Pineapple Pork Roast

*Fresh pineapple should not be used in this recipe as the enzymes in the fresh fruit will make the pork a little mushy.*

**PREP TIME:** 10 minutes
**COOK TIME:** 3 hours 15 minutes

**INGREDIENTS | SERVES 8**

1 (3-pound) pork roast
¼ cup all-purpose flour
½ teaspoon salt
½ teaspoon freshly cracked black pepper
2 tablespoons vegetable oil
1 medium onion, peeled and sliced
2 cloves garlic, peeled and minced
1 teaspoon fresh grated ginger
1 (16-ounce) can pineapple chunks in juice, undrained
2 tablespoons soy sauce
2 tablespoons mirin, or 1 tablespoon sugar mixed with 1 tablespoon sake
Water, to cover

## Tenderizing with Pineapple

Pineapple, especially the stem, contains an enzyme called bromelain. This enzyme is very effective at tenderizing meat by breaking down the collagen and connective tissue in the meat. The dry, powdered form of bromelain is sold as a meat tenderizer under several brand names. The enzyme is only active in fresh pineapple or in the dry powder as it is heat sensitive and is destroyed in the canning process.

1. Pat pork roast dry with paper towels. In a small bowl combine flour, salt, and pepper. Coat the roast with flour mixture, reserving any remaining mixture. Set aside.

2. Heat oven to 375°F.

3. In an ovenproof 6- or 8-quart Dutch oven over medium heat add oil. Once it shimmers add roast and brown well on all sides, about 5 minutes per side. Remove roast to a plate to rest.

4. To the Dutch oven add onion and cook until tender, about 5 minutes. Add garlic and ginger and cook until fragrant, about 30 seconds. Add any reserved flour and stir to coat onions.

5. Add pineapple chunks with their juice, soy sauce, and mirin. With a wooden spoon or heatproof spatula, scrape up any browned bits from the bottom of the Dutch oven. Add roast back to the pot and add enough water so it comes halfway up the side of roast. Cover and bake 1 hour, then flip the roast and cook another hour.

6. Remove the lid and cook another 40–50 minutes, or until roast is tender and sauce has thickened slightly. Remove roast from the liquid and allow to rest, tented with foil, 10 minutes, before slicing and arranging on a platter. Pour the braising liquid over the pork. Serve hot.

# Roast Pork Loin with Apples

*Herbes de Provence is a mixture of equal amounts of thyme, savory, marjoram, and oregano. It sometimes also includes some sage, rosemary, dried lavender flowers, and/or fennel seeds.*

**PREP TIME:** 10 minutes
**COOK TIME:** 1 hour 35 minutes

**INGREDIENTS | SERVES 8**

1 teaspoon salt

¼ teaspoon freshly cracked black pepper

2 teaspoons herbes de Provence

1 (4-pound) pork loin, trimmed of fat and silver skin

2 tablespoons unsalted butter

1 tablespoon vegetable oil

3 large Golden Delicious apples, cored and cut into wedges

¼ teaspoon granulated sugar

4 large Yukon gold potatoes, peeled and quartered

## Pan Size

The amount of air space between the food and the lid may add to the cooking time, but when in doubt, go bigger. It saves you the aggravation of having to move the ingredients to a bigger pot if the one you picked doesn't have enough room to hold all of the ingredients, and it prevents boil-overs in the oven.

1. Heat oven to 375°F.

2. In a small bowl, mix salt, pepper, and herbes de Provence together and rub it into meat.

3. Add butter and oil to an ovenproof 9-quart Dutch oven over medium-high heat. Once the butter melts and starts to foam add the roast and brown it 2 minutes on each sides, or about 8 minutes total.

4. Remove meat from the pan and arrange apple slices over the bottom of the pan. Sprinkle apples with sugar. Nestle meat on top of apples. Arrange potato wedges around meat.

5. Cover and bake 30 minutes. Remove the cover and baste meat with the pan juices. Continue to bake uncovered 45 minutes, or until the internal temperature of roast is 150°F. Remove roast to a serving platter and tent with aluminum foil; let rest 10 minutes.

6. Slice pork crosswise into 8 slices. Arrange apples and potatoes around roast. Ladle the pan juices over roast. Serve immediately.

# BBQ Pulled Pork

*This pork makes excellent pork sandwiches or sliders, or can be used as a topping for baked potatoes. You can also serve this on top of Baked Five-Cheese Macaroni and Cheese (Chapter 6) for a decadent meal!*

**PREP TIME:** 10 minutes
**COOK TIME:** 3 hours 30 minutes

**INGREDIENTS | SERVES 8**

1 (3-pound) pork shoulder
1 teaspoon cumin
½ teaspoon smoked paprika
½ teaspoon salt
½ teaspoon freshly cracked black pepper
2 tablespoons vegetable oil
2 large onions, peeled and sliced
2 cloves garlic, peeled and minced
2 cups beer, ale or lager
1 cup barbecue sauce, divided
Water, to cover

1. Pat pork shoulder dry with paper towels. In a small bowl combine cumin, smoked paprika, salt, and pepper. Rub spices on all sides of pork shoulder. Set aside.

2. In an ovenproof 6- or 8-quart Dutch oven over medium heat add oil. Brown pork well on all sides, about 5 minutes per side. Remove to a plate to rest.

3. Heat oven to 350°F.

4. To the Dutch oven add onion. Cook until onions are tender, about 5 minutes. Add garlic and cook until fragrant, about 30 seconds.

5. Add beer to the pot and, with a wooden spoon or heatproof spatula, scrape any browned bits off the bottom of the Dutch oven. Stir in half of barbecue sauce. Add pork back to the Dutch oven and coat the top with reserved barbecue sauce. Add enough water to come halfway up the side of roast. Cover and bake 1 hour, then turn pork over and cook 1 hour more.

6. Turn pork roast back over, uncover, and roast another 45–55 minutes, or until pork is fork tender and braising liquid has reduced. Remove pork from liquid and allow to rest on a cutting board tented with foil 10 minutes. Once rested shred pork with two forks and place on a platter. Keep warm.

7. Heat the Dutch oven with the braising liquid over high heat. Bring the liquid to a boil and reduce until thick, about 8–10 minutes. Pour over shredded pork. Serve hot.

# Crispy Pork Belly

*Pork belly can be difficult to find with the skin on. Check with your butcher, or go to your local Asian market and ask for 3-layer pork belly.*

**PREP TIME:** 6 hours
**COOK TIME:** 1 hour 20 minutes

**INGREDIENTS | SERVES 4–6**

2 pounds skin-on pork belly, cut into 4 pieces

1 teaspoon salt

½ teaspoon freshly cracked black pepper

½ teaspoon Chinese five spice powder

1 medium onion, peeled and sliced

4 cloves garlic, whole

## Drying Out the Pork Skin

The secret to pork skin so crisp it is more like pork crackling is to let the skin and fat dry out for a few hours. Reducing the water in the fat and skin will help them render more effectively in the oven and result in skin so crunchy it bubbles and cracks in the oven. Don't dry the meat for longer than a day or the meat will dry out too much and be slightly chewy around the edges.

1. With a sharp paring knife score the skin of the pork belly until you reach the fat. In a small bowl combine salt, pepper, and five spice powder, and season all sides of pork. Place pork belly steaks on a wire rack over a baking sheet and refrigerate, uncovered, 6 hours, or overnight.

2. Heat oven to 450°F.

3. In an ovenproof 6- or 8-quart Dutch oven place pork belly steaks skin side up. Roast, uncovered, 40–50 minutes or until the skin on the pork is golden brown and bubbled up. Reduce heat to 350°F.

4. Remove the pot from the oven and carefully remove pork belly steaks. Add onions and garlic to the pot and stir to coat in the rendered pork fat, then place pork belly on top skin side up. Return to the oven to roast for an additional 30–40 minutes or until meat of the steaks is fork tender and onions are soft.

5. Remove pork belly from the Dutch oven. Smash garlic and mix with onions. Serve pork belly on a bed of cooked onions.

# Seared and Roasted Pork Belly

*Pork belly is the cut of meat that is used to make bacon. For this dish it is not cured or smoked.*

**PREP TIME:** 12–24 hours
**COOK TIME:** 2 hours 35 minutes

**INGREDIENTS | SERVES 4**

1¼ pounds skinless, boneless pork belly
¼ cup salt
½ cup sugar
4½ cups water, divided
2 cups ice
½ cup chicken broth
5 cloves garlic, peeled
10 peppercorns

## Go Belly Up

You may not find pork belly in the butcher case, but your butcher should be able to get it for you. Ask for a piece that is equally fatty and meaty. It may be easier to locate pork belly at a Chinese butcher shop.

1. Rinse pork belly and remove any loose pieces along the edges.

2. Place salt, sugar, and 4 cups water into a small saucepan over medium heat. Stir frequently until the salt and sugar are dissolved. Place the pork belly into a sealable container that is deeper than the pork belly, but not much wider. Stir ice into the pan of water. Once ice is melted, pour mixture over pork. Refrigerate 12–24 hours.

3. Heat oven to 300°F.

4. Remove pork from the brine and rinse it. Pat it dry and cut it into four even pieces. Place pieces in the bottom of 6-quart Dutch oven. Pour in ½ cup water and broth. Sprinkle garlic cloves and peppercorns around the pan. Cover with a lid, place in the middle of the oven, and cook 2½ hours. The pork should be very tender.

5. Remove the pork from the Dutch oven, then drain the liquid and peppercorns from the pan. Save garlic cloves. Return the pork to the Dutch oven so it is fat-side down. Smear a garlic clove over the meaty side of each slice of pork. Place the Dutch oven over high heat and cook about 3–5 minutes, or until fat is crispy and golden brown. Serve immediately.

# Asian Pork Tenderloin

*Pork tenderloin marinates beautifully; the meat absorbs flavors and becomes very tender and juicy.*

**PREP TIME:** 12–24 hours
**COOK TIME:** 30 minutes

**INGREDIENTS | SERVES 6**

½ cup low-sodium soy sauce
2 tablespoons hoisin sauce
2 tablespoons honey
3 cloves garlic, peeled and minced
1 cup chicken broth, divided
1 tablespoon brown sugar
1 tablespoon grated gingerroot
¼ teaspoon pepper
2 (1-pound) pork tenderloins
2 tablespoons unsalted butter

1. In a large zip-top bag, combine soy sauce, hoisin sauce, honey, garlic, ½ cup broth, brown sugar, gingerroot, and pepper. If necessary, pull the silver skin off pork and discard.

2. Add pork to the bag, close, and massage the bag to mix marinade into pork. Place in casserole dish and refrigerate 12–24 hours.

3. Heat oven to 425°F.

4. Pour tenderloin and marinade into an ovenproof 6- or 8-quart Dutch oven lightly coated with nonstick cooking spray. Bake 20–30 minutes, or until a meat thermometer registers 155°F.

5. Remove pork and cover to keep warm. Place the Dutch oven on stovetop over medium heat and add ½ cup chicken broth. Bring to a boil, scraping to remove pan drippings, until reduced by half. Add butter, swirl to coat, and pour over pork. Serve immediately.

# Bacon-Wrapped Stuffed Pork Tenderloin

*A little apple butter and some tart diced apple mixed into the stuffing
play well against the salty bacon wrapping this roast.*

**PREP TIME:** 1 hour 20 minutes
**COOK TIME:** 1 hour
**INGREDIENTS | SERVES 4**

1 (2-pound) pork tenderloin
¼ teaspoon salt
¼ teaspoon freshly cracked
black pepper
8 strips thick-cut bacon
¼ cup apple butter
3 tablespoons unsalted butter
1 medium onion, peeled and chopped
1 stalk celery, chopped
½ Granny Smith apple, cored and cubed
2 cups cubed stale bread
½ teaspoon sage
¼ teaspoon fresh minced rosemary
1 large egg, beaten

1. Make a lengthwise slit into pork loin about ¾ of the way through meat. Open tenderloin so it lies flat and with a meat mallet pound tenderloin until it is ¼" thick. If you do not have a meat mallet, place the pork loin between two pieces of plastic wrap and use a wooden rolling pin or a heavy skillet. Season both sides with salt and pepper.

2. On a large sheet of plastic wrap lay out bacon strips vertically so they overlap slightly. Lay seasoned pork tenderloin horizontally over bacon and brush the inside of the tenderloin with apple butter. Set aside.

3. In an ovenproof 6- or 8-quart Dutch oven over medium-high heat add butter. Once the butter has melted and starts to foam add onion, celery, and apple. Cook until everything is tender, about 5 minutes, then remove the pot from the heat and fold in bread cubes, sage, and rosemary. Fold in beaten egg and set aside 5 minutes to absorb.

4. Spread bread mixture inside the pork tenderloin, leaving a ½" border around the edges of pork. Roll tenderloin so the filling is covered. Using the plastic, wrap bacon around tenderloin. Wrap tenderloin tightly in the plastic and refrigerate 1 hour.

5. Heat oven to 350°F and clean out the Dutch oven.

6. Unwrap tenderloin and place seam side down into the Dutch oven. Bake, uncovered, 45–55 minutes, or until pork is cooked through and the stuffing reaches an internal temperature of 160°F. Let roast rest 10 minutes before removing from the Dutch oven and slicing.

# Sweet and Sour Pork

*You may never call for take-out again after you find out how easy and delicious homemade Sweet and Sour Pork is to make at home!*

**PREP TIME:** 10 minutes
**COOK TIME:** 25 minutes

**INGREDIENTS | SERVES 8**

1 cup water, divided
¾ cup pineapple juice
½ cup sugar
2 tablespoons rice wine vinegar
1 tablespoon soy sauce
2 tablespoons ketchup
2 cloves garlic, peeled and minced
1 teaspoon fresh grated ginger
⅓ cup plus 1 tablespoon cornstarch, divided
1 (1-pound) pork tenderloin, cut into 1" cubes
½ teaspoon salt
½ cup vegetable oil
2 medium red bell peppers, seeded and cut into ½" pieces
1 medium onion, peeled and cut into ½" chunks
1 pint sliced button mushrooms
1 (15-ounce) can pineapple chunks, drained

## Sweet and Sour Sauce

Western-style sweet and sour sauce originated in China, and is descended from a Cantonese sauce used for pork. Traditional sweet and sour sauce is a mixture of sugar or honey, rice vinegar, and aromatic ingredients like garlic and ginger. Western sweet and sour sauce often adds tomato or ketchup, but this is rarely seen in China. Making your own sweet and sour sauce is easy, and it is much better for you than the bottled sauces at most stores. Homemade sweet and sour sauce keeps for one week in the refrigerator.

1. In a medium saucepan combine ¾ cup water, pineapple juice, sugar, vinegar, soy sauce, ketchup, garlic, and ginger. Bring to a boil over medium heat then reduce to a simmer and allow the sauce to reduce by half, about 10 minutes. Once reduced, combine the remaining water with 1 tablespoon cornstarch and whisk into the sauce. Bring to a boil and cook 20 seconds or until thick, then remove from heat and reserve.

2. In a large zip-top bag combine the remaining cornstarch with cubed pork and salt. Seal the bag and shake well to coat.

3. In a 6- or 8-quart Dutch oven over medium-high heat add oil. Once oil shimmers add half of pork cubes and brown them on all sides, about 1 minute per side. Remove from the pot to a paper towel–lined plate to drain and repeat with remaining pork. Add the second batch to the first and set aside.

4. To the Dutch oven add bell peppers, onion, and mushrooms. Cook until the vegetables are tender, about 5 minutes.

5. Return pork to the Dutch oven and cook, stirring often, until cooked through, about 5 minutes. Pour in the prepared sauce and pineapple chunks; stir until everything is coated and the sauce is hot, about 2 minutes. Serve immediately.

# Bacon Meatloaf

*Bacon lovers, rejoice! This meatloaf is made of almost ⅓ ground bacon, and it is stuffed with mozzarella cheese. Instead of ketchup, this meatloaf is coated with marinara sauce for a brighter flavor.*

**PREP TIME:** 1 hour 10 minutes
**COOK TIME:** 1 hour 20 minutes

**INGREDIENTS | SERVES 8**

½ pound smoked bacon, cut into 1" pieces
½ pound ground pork
½ pound $9\frac{3}{7}$ lean ground beef
½ cup panko bread crumbs
1 large egg
1 teaspoon oregano
½ teaspoon ground fennel
½ teaspoon smoked paprika
¼ teaspoon salt
¼ teaspoon freshly ground black pepper
1 cup shredded mozzarella cheese
½ cup marinara sauce

1. In the work bowl of a food processor add bacon and pulse until bacon is ground but not a paste, about 20 pulses.

2. Transfer ground bacon to a large bowl along with the ground pork, ground beef, bread crumbs, egg, oregano, fennel, smoked paprika, salt, and pepper. Mix until everything is uniformly mixed. Cover and refrigerate 1 hour.

3. Heat oven to 400°F. Lightly spray an ovenproof 6- or 8-quart Dutch oven with nonstick cooking spray.

4. Once chilled, place half the meat mixture into the bottom of the prepared Dutch oven, creating a circle with a 1" lip around the edge. Fill in the center of the meat with shredded cheese, then top with remaining meat, pressing the edges to seal. Using a spatula, go around the edges of meatloaf to form a smooth, round loaf. Brush the top with marinara sauce.

5. Bake 20 minutes, then reduce heat to 350°F and bake an additional 35–40 minutes or until the juice from meatloaf runs clear and the center of meatloaf reaches 160°F. Allow meatloaf to rest 20 minutes before serving.

# Kielbasa, Potatoes, and Peppers

*This dish, using Polish smoked sausage, is quick to make and comforting. If you like mustard with your sausages, add 3 tablespoons of mustard with the chicken broth.*

**PREP TIME:** 15 minutes
**COOK TIME:** 20 minutes

**INGREDIENTS | SERVES 4**

3 tablespoons vegetable oil
4 medium potatoes, cut into ¼" slices
1 small onion, peeled and chopped
1 large bell pepper, seeded and cubed
1 pound kielbasa, cut into 1" pieces
½ cup chicken broth
1 tablespoon Worcestershire sauce
2 teaspoons salt
¼ teaspoon freshly ground black pepper

1. Place a 6- or 8-quart Dutch oven over medium heat. Once it is heated, add oil and potatoes. Cook 3 minutes. Stir and cover with a lid. Cook another 5 minutes, stirring occasionally.

2. Add onions and the peppers. Cook 3 minutes, covered. Add kielbasa and chicken broth. Cook 8–10 minutes, or until the kielbasa is cooked through and the potatoes are browned. Stir in Worcestershire sauce, and season with the salt and pepper.

# Grits and Ham Bake

*This dish is an excellent recipe for using leftover spiral-sliced ham.*

**PREP TIME:** 15 minutes
**COOK TIME:** 1 hour

**INGREDIENTS | SERVES 4**

3 cups water
¾ cups instant grits
6 ounces evaporated milk
1½ cups shredded Cheddar cheese
1 teaspoon garlic powder
¼ teaspoon ground black pepper
Several dashes Tabasco sauce
8 ounces ham, cubed
1 large egg, beaten well
¼ cup shredded Monterey jack cheese

1. Heat oven to 350°F.

2. In an ovenproof 6- or 8-quart Dutch oven boil water over medium heat, add grits, and cook according to the package directions until done. Stir in milk, Cheddar cheese, seasonings, and ham. Stir egg into mixture.

3. Bake in the middle of the oven 45 minutes. Sprinkle Monterey jack cheese on top and bake 5–10 minutes. Let mixture cool in the Dutch oven 10 minutes before serving. Leftovers can be refrigerated for several days.

# Gnocchi with Fennel, Sausage, and Peppers in Broth

*Gnocchi are tender little potato dumplings that make a tasty alternative to pasta.*
*Always cook gnocchi in boiling water before adding to soups or sauces.*

**PREP TIME:** 10 minutes
**COOK TIME:** 30 minutes

**INGREDIENTS | SERVES 4**

2 cups frozen or vacuum-packed gnocchi

1 tablespoon olive oil

½ pound Italian sausage

6 cups strong chicken broth

1 cup thinly sliced fennel

1 medium red bell pepper, seeded and sliced

¼ teaspoon salt

¼ teaspoon freshly cracked black pepper

½ cup freshly grated Parmesan cheese

1. Bring a 6- or 8-quart Dutch oven filled with water to a boil over high heat. Add gnocchi, and cook until dumplings float to surface, then drain and transfer the gnocchi to a bowl and drizzle with olive oil.

2. Return the Dutch oven to medium-high heat and add Italian sausage. Brown on both sides, piercing the casing to let fat escape, about 5 minutes per side. When cooked, remove from the pan to cool slightly, then remove the casing and chop sausage into small pieces.

3. To the Dutch oven add broth and bring to a boil. Add fennel and cook 3 minutes.

4. Reduce heat to medium. Add bell pepper and sausage, and simmer 5 minutes.

5. Add gnocchi, salt, and pepper, toss to coat, and then remove from the heat. Cover with the lid and let rest 1 minute. Ladle into bowls and serve with freshly grated Parmesan.

# Pork Meatballs with Orange Glaze

*These are big meatballs, but if you wanted to convert this to an appetizer you can make the meatballs about 1" each. Serve these meatballs with cooked rice or buttered egg noodles.*

**PREP TIME:** 1 hour 10 minutes
**COOK TIME:** 50 minutes

**INGREDIENTS | SERVES 8**

2 pounds ground pork

½ cup panko bread crumbs

½ medium onion, peeled and finely chopped

1 large egg

1 teaspoon salt

½ teaspoon ground fennel

½ teaspoon oregano

¼ teaspoon freshly cracked black pepper

¼ cup olive oil, divided

½ cup orange marmalade

¼ cup orange juice

1 teaspoon packed light brown sugar

1. In a large bowl combine ground pork, bread crumbs, onion, egg, salt, fennel, oregano, and pepper. Mix until well combined. Shape meat mixture into 16 balls and place on a parchment-lined baking sheet. Refrigerate uncovered 1 hour.

2. Heat oven to 350°F.

3. In an ovenproof 6- or 8-quart Dutch oven add half the oil. Brown meatballs on all sides in batches, adding additional oil as needed to prevent sticking, about 2 minutes per side. Once all the meatballs are browned add them all back to the Dutch oven.

4. In a small bowl combine marmalade, orange juice, and sugar. Pour mixture over the meatballs and toss gently to coat. Cover and bake 30 minutes, then uncover and bake 10 minutes more, stirring the meatballs every 3 minutes, until they are coated in the orange glaze and cooked through. Serve hot.

# Choucroute

*This dish is pronounced "shoe-croote" and is French for "sauerkraut." As the sauerkraut cooks, the taste becomes very mild. Because of the acidic nature of sauerkraut, it's better to use an enameled Dutch oven for this dish. Serve this dish with boiled and buttered potatoes.*

**PREP TIME:** 10 minutes
**COOK TIME:** 2 hours 45 minutes

**INGREDIENTS | SERVES 6–8**

4 slices bacon, cut into 1" pieces

1 large yellow onion, peeled and chopped

3 cloves garlic, peeled and sliced

2 medium apples, cored and sliced

1 quart sauerkraut, fresh, jarred, or bagged

1 bottle non-bitter beer, or ½ bottle Riesling

7 juniper berries, or ½ cup gin

8 peppercorns

2 bay leaves

1 tablespoon brown sugar

¼ pound ham, cubed

1½ pounds German sausage (knackwurst, bratwurst, garlic sausage)

1. Place a 6- or 8-quart Dutch oven over medium heat. Once it is heated, add bacon and fry until is cooked through but not crispy. Add onion and cook 5–7 minutes or until onion starts to brown. Add garlic and cook 1 minute, stirring continually.

2. Add apples, sauerkraut, and beer. Stir to combine. Add juniper berries, peppercorns, bay leaves, and sugar. Reduce heat to low, cover, and simmer 1 hour.

3. Stir ham into the pot and add sausages. Cook 1½ hours, covered. Add water to the pot if it seems like it is getting too dry. When sausages are cooked through, serve warm.

# Ground Pork and Eggplant Casserole

*If you prefer, this dish will fit in a 2-quart baking dish, but using a 4-quart Dutch oven will give you plenty of room to mix the meat and vegetables together and let you do the stovetop cooking and baking in one pot.*

**PREP TIME:** 15 minutes
**COOK TIME:** 1 hour 20 minutes

**INGREDIENTS | SERVES 8**

2 pounds lean ground pork

2 tablespoons peanut or extra-virgin olive oil

2 large yellow onions, peeled and chopped

3 celery stalks, chopped

1 green pepper, seeded and chopped

6 cloves garlic, chopped

4 medium eggplants, cut into ½" dice

⅛ teaspoon dried thyme, crushed

1 tablespoon freeze-dried parsley

3 tablespoons tomato paste

1 teaspoon hot sauce, optional

2 teaspoons Worcestershire sauce

½ teaspoon salt

½ teaspoon freshly cracked black pepper

1 large egg, beaten

½ cup bread crumbs

1 tablespoon melted unsalted butter

1. Heat oven to 350°F.

2. Place 6- or 8-quart Dutch oven over medium-high heat. Add ground pork and fry until done, breaking it apart as it cooks. Remove from pan and keep warm.

3. Drain off and discard any pork fat from the pan, then add the oil over medium heat. Once the oil is hot and starts to shimmer add onion, celery, and green pepper; sauté until onion is transparent, about 5 minutes. Add garlic, eggplant, thyme, parsley, and tomato paste. Stir to combine. Cover and sauté, stirring often, 20 minutes or until vegetables are tender.

4. Return ground pork to pan. Add hot sauce (if using), Worcestershire sauce, salt, pepper, and egg; stir to combine. Sprinkle bread crumbs over the top and drizzle with melted butter. Bake 40 minutes, or until the crumb topping is lightly browned and casserole is hot in the center.

## Why Freshly Cracked Black Pepper?

Bottled ground black pepper contains anti-caking agents that can cause stomach upset for some people and can also change the flavor. That last reason is why dishes always taste more peppery when you grind the pepper yourself.

# Spicy Pork and Apricot Tajine

*This dish can be made with boneless lamb or chicken in place of pork. Serve this dish over steamed couscous.*

**PREP TIME:** 15 minutes
**COOK TIME:** 2 hours 30 minutes

**INGREDIENTS | SERVES 6–8**

1 teaspoon cinnamon
½ teaspoon ground ginger
½ teaspoon cumin
½ teaspoon cayenne
1 teaspoon paprika
1 teaspoon kosher salt
¼ teaspoon cardamom
2 pounds boneless pork roast, cut into 2" cubes
2 tablespoons olive oil
1 large onion, peeled and diced
3 cloves garlic, peeled and minced
¼ teaspoon saffron
¼ cup hot water
1 (16-ounce) can diced tomatoes, undrained
1 tablespoon brown sugar
2 cups chicken or pork broth
8 dried apricots, quartered
¼ cup minced fresh cilantro

1. Combine cinnamon, ginger, cumin, cayenne, paprika, kosher salt, and cardamom, then sprinkle half of the spice mixture over the pork cubes.

2. In a 6- or 8-quart Dutch oven heat oil over medium-high heat. Brown pork on all sides, about 3 minutes per side, then remove to a platter. Add onion and garlic, and cook until tender, about 5 minutes.

3. Dissolve saffron in hot water. Add saffron, tomatoes, and brown sugar to the pot, and stir well. Return pork to pot, and add broth and apricots. Stir in remaining spices, and then bring to a boil. Reduce heat to medium-low, cover, and simmer 2 hours, adding more liquid if necessary.

4. Stir in cilantro. Remove from heat and let stand 10 minutes.

# Swedish Sauerkraut Dinner

*Serve this dinner with crusty rolls or pumpernickel bread and some cheese.*

**PREP TIME:** 10 minutes
**COOK TIME:** 1 hour 20 minutes

**INGREDIENTS | SERVES 8**

1 pound slab bacon or smoked pork jowl, diced

2 medium yellow onions, peeled and sliced

4 large russet or red potatoes, peeled or unpeeled, diced

1 pound green cabbage, cored and shredded

1 (2-pound) bag sauerkraut, rinsed and well drained

1 apple, cored and chopped

2 cups dry white wine, apple juice, or chicken broth

1 tablespoon light brown sugar

1 teaspoon caraway seeds

1 teaspoon freshly cracked black pepper

1. Put bacon or pork jowl in a 6-quart Dutch oven and fry over medium heat to render out most of the fat. Spoon out some of the excess fat, leaving at least 2 tablespoons of fat in the pan.

2. Add onion and sauté until transparent, about 8 minutes. Add potatoes and mix with bacon and onion. Add cabbage and cook, covered, 5 minutes, or until cabbage wilts.

3. Squeeze any excess moisture out of sauerkraut and add it to the pan, along with the remaining ingredients. Lower heat, cover, and simmer gently 1 hour, stirring occasionally.

# Jambalaya

*There are as many versions of Jambalaya as there are Southern cooks. Originally created as a dish to use up leftovers, it's a versatile recipe that you can adjust according to your tastes.*

**PREP TIME:** 15 minutes
**COOK TIME:** 40 minutes
**INGREDIENTS | SERVES 6–8**

3 tablespoons bacon fat or peanut oil

1 (1-pound) bag baby carrots, divided

4 stalks celery, diced

2 medium green bell peppers, seeded and chopped

1 large yellow onion, peeled and diced

6 green onions, chopped

3 cloves garlic, peeled and minced

½ pound smoked sausage, thinly sliced

½ pound cooked ham, diced

2 (15-ounce) cans diced tomatoes, drained

4 cups Braised Pork Shoulder (see recipe in this chapter) or 4 cups ready-cooked pork shoulder

3 cups chicken broth

1 tablespoon dried parsley

1 teaspoon dried thyme

½ teaspoon hot sauce, or to taste

¼ cup Worcestershire sauce

2 cups long-grain rice, uncooked

¼ teaspoon salt

¼ teaspoon freshly cracked black pepper

Water, as needed

1 pound shrimp, peeled and deveined, cut in half if large

1. Add bacon fat or oil to a 6- or 8-quart Dutch oven and bring it to temperature over medium heat. Shred 8 of the baby carrots. Add shredded carrots, celery, and green peppers to the pan; sauté 3–5 minutes, or until soft.

2. Add the yellow and green onions and sauté until transparent, about 5 minutes. Add garlic and sauté an additional 30 seconds.

3. Stir in smoked sausage and stir-fry 3 minutes; add ham and stir-fry 1 minute. Chop remaining carrots and add to the pan.

4. Stir in tomatoes, pork, broth, parsley, thyme, hot sauce, and Worcestershire sauce. Bring to a boil, then stir in rice, salt, and pepper; reduce heat, cover, and simmer 20 minutes. Fluff the rice; add additional water, if needed.

5. Add shrimp to the pot, cover, and cook another 3–5 minutes, or until shrimp are bright pink and opaque. If excess moisture remains in the dish, uncover and cook until it's evaporated, stirring often to keep rice from sticking.

# Spring Pork Stew with Orange Gremolata

*Orange gremolata—a blend of minced parsley, garlic, and orange peel—gives this stew a fresh, light flavor. Serve this dish with cooked rice or mashed potatoes.*

**PREP TIME:** 15 minutes
**COOK TIME:** 2 hours 15 minutes

**INGREDIENTS | SERVES 6–8**

¼ cup sauce and gravy flour

1 teaspoon kosher salt

1 teaspoon coarsely ground black pepper, divided

½ teaspoon garlic powder

3 pounds boneless pork loin, trimmed and cut into 1"-thick pieces

⅓ cup olive oil

1 (14-ounce) can diced tomatoes

1 cup pork or chicken broth

1 cup white wine

2 bay leaves

2 cups julienned carrots

2 cups sugar snap peas

12 cippolini onions, quartered

1 cup loosely packed flat parsley leaves

4 cloves garlic, peeled

Zest of 1 large orange

1. Heat oven to 350°F.

2. Combine flour, salt, ½ teaspoon pepper, and garlic powder in a medium bowl. Dredge pork pieces in mixture until well coated.

3. Heat oil in an ovenproof 6- or 8-quart Dutch oven over medium-high heat. Once oil shimmers add pork in batches and brown well on both sides, about 4–5 minutes per side. Remove from the Dutch oven to a plate to rest.

4. Add tomatoes to the Dutch oven, stirring up any browned bits from bottom of pot. Add broth, wine, and bay leaves; bring to a boil and cook for 5 minutes.

5. Remove the Dutch oven from heat. Arrange a layer of pork on bottom of pot, followed by carrots, sugar snap peas, and onions. Place remaining pork on top layer, cover with the lid, and bake 1½ hours.

6. In a food processor combine parsley, garlic, and orange. Pulse until finely minced.

7. Carefully open the Dutch oven and stir in parsley mixture. Be sure to stir up the pork from the bottom of the Dutch oven. Cover and bake 30 minutes more, or until pork is fork tender. Top with the reserved pepper.

# Spiced Wild Boar with Prunes

*Sweet prunes make a nice foil for rich wild boar meat in this fall favorite. If you don't have access to wild boar, you can substitute pork or even venison. Serve this dish with boiled sliced potatoes.*

**PREP TIME:** 10 minutes
**COOK TIME:** 1 hour 25 minutes
**INGREDIENTS | SERVES 6**

1½ cups dried pitted prunes
1½ cups red wine
1 small orange, quartered
4 tablespoons unsalted butter, divided
3 pounds wild boar loin, cut into 1" cubes
½ cup all-purpose flour
½ teaspoon salt
½ teaspoon freshly cracked black pepper
1 small onion, peeled and diced
3 cloves garlic, peeled and minced
4 cups beef or chicken broth
2 bay leaves
¼ cup brandy
⅓ cup heavy cream
Pinch thyme

1. In a small bowl, combine prunes, wine, and orange quarters. In a 6- or 8-quart Dutch oven melt 3 tablespoons butter over medium-high heat.

2. Toss boar cubes in flour and season with salt and pepper. Working in batches, brown meat on all sides, about 3 minutes per side, then remove to a bowl. Add remaining butter to pot along with onion and garlic; cook until just tender, about 3 minutes.

3. Add broth and stir well, scraping up browned bits from bottom of the Dutch oven. Add bay leaves and bring the mixture to a boil. Reduce heat to medium and return boar to the Dutch oven. Remove orange quarters from prune and wine mixture; pour mixture into the pot. Stir well, then simmer 1 hour or until the boar is tender.

4. Add brandy, cream, and thyme and stir well, then cook an additional 5 minutes.

## This Little Piggy Went to Market

Boar, a type of pig, are not native to North America; they were brought to the continent by early Spanish settlers. Escapees made themselves quite at home in low-lying coastal brush and forests, and today their descendants are considered an invasive species. They're a favorite target for hunters, both for sport and meat. For non-hunters, boar is now farmed at various locations in the United States. Wild boar meat can be found at specialty stores and through some online purveyors. In general, boar can be used in place of pork in any recipe.

# CHAPTER 11

# Seafood and Fish

# Baked Shrimp Scampi

*This dish is perfect as a topping for fettuccini alfredo, or served with a crisp green salad with a lemony dressing.*

**PREP TIME:** 10 minutes
**COOK TIME:** 25 minutes

**INGREDIENTS | SERVES 4**

½ cup panko bread crumbs
6 tablespoons salted butter, divided
1 shallot, peeled and minced
1 clove garlic, peeled and minced
1 tablespoon finely chopped fresh chives
1 teaspoon finely chopped fresh parsley
½ teaspoon finely chopped fresh dill
¼ teaspoon smoked paprika
¼ teaspoon salt
¼ teaspoon freshly cracked black pepper
1 pound ($^{23}/_{30}$) tail-on shrimp

## Shrimp Sizes

Shrimp is labeled for size based on how many shrimp it will take to make 1 pound. For example, if you buy 51/60 shrimp, it will take somewhere between 51 and 60 shrimp to equal 1 pound. For frying, boiling, roasting, or grilling look for shrimp that are 26/30, also called extra-large, and 16/20, or extra-jumbo. Some shrimp are very large, or U/10, meaning it takes 10 or less to make 1 pound.

1. Heat oven to 350°F.

2. In a small bowl add bread crumbs. Melt 2 tablespoons butter and toss until the crumbs are evenly coated. Set aside.

3. In an ovenproof 6- or 8-quart Dutch oven over medium heat add remaining butter. Once it melts and starts to foam add shallots and cook until tender, about 1 minute. Add remaining ingredients except the shrimp and cook until fragrant, about 30 seconds. Remove the Dutch oven from heat.

4. Add shrimp and toss to coat, then sprinkle the bread crumbs over the shrimp and bake 15–20 minutes, or until the shrimp are cooked through and the bread crumbs are golden brown. Serve immediately.

# French or Belgian Steamed Mussels

*Some mussels won't open during cooking, which means they are unsafe to eat and should be discarded before serving. Serve this dish with crusty bread.*

**PREP TIME:** 40 minutes
**COOK TIME:** 25 minutes

**INGREDIENTS | SERVES 2**

Water, as needed

1 cup cornmeal

2 pounds fresh mussels

2 tablespoons unsalted butter

1 medium yellow onion, peeled and thinly sliced

1 large clove garlic, peeled and minced

2 cups dry white wine or ale

3 tablespoons chopped fresh tarragon or thyme

## Caring for Your Mussels

Discard any mussels with cracked shells. If you tap an open mussel, it should close; if it doesn't, discard it. Make sure they are wrapped in something damp and placed in a mesh bag since they need airflow. You can keep them in the bottom of your refrigerator wrapped in wet newspaper for up to 48 hours, but they're best the day they're purchased.

1. Fill a very large bowl half full of water that is cool to the touch. Sprinkle cornmeal across the top of the water and let it settle. Use a plastic bristle brush to remove any dirt or other unwanted debris from mussels. To remove the beard, place the back of a butter knife on one side of the beard and your thumb on the other side. Pinch the beard between your thumb and the knife and pull using a side-to-side motion.

2. Place mussels into the bowl of water. Shake the bowl every few minutes to keep the cornmeal floating. Let them sit in the water 30 minutes. Every 10 minutes gently nudge the bowl to create waves. The mussels should expel any dirt they have stored and replace it with the cornmeal.

3. Place a 6- or 8-quart Dutch oven over medium heat and add butter. Add onions and stir to coat in butter. Stir frequently until they are mostly translucent. Add garlic and stir. Cook 3–4 minutes. Add wine and herbs. Cover and bring to a boil.

4. Remove the lid and gently add mussels to the pan, leaving the dirt in the bottom of the bowl. When all mussels are added, increase heat to high and cook 3–4 minutes.

5. Scoop mussels into bowls and keep them warm. Let the liquid in the pan continue to boil 5–10 minutes until reduced by half. Pour liquid and onions over mussels.

# Mussels with White Wine and Shallots

*Nothing beats a big pot of steamed mussels. Serve these mussels with
lemon wedges and crusty garlic bread with lots of butter!*

**PREP TIME:** 25 minutes
**COOK TIME:** 20 minutes

**INGREDIENTS | SERVES 6**

6 tablespoons unsalted butter, divided

2 shallots, peeled and minced

2 cloves garlic, peeled and minced

½ teaspoon salt

½ teaspoon freshly cracked
black pepper

3 cups white wine

3 pounds cultivated mussels, scrubbed
and beards removed

¼ cup chopped fresh chives

1 tablespoon chopped fresh tarragon

## Cleaning Mussels

When you bring your mussels home be
sure to remove the wrapping and transfer
to a bowl so they can breathe. Discard any
open or broken mussels. To clean, first soak
your mussels in cold water for about
20 minutes. This will reduce the salt they
are retaining. Next, remove the beard by
holding the mussel in your hand, and with a
dry hand towel grab the beard and sharply
tug it toward the hinge of the shell. Pulling
away from the hinge will kill the mussel.
Finally, use a brush to scrub the outside of
the shells to remove any dirt or sand. Now
your mussels are ready to cook!

1. In a 6- or 8-quart Dutch oven over medium heat add
   2 tablespoons butter. Once butter melts and starts to
   foam add shallots and cook until tender, about
   1 minute. Add garlic, salt, and pepper and cook until
   the garlic is fragrant, about 30 seconds.

2. Add white wine and bring to a boil, then add mussels
   and stir to combine. Cover and cook 6–8 minutes. With
   a slotted spoon remove and discard any mussels that
   did not open. Transfer remaining mussels to a
   serving bowl.

3. Bring the cooking liquid to a simmer and whisk in
   remaining butter and herbs. Pour liquid over the
   mussels and serve immediately.

# Crab and Fish Casserole

*Use mild whitefish fillets in this easy casserole; orange roughy or cod would be perfect.*

**PREP TIME:** 10 minutes
**COOK TIME:** 50 minutes

**INGREDIENTS | SERVES 6**

2 tablespoons unsalted butter

1 medium onion, peeled and minced

3 cloves garlic, peeled and minced

1 (16-ounce) jar Alfredo sauce

½ pound fish fillets

3 tablespoons orange juice

½ cup ground almonds

1 cup shredded Havarti cheese

½ pound crabmeat

1 cup soft whole-wheat bread crumbs

3 tablespoons grated Parmesan cheese

3 tablespoons unsalted butter, melted

## Make It Ahead

This is an ideal casserole to make ahead of time. Prepare it through Step 3, then cover and refrigerate. Make the bread crumb and cheese topping and place in small plastic bag; refrigerate. To finish, sprinkle casserole with the topping and bake, adding 10–15 minutes to the baking time.

1. Heat oven to 350°F.

2. In an ovenproof 6- or 8-quart Dutch oven melt butter over medium heat. Once melted add onion and garlic, and cook 5 minutes or until tender. Add Alfredo sauce and bring to a simmer. Add fish fillets and simmer 4–5 minutes, or until fish flakes. Stir to break up fish.

3. Stir in orange juice and almonds and remove from heat. Add Havarti cheese and crabmeat.

4. In a small bowl, combine the bread crumbs, Parmesan cheese, and melted butter; mix well. Sprinkle over fish mixture. Bake 30–40 minutes, or until the bread crumbs have browned. Serve immediately.

# Cioppino

*This is a distinctly San Francisco dish believed to have been created by Italian fishermen as a way to use each day's catch. It goes perfectly with sourdough bread.*

**PREP TIME:** 20 minutes
**COOK TIME:** 2 hours 30 minutes
**INGREDIENTS | SERVES 8–10**

¼ cup unsalted butter or olive oil

2 medium onions, peeled and chopped

4 cloves garlic, peeled and minced

¼ cup parsley leaves

¼ cup oregano leaves

2 (28-ounce) cans whole tomatoes, peel removed

2 (10-ounce) cans of clams

2 bay leaves

2 tablespoons dried basil leaves

2 cups dry white wine

16 fresh clams

16 mussels

1½ pounds salmon, cut into bite-sized chunks

1 pound fresh crabmeat or imitation crab stick, cut into chunks

1½ pounds small bay scallops

½ teaspoon salt

¼ teaspoon freshly cracked black pepper

1. Place a 6- or 8-quart Dutch oven over medium heat. Once it's heated through add butter and onion. Cook 10–12 minutes. Add the garlic and stir continually 1 minute. Stir in parsley and oregano.

2. Add juice from the tomatoes to the Dutch oven. Squeeze each tomato in your hand to break apart. Add to pan and press each tomato against the side to break it into smaller pieces. Pour clam juice into pan and refrigerate clams for later. Stir in dried herbs and wine.

3. Cover with a lid, reduce the heat to low, and simmer 2 hours. (If necessary, you can complete this part up to 2 days ahead and refrigerate. Return it to the pan and bring to a boil before turning the flame to low.)

4. Scrub clams and mussels with a bristle brush. Remove beards from mussels. Soak in cold water 20 minutes. Gently add shellfish and reserved canned clams to the pan. Stir them into the sauce.

5. Stir in fish chunks, then crabmeat. Stir in scallops. Cover and steam 5–8 minutes until clams and mussels have opened.

6. Remove bay leaves and season dish with salt and pepper. Serve directly from the Dutch oven while hot.

# Seafood Paella

*Use a very large 16-inch Dutch oven if you have one available for this recipe. Paella is typically cooked in a very wide pan made specifically for this dish, but as most home cooks do not have one, a large Dutch oven makes an excellent substitute.*

**PREP TIME:** 8–12 hours
**COOK TIME:** 45 minutes

**INGREDIENTS | SERVES 4–6**

2 quarts plus 1 cup water, divided
¼ cup salt plus 2 pinches, divided
¼ cup sugar
Ice cubes, as needed
1 pound large shrimp, peeled and deveined
4 tablespoons olive oil, divided
6 cloves garlic, peeled and minced, divided
Pinch pepper
1 large red bell pepper, seeded and sliced
1 medium white onion, peeled and finely chopped
1 (15-ounce) can diced tomatoes, drained
1 (15-ounce) can chicken broth
2 cups uncooked white rice
½ cup dry white wine
3 bay leaves
1 large pinch saffron threads
12 mussels, cleaned and debearded
1 cup cleaned squid, sliced in rings
2 cups crabmeat
1 cup frozen peas, thawed
¼ cup chopped parsley
1 large lemon, cut in wedges

1. Bring 2 quarts water to a boil in an ovenproof 10- or 12-quart Dutch oven. Stir in ¼ cup salt and sugar until dissolved. Add several cups of ice cubes until chilled. Add shrimp to the brine, cover, and refrigerate overnight. Remove shrimp from brine and pat dry. Sprinkle with 1 tablespoon oil, ⅓ of the garlic, 1 pinch salt, and pepper. Let sit at room temperature 30 minutes. Discard the brine.

2. Heat oven to 350°F with a rack just below the middle position.

3. Place the Dutch oven over medium heat. Add 1 tablespoon oil and bell pepper. Cook 5–7 minutes. Spoon pepper out and set aside, but leave as much of the oil in the pan as possible.

4. Add 2 tablespoons oil and onions to the pan and cook 5–7 minutes. Add remaining garlic, stirring continually 1 minute. Stir in 1 cup water, tomatoes, chicken broth, rice, wine, bay leaves, saffron, and 1 pinch salt. Increase heat to medium-high and bring to a boil.

5. When the contents boil, cover and cook in the middle of oven 15–20 minutes. Remove from oven and gently stir seafood into rice. Lay pepper strips in a pinwheel on top and sprinkle peas across the top. Cook in the oven, uncovered, for 8–12 minutes.

6. Rest dish 5 minutes before serving. Discard bay leaves and any unopened mussels. Serve with parsley and lemon wedges.

# Lobster Paella

*If your budget is tight, you can substitute cooked shrimp for the lobster.*

**PREP TIME:** 10 minutes
**COOK TIME:** 45 minutes

**INGREDIENTS | SERVES 6**

¼ cup extra-virgin olive oil

2 large yellow onions, peeled and diced

2 medium red bell peppers, seeded and sliced into ½" strips

4 cloves garlic, peeled and minced

2 cups uncooked white basmati rice

5 cups chicken broth

½ teaspoon saffron threads, crushed

¼ teaspoon crushed red pepper flakes

1 teaspoon sea or kosher salt

½ teaspoon freshly cracked black pepper

⅓ cup licorice-flavored liqueur, such as Pernod

1½ pounds cooked lobster meat

1 pound kielbasa, cut into ¼" rounds

1 (10-ounce) package frozen peas

2 tablespoons chopped fresh parsley

2 medium lemons, cut into wedges

1. Heat oven to 425°F.

2. Add oil to an ovenproof 6- or 8-quart Dutch oven and bring it to temperature over medium heat. Add onions and sauté 5 minutes, stirring occasionally. Add bell peppers; sauté 5 minutes. Lower the heat; add garlic and sauté 1 minute.

3. Stir in rice, chicken broth, saffron, red pepper flakes, salt, and pepper; bring to a boil over medium-high heat. Cover, move the pot to the oven, and bake 15 minutes.

4. Take the pot out of the oven and remove the lid; gently stir rice using a wooden spoon. Return the pot to the oven and bake uncovered 10–15 minutes, or until rice is fully cooked.

5. Move the paella back to the stovetop; add liqueur. Cook over medium heat 1 minute or until liqueur is absorbed by rice. Turn off heat and add lobster, kielbasa, and peas, gently stirring to mix in added ingredients. Cover and let it set 10 minutes. Uncover, sprinkle with parsley, garnish with lemon wedges, and serve hot.

# Lobster Ragu

*Tasso is a Cajun ham that comes from the shoulder (pork butt), which makes it a fattier cut of meat with a great deal of flavor. If you're not sure how to cook a whole lobster, you can have the seafood department in your grocery store steam it for you.*

**PREP TIME:** 15 minutes
**COOK TIME:** 40 minutes

**INGREDIENTS | SERVES 6–8**

1½ pounds dried pappardelle or fettuccine

3 tablespoons extra-virgin olive oil

3 stalks celery, diced

3 large carrots, peeled and diced

2 medium red onions, peeled and sliced

½ teaspoon freshly cracked black pepper

¼ teaspoon salt

8 ounces tasso, salt pork, or bacon, diced

8 ounces cremini mushrooms, cleaned and sliced

8 ounces portobello mushrooms, cleaned and sliced

8 ounces button mushrooms, cleaned and sliced

2 tablespoons tomato paste

2 teaspoons dried oregano

2 teaspoons dried thyme

1 tablespoon dried parsley

1 cup red wine

4 cups beef broth

2 (1¼-pound) cooked lobsters

¼ cup chopped fresh basil

1. In a 6- or 8-quart Dutch oven cook pasta in boiling water according to the package directions until al dente. Drain in a colander, set aside, and keep warm.

2. Wipe out the Dutch oven, then add the oil over medium heat. Once the oil is hot and starts to shimmer add the celery and carrot and sauté 3–5 minutes, or until soft. Add onion, pepper, and salt and sauté until transparent, about 5 minutes. If using tasso, add to pan and sauté 1 minute; if using salt pork or bacon, sauté 3 minutes, or until it renders some of its fat.

3. Add all mushrooms. Stirring frequently, cook until all of mushroom liquid is rendered out. Push mushrooms to the sides of the pan; add tomato paste to center of pan and sauté 2 minutes, then stir it into mushrooms along with oregano, thyme, parsley, wine, and broth, scraping the bottom of the pot to loosen any browned bits as you stir.

4. Reduce heat and simmer 20 minutes. Toss drained pasta into the sauce.

5. Remove meat from the lobster shells; chop into large pieces. Gently stir lobster meat into the pasta and sauce. Garnish with chopped basil.

## Lobster Shell Uses

Freeze the lobster shells and use them later to make a broth to add to your favorite seafood stew or soup. Lobster broth is delicious, and it's easy to make—just simmer the shells with a roughly chopped onion, a few bay leaves, and enough water to cover everything for about 45 minutes.

# Shrimp and Chanterelle Stroganoff

*This dish looks impressive and it's very easy to make. The sauce can be prepared up to a day in advance; just reheat it and add the shrimp, tarragon, sour cream, and seasonings the next day. Serve this dish over fresh cooked rice.*

**PREP TIME:** 15 minutes
**COOK TIME:** 15 minutes

**INGREDIENTS | SERVES 8**

4 tablespoons unsalted butter

2 shallots, peeled and minced

2 cloves garlic, peeled and minced

4 plum tomatoes, diced

1 pound chanterelle mushrooms, separated into individual pieces

4 ounces portobello mushrooms, finely chopped

1 cup dry white wine

1 cup heavy cream

3 pounds shrimp, peeled and deveined

1 tablespoon chopped fresh tarragon

1 cup sour cream, room temperature

½ teaspoon salt

¼ teaspoon freshly cracked black pepper

1. Melt butter in a 6- or 8-quart Dutch oven over medium-high heat. Add shallots and garlic and cook until just tender, about 2 minutes.

2. Add diced tomatoes and cook an additional 2 minutes. Add mushrooms and cook, stirring frequently, until the mushrooms soften, about 5 minutes.

3. Add white wine and heavy cream to mushroom mixture. Bring to a boil and stir well. Add shrimp and cook just until they begin to turn opaque, about 2 minutes.

4. Remove the Dutch oven from heat; stir in chopped tarragon, sour cream, salt, and pepper. Serve immediately.

# Creamy Shrimp and Grits

*This classic South Carolina brunch dish can be prepared with a creamy sauce or shrimp sauté over cream-infused grits. This is the creamy stew version.*

**PREP TIME:** 15 minutes
**COOK TIME:** 25 minutes

**INGREDIENTS | SERVES 4**

4 strips bacon

1 tablespoon unsalted butter

1 small onion, peeled and finely chopped

2 tablespoons all-purpose flour

1 cup shrimp or chicken broth

1½ pounds shrimp, peeled and deveined

1 cup heavy cream

¼ teaspoon thyme

¼ teaspoon cayenne

¼ teaspoon lemon zest

2 green onions, sliced

2 tablespoons minced fresh parsley

½ teaspoon salt

¼ teaspoon freshly cracked black pepper

1 recipe Classic Breakfast Grits or Easy Baked Cheese Grits (Chapter 2)

1. In a 6- or 8-quart Dutch oven fry bacon over medium-high heat until crisp. Remove to a plate and reserve. Add butter and onion to bacon fat and cook until onion is tender, about 5 minutes.

2. Sprinkle flour over onions and stir well to blend. Slowly add broth and stir until the mixture is smooth and thickened, about 5–8 minutes. Reduce heat to medium and cook 5 minutes, stirring frequently.

3. Add shrimp and cook just until shrimp turn pink. Stir in cream, thyme, cayenne, lemon zest, green onions, and parsley. Crumble bacon into sauce and add salt and pepper. Remove from heat.

4. Divide grits over 4 shallow soup plates. Ladle shrimp sauce over grits; serve immediately.

## Glorified Grits

Grits are ground hominy; that is, the dried corn kernel from which the hull and germ have been removed. Corn grits are ground dried corn kernels with the hull and germ still intact. Southerners love both, but insist the best grits are stone ground and slow cooked. Although one can make grits by boiling the grains in water, grits are often augmented with butter, cream, and cheese. Oh, and there's an ongoing debate as to whether the term grits is singular or plural, as in "grits are" versus "grits is."

# Shrimp Étouffée

*The secret of a good Shrimp Étouffée is in the sauce, which requires a dark roux. It takes a little extra work, but it's worth the effort. Serve the results over cooked rice.*

**PREP TIME:** 15 minutes
**COOK TIME:** 1 hour 35 minutes

**INGREDIENTS | SERVES 6**

3 tablespoons bacon fat or peanut oil

3 tablespoons all-purpose flour

1 small green pepper, seeded and chopped

3 stalks celery, diced

1 large carrot, peeled and shredded

1 large yellow onion, peeled and diced

4 green onions, chopped

3 cloves garlic, peeled and minced

3 tablespoons tomato paste

1¼ cups beef broth

1 cup dry white wine

2 bay leaves

¼ teaspoon dried basil

¼ teaspoon dried thyme

1 teaspoon hot sauce, or to taste

1½ pounds shrimp, peeled and deveined

¼ teaspoon salt

¼ teaspoon freshly cracked black pepper

3 cups cooked rice

¼ cup chopped fresh parsley

1. Add bacon fat or oil and flour to a 6- or 8-quart Dutch oven over medium heat. Cook, stirring constantly so roux doesn't burn, 15 minutes, or until roux is the color of peanut butter.

2. Stir in green pepper, celery, carrot, and yellow and green onions. Sauté 10 minutes or until the vegetables are tender. Add the garlic and cook until fragrant, about 30 seconds.

3. Add tomato paste, broth, and wine, stirring constantly until mixture thickens. Add bay leaves, basil, thyme, and hot sauce; stir to combine. Cover, reduce the heat, and simmer 45 minutes.

4. Add shrimp and simmer 20 minutes, uncovered. Remove and discard bay leaves. Season with salt and pepper along with additional hot sauce, if desired. Serve over cooked rice, garnished with chopped fresh parsley.

## Cooked Long-Grain White Rice

For 8 servings, add 3 cups long-grain rice and 4½ cups water or broth to a large saucepan; bring to a boil over medium-high heat. Reduce heat to medium-low; cover and cook for 15 minutes. Remove the lid, add butter or extra-virgin olive oil to taste, and fluff with a fork until the butter or oil is mixed into the rice and all of the liquid is absorbed.

# Halibut Creole

*If the fillet comes with the skin on it, don't try to remove it while the fish is raw. After it cooks, you should be able to carefully grab the skin and pull it off. The skin is edible, but many people find the texture and taste off-putting.*

**PREP TIME:** 10 minutes
**COOK TIME:** 30 minutes

**INGREDIENTS | SERVES 4**

4 tablespoons unsalted butter
Juice from 2 medium lemons
Several dashes Tabasco sauce
4 (8-ounce) halibut steaks
Pinch salt
Pinch pepper
1 small onion, peeled and chopped
½ large red bell pepper, seeded and chopped
3 large tomatoes, peeled, seeded, and chopped

1. Heat oven to 400°F.

2. Place an ovenproof 6- or 8-quart Dutch oven over medium heat. Add butter, lemon juice, and Tabasco sauce. Stir until butter has melted. Turn off heat.

3. Season fish on each side with salt and pepper. Sprinkle onion and bell pepper over the bottom of the Dutch oven. Add fish and scatter tomatoes over the top.

4. Bake 20–25 minutes or until the thickest part of fish is opaque. Spoon the pan juices over fish every 10 minutes. Remove fish from pan and spoon sauce over it to serve.

# Whole Roasted Fish with Lemons and Herbs

*A whole roasted fish makes for a pretty presentation tableside, but if you prefer you can remove the head and tail before roasting.*

**PREP TIME:** 20 minutes
**COOK TIME:** 40 minutes

**INGREDIENTS | SERVES 4**

1 (4-pound) whole fish, such as snapper or sea bass, cleaned and scaled
1 tablespoon olive oil
½ teaspoon sea salt
½ teaspoon freshly cracked black pepper
2 medium lemons, sliced ⅛" thick
4 dill fronds
2 sprigs thyme
1 clove garlic, peeled and thinly sliced

1. Heat oven to 450°F and lightly spray an ovenproof 12-inch Dutch oven with nonstick cooking spray.

2. Brush the outside of the fish with olive oil and season with salt and pepper. Open the fish slightly and fill the center with 3 slices of lemon, along with dill, thyme, and garlic slices.

3. Place fish into the Dutch oven and top with a few slices of lemon. Roast 30 minutes, occasionally spooning juices in the bottom of the Dutch oven over fish. The fish is ready when the flesh flakes easily and reaches an internal temperature of 130°F. Let fish rest 10 minutes, and then carefully transfer to a platter to serve.

# New Orleans–Style Oysters and Shrimp Salad

*You can serve the pasta and the salad separately, but the contrast between the warm soft pasta and the cool crisp salad makes for a delightful dish.*

**PREP TIME:** 10 minutes
**COOK TIME:** 30 minutes

**INGREDIENTS | SERVES 8**

1 pound dried penne pasta

2 tablespoons peanut or vegetable oil

2 tablespoons all-purpose flour

1 large yellow onion, peeled and diced

1 teaspoon anchovy paste

1 cup milk

1 cup heavy cream

½ teaspoon hot sauce

1 teaspoon Worcestershire sauce

Pinch dried thyme

2 pints small oysters, drained, liquid reserved

2 pounds medium shrimp, cooked, peeled, and deveined

½ teaspoon salt

½ teaspoon freshly cracked black pepper

8 cups salad mix

8 green onions, chopped

1. In a 6- or 8-quart Dutch oven, cook penne according to package directions; drain, set aside, and keep warm.

2. Wipe out the Dutch oven; add oil over medium heat. Once the oil is hot, stir in flour and cook until it begins to turn light brown, about 5–6 minutes. Add onion and sauté 3 minutes or until soft. Whisk in anchovy paste, milk, and cream.

3. Bring to a simmer and stir in hot sauce, Worcestershire sauce, and thyme; simmer 10 minutes.

4. Stir oysters and shrimp into the cream sauce. Simmer just long enough to heat the seafood, about 2 minutes, then stir in pasta. If pasta mixture is too thick, stir in a little extra milk, cream, or liquid drained from the oysters. Taste for seasoning and add salt and pepper if needed.

5. To serve, spread 1 cup salad mix over the top of a plate, ladle pasta mixture over the salad greens, and garnish with chopped green onion.

# Shrimp Provençal

*This easy meal, with a twist from France, is full of flavor and good for you too.*

**PREP TIME:** 20 minutes
**COOK TIME:** 1 hour 5 minutes
**INGREDIENTS | SERVES 6**

1 tablespoon olive oil
3 tablespoons unsalted butter
2 medium onions, peeled and chopped
4 cloves garlic, peeled and minced
1 (14-ounce) can diced tomatoes, undrained
1 (8-ounce) can tomato sauce
¼ cup dry sherry, if desired
½ teaspoon fennel seeds
1 teaspoon sugar
½ teaspoon salt
⅛ teaspoon cayenne pepper
1 teaspoon dried thyme leaves
1½ pounds raw medium shrimp, shelled
3 cups hot cooked brown rice
½ cup crumbled goat cheese

1. In large 4- or 6-quart Dutch oven combine olive oil and butter over medium heat. Once butter melts add onion and garlic; cook 5–6 minutes or until tender.

2. Add all remaining ingredients except shrimp, rice, and cheese. Bring to a simmer, stirring frequently. Reduce heat to low, partially cover, and simmer 50 minutes, stirring occasionally.

3. Just before serving, stir in shrimp and cook until shrimp curl and turn pink, about 3–4 minutes. Serve over rice and sprinkle with cheese.

# Southern-Style Fried Catfish

*Cornmeal mixed with fine cracker crumbs is the secret to a good Southern fried catfish. Serve this with French Fries or Onions Rings (Chapter 7), lemon wedges, and Tartar Sauce (see recipe in the sidebar).*

**PREP TIME:** 1 hour 15 minutes
**COOK TIME:** 15 minutes

**INGREDIENTS | SERVES 8**

2 pounds catfish fillets, about 4 ounces each

2 (12-ounce) beers, lager or ale preferred

Oil, for frying

1 cup all-purpose flour

1 teaspoon salt

½ teaspoon freshly cracked black pepper

2 large eggs, beaten

1 cup buttermilk

1 teaspoon hot sauce

1 cup yellow cornmeal

1 cup fine saltine cracker crumbs

## Tartar Sauce

This is a classic tartar sauce that can be used for all kinds of fried seafood. Mix 1 cup mayonnaise with ¼ cup minced sweet gherkins, ¼ cup minced onion, and ½ teaspoon Worcestershire sauce. Add ¼ teaspoon salt and freshly cracked black pepper, and mix well. Refrigerate 1 hour before serving. This sauce lasts 1 week when stored in an airtight container in the refrigerator.

1. In a large bowl combine catfish fillets and beer. Refrigerate 1 hour, then drain well and pat the fillets dry.

2. In a 6- or 8-quart deep Dutch oven add 3" oil, making sure there is at least a 3" air gap at the top of the pot. Heat oil to 350°F.

3. In a large zip-top bag combine flour, salt, and pepper. Seal the bag and shake to mix. In a shallow dish combine eggs, buttermilk, and hot sauce. Whisk to combine. Finally, in a second large zip-top bag combine cornmeal and cracker crumbs. Seal and shake to combine.

4. Working in batches, add a few fillets to flour and toss to coat. Remove from flour and tap off any excess. Dip fillets into egg mixture, allowing any excess to drip off. Finally, add fillets to cornmeal mixture and toss to coat. Transfer coated fillets to a wire rack to hold.

5. Fry fillets 2–3 at a time until they are golden brown on both sides, about 3 minutes per side. While first batch is frying, heat oven to 175°F. Transfer cooked fillets to a wire rack over a sheet pan and place in warm oven to hold while you fry remaining fillets. Serve hot.

# Beer-Battered Fish Planks

*This beer batter is perfect for firm whitefish like cod. Serve this with French Fries (Chapter 7) and a little malt vinegar for some tasty fish and chips!*

**PREP TIME:** 1 hour 15 minutes
**COOK TIME:** 25 minutes

**INGREDIENTS | SERVES 8**

2 cups all-purpose flour

1 teaspoon salt

½ teaspoon freshly cracked black pepper

½ teaspoon smoked paprika

½ teaspoon garlic powder

¼ teaspoon onion powder

1 large egg, beaten

1 (12-ounce) beer, lager preferred

Oil, for frying

2 pounds cod fillets, about 4 ounces each

1. In a large bowl combine flour, salt, pepper, paprika, garlic powder, and onion powder. Whisk to combine, then add egg and beer and whisk until a smooth batter forms. Allow to rest at room temperature for 1 hour.

2. In a 6- or 8-quart deep Dutch oven add 3" oil, making sure there is a 3" air gap at the top of the pot. Heat oil to 350°F.

3. Heat oven to 175°F. Pat the fish fillets dry. Working with one fillet at a time, dip into batter and immediately add to hot oil. Fry until fish is golden brown on both sides, about 5–6 minutes. Remove fillet from the oil and transfer to a wire rack over a sheet pan to drain, then transfer to warm oven to keep warm while you fry remaining fish. Serve hot.

## Beer for the Batter

Lighter beers work better for batters than darker beers do. A stout, for example, would be too strong in flavor and would compete with your fish. Also, the natural sugar in the stout would result in very dark fish because the sugars would caramelize as the fish fries. You want a light, crisp beer that will add a nutty, buttery flavor to your batter without overpowering it.

# Crunchy Fried Shrimp

*These shrimp are very crunchy, but not heavily breaded so they are great for dinner, as an appetizer, or as a snack during the big game.*

**PREP TIME:** 15 minutes
**COOK TIME:** 15 minutes

**INGREDIENTS | SERVES 8**

Oil, for frying

1 cup all-purpose flour

1 teaspoon salt

½ teaspoon seafood seasoning, such as Old Bay

2 large eggs, beaten

½ cup milk

2 cups panko bread crumbs

2 pounds ($^{21}/_{25}$ or $^{26}/_{30}$) shrimp, peeled and tail on

1. In a 6- or 8-quart deep Dutch oven add 3" oil, making sure there is a 3" air gap at the top of the pot. Heat oil to 350°F.

2. In a large zip-top bag combine flour, salt, and seafood seasoning. Seal the bag and shake to mix. In a shallow dish combine eggs and milk and whisk to combine. Finally, spread bread crumbs into a shallow dish.

3. Pat shrimp dry with paper towel. Working in batches, add the shrimp to flour mixture and shake to coat. Tap off any excess flour, then dip into egg mixture, letting any excess drip off. Finally roll shrimp in bread crumbs and transfer to a plate while you coat remaining shrimp.

4. Fry shrimp 5 or 6 at a time, until golden brown all over and floating, about 3–4 minutes. Remove shrimp to a wire rack over a sheet pan to drain, and then repeat with remaining shrimp. You can hold shrimp in a warm oven (175°F) if desired while you finish frying. Serve hot.

# Deep-Fried Calamari

*This dish is often served with marinara sauce, but can also be served with a spicy or garlicky mayonnaise or a remoulade sauce.*

**PREP TIME:** 15 minutes
**COOK TIME:** 20 minutes

**INGREDIENTS | SERVES 2–3**

1 pound frozen calamari, cleaned
¼ cup fine cornmeal
2 tablespoons cornstarch
2 teaspoons seafood seasoning, such as Old Bay
½ teaspoon salt
1 quart canola or safflower oil

1. Thaw calamari. Slice off the tentacles. Slice the tubes into ½"-wide rings. Pat dry with paper towels.

2. Combine cornmeal, cornstarch, seasoning, and salt in a plastic bag. Add calamari to the bag and shake until coated evenly.

3. Heat oven to 175°F. Place a wire rack over a baking sheet in the middle of the oven.

4. Place 2" oil in a 6- or 8-quart Dutch oven over medium-high heat. Once oil reaches 350°F, carefully add a handful of calamari pieces. Cook 2–3 minutes or until they're lightly golden brown.

5. Remove cooked calamari with a slotted spoon or wire skimmer and place on wire rack in warm oven to drain.

# Coconut Shrimp with Pineapple Dipping Sauce

*These shrimp are sweet and savory, and go well with a juicy steak, crab cakes, or grilled chicken!*

**PREP TIME:** 15 minutes
**COOK TIME:** 20 minutes

**INGREDIENTS | SERVES 8**

2 pounds (²¹/₂₅) shrimp, peeled and tail on

1 cup all-purpose flour

1 teaspoon salt

2 large eggs, beaten

½ cup full-fat coconut milk

1 cup panko bread crumbs

1 cup unsweetened flaked coconut

Oil, for frying

1 (4-ounce) can crushed pineapple in juice, drained

½ cup cream of coconut, such as Coco Lopez

### Coconut Milk versus Cream of Coconut

Coconut milk and cream of coconut are two very different things. Coconut milk is the liquid that is produced when the flesh of fresh coconut is pressed. This liquid is thick and fatty and is used for making sauces, smoothies, and curries. Cream of coconut is a sweet coconut-flavored syrup that is used for making drinks and, in this case, dipping sauces.

1. Pat shrimp dry with paper towels. Set aside.

2. In a large zip-top bag combine flour and salt. Seal the bag and shake to combine. In a shallow dish combine eggs and coconut milk. Whisk to combine. Finally, in a shallow dish combine bread crumbs and coconut. Mix well.

3. In a 6- or 8-quart deep Dutch oven add 3" oil, making sure there is a 3" air gap at the top of the pot. Heat oil to 350°F.

4. Working in batches, add shrimp to flour mixture and shake to coat. Tap off any excess flour, then dip into egg mixture, letting any excess drip off. Finally roll shrimp in bread crumb and coconut mixture and transfer to a plate while you coat remaining shrimp.

5. Fry shrimp 5 or 6 at a time until golden brown all over and floating, about 3 minutes. Transfer to a wire rack over a sheet pan to drain. You can hold shrimp in a warm (175°F) oven, if desired, while you fry remaining shrimp.

6. In a small bowl combine pineapple and cream of coconut. Serve this with hot shrimp for dipping.

# CHAPTER 12

# Vegetarian and Vegan

# Roasted Vegetable Deep Dish Pizza

*This hearty pizza is sure to please everyone—even the carnivores! This recipe is flexible, so use whatever vegetables look best at your local market.*

**PREP TIME:** 40 minutes
**COOK TIME:** 1 hour

**INGREDIENTS | SERVES 8**

2 tablespoons olive oil

1 medium red or green bell pepper, cut into ½" pieces

1 medium zucchini, cut into ½" slices

1 medium yellow squash, cut into ½" slices

½ pint sliced button mushrooms

½ teaspoon salt

½ teaspoon freshly cracked black pepper

1 tablespoon unsalted butter

1 (12-ounce) can diced fire-roasted tomatoes

1 clove garlic, peeled and minced

½ teaspoon ground fennel

¼ teaspoon oregano

1 recipe Dutch Oven Pizza Crust (Chapter 3)

Cornmeal, for dusting pan

2 cups shredded mozzarella cheese

1. In a large zip-top bag add olive oil, bell pepper, zucchini, squash, mushrooms, salt, and pepper. Let stand at room temperature 30 minutes.

2. Heat oven to 425°F.

3. Spread vegetables out on a baking sheet in a single layer. Roast until vegetables are tender, about 10 minutes. Remove from oven and let cool.

4. In an ovenproof 6- or 8-quart Dutch oven over medium heat combine butter, tomatoes, garlic, fennel, and oregano. Cook, stirring often, until mixture comes to a boil and reduces slightly, about 20 minutes. Transfer sauce to a bowl to cool. Rinse the Dutch oven and wipe dry.

5. Roll out pizza crust 2" wider than your Dutch oven. Sprinkle a little cornmeal onto the bottom of the Dutch oven. Place crust into the Dutch oven and form a lip around the sides of the pot that is at least 2" deep.

6. Spread shredded cheese into the bottom of crust, then add roasted vegetables, and finally spread sauce over top.

7. Bake pizza 18–25 minutes or until crust is golden brown and toppings are bubbling. Rest pizza 10 minutes, then transfer to a cutting board to slice and serve.

# Brown Rice and Quinoa Stuffed Peppers

*These peppers are generously stuffed with a brown rice and quinoa pilaf. If you like you can add some shredded cheese to the tops of these peppers if you are not serving vegans.*

**PREP TIME:** 10 minutes
**COOK TIME:** 35 minutes

**INGREDIENTS | SERVES 4**

2 tablespoons olive oil, divided

4 medium bell peppers, red, green, or yellow, tops removed and cored

1 medium onion, peeled and chopped

1 clove garlic, peeled and minced

1 (14.5-ounce) can diced tomatoes, drained

¼ teaspoon cumin

¼ teaspoon salt

¼ teaspoon freshly cracked black pepper

1 cup cooked brown rice

1 cup cooked quinoa

1. Heat oven to 375°F.

2. Lightly brush bell peppers inside and out with 1 tablespoon olive oil. Place peppers into an ovenproof 6- or 8-quart Dutch oven and roast 8–10 minutes, or until peppers are just starting to become tender. Remove from oven and set aside.

3. Heat the Dutch oven over medium heat add remaining olive oil. Once oil shimmers add onion and cook until tender, about 5 minutes. Add garlic, tomato, cumin, salt, and pepper and cook until tomatoes are heated and the garlic is fragrant, about 3 minutes. Fold in rice and quinoa, then turn off heat.

4. Divide rice mixture evenly among peppers and clean out the Dutch oven, then return the peppers to the Dutch oven and bake, uncovered, for 10–15 minutes or until peppers are very tender and filling is hot.

# Barley Risotto

*When you are hungry, nothing beats a bowl of this hearty barley risotto. During the summer you can substitute summer squash or zucchini for the butternut squash.*

**PREP TIME:** 10 minutes
**COOK TIME:** 1 hour 45 minutes

**INGREDIENTS | SERVES 8**

1 butternut squash, peeled and cut into ½" cubes

3 tablespoons olive oil, divided

1 teaspoon salt, divided

1 teaspoon freshly cracked black pepper, divided

6 cups vegetable broth

1 medium onion, peeled and finely chopped

1 clove garlic, peeled and minced

1½ cups pearl barley

½ cup white wine

2 tablespoons finely chopped fresh parsley

### Pearled Barley versus Hulled Barley

Barley is processed using a process called pearling. This process removes the outer hull, and if the barley is pearled long enough it also removes the endosperm, bran, and germ. Hulled barley, also called pot barley, has only the hull removed; most of the bran and germ are intact, making it a whole grain. Barley that is labeled as pearled has almost all of the bran and germ removed and is not a whole grain. You can substitute hulled barley for most recipes that call for barley, but it will take a little longer to cook thoroughly.

1. Heat oven to 400°F.

2. In a large bowl combine butternut squash, 1 tablespoon olive oil, ¼ teaspoon salt, and ¼ teaspoon pepper. Toss to thoroughly coat squash, then transfer to a baking sheet and roast until squash is tender, about 25–30 minutes. Remove from the oven and set aside to cool.

3. In a medium saucepan bring vegetable broth to a simmer.

4. In an ovenproof 6- or 8-quart Dutch oven over medium heat add remaining olive oil. Once it shimmers add onion and cook, stirring often, until tender, about 5 minutes. Add garlic and remaining salt and pepper, and cook until the garlic is fragrant, about 30 seconds.

5. Add barley and cook, stirring frequently, until barley is coated in oil and is lightly toasted, about 5 minutes. Add white wine and cook, stirring constantly, until wine is absorbed, about 2 minutes.

6. Begin ladling in vegetable broth ½ cup at a time, stirring frequently, allowing broth to be absorbed by barley after each addition, about 45–50 minutes.

7. Once all the broth is absorbed fold in roasted squash and chopped parsley. Serve immediately.

# Barley Mushroom Casserole

*Barley is a delicious, nutty, and mild grain that's very healthy. Cooked with vegetables, it makes an excellent vegetarian main dish or side dish for grilled meats.*

**PREP TIME:** 10 minutes
**COOK TIME:** 1 hour 10 minutes

**INGREDIENTS | SERVES 6**

2 tablespoons unsalted butter
1 medium onion, peeled and chopped
3 cloves garlic, peeled and minced
2 cups sliced cremini mushrooms
1 cup sliced button mushrooms
1½ cups pearl barley
½ cup chopped celery
1 teaspoon salt
¼ teaspoon pepper
1 teaspoon dried thyme leaves
3½ cups vegetable broth
¼ cup chopped flat-leaf parsley
½ cup grated Parmesan cheese

1. Heat oven to 350°F.

2. In an ovenproof 6- or 8-quart Dutch oven melt butter over medium heat. Add onion and garlic, and cook until just softened, about 3 minutes. Add mushrooms and cook 4 minutes longer.

3. Add barley and cook 5–6 minutes, stirring often, until barley is lightly browned. Add celery, salt, pepper, thyme, and broth and bring to a simmer.

4. Bake 50–65 minutes, or until barley is tender. Mix in chopped parsley and cheese and serve.

# Pearl Couscous with Corn, Black Beans, and Tomatoes

*This can be served warm as a main dish, or can be served cold as a salad or side dish for a barbecue.*

**PREP TIME:** 10 minutes
**COOK TIME:** 25 minutes

**INGREDIENTS | SERVES 8**

2 tablespoons olive oil

1 (10-ounce) bag frozen whole kernel corn

1 medium onion, peeled and finely chopped

1 medium red bell pepper, seeded and finely chopped

2 cloves garlic, peeled and minced

¼ teaspoon chili powder

¼ teaspoon salt

¼ teaspoon freshly cracked black pepper

1 cup pearl or Israeli couscous

1½ cups vegetable broth

1 (14.5-ounce) can low-sodium black beans, rinsed and drained

2 roma tomatoes, seeded and chopped

1. In a 6-quart Dutch oven over medium heat add olive oil. Once oil starts to shimmer add corn. Cook, stirring often, until corn starts to brown, about 10 minutes. Add onion and bell pepper and cook until they soften slightly, about 5 minutes. Add garlic, chili powder, salt, and pepper and cook until fragrant, about 1 minute.

2. Add couscous and stir well to mix with the vegetables. Add vegetable broth, bring to a boil, then reduce heat to low and cover with the lid. Cook until couscous has absorbed all the liquid, about 10–15 minutes.

3. Once couscous has absorbed the liquid remove the lid and fluff with a spoon. Fold in black beans and tomatoes. Serve warm or at room temperature.

# Roasted Chickpeas and Zucchini

*This dish is earthy from the curry powder, but it is kept from being too heavy by a little fresh lemon juice. If you like you can add a little pan-fried paneer cheese to this dish.*

**PREP TIME:** 10 minutes
**COOK TIME:** 20 minutes

**INGREDIENTS | SERVES 6**

4 medium zucchini, cut into ½"-thick slices

1 (15-ounce) can chickpeas, drained and rinsed

1 medium onion, peeled and roughly chopped

3 tablespoons olive oil

1 tablespoon fresh lemon juice

½ teaspoon curry powder

¼ teaspoon salt

¼ teaspoon freshly cracked black pepper

2 tablespoons chopped fresh parsley

1. Heat oven to 400°F.

2. In an ovenproof 6- or 8-quart Dutch oven combine all ingredients expect chopped parsley. Toss until everything is evenly coated.

3. Roast 20 minutes, stirring halfway through the cooking time, or until zucchini and onion are tender. Garnish with chopped parsley. Serve immediately.

# Vegetable Green Curry

*Green curry is named for its color, and originates from central Thailand. Green curry paste is available in jars or sealed packets at most Asian markets. Serve this dish in bowls with cooked white rice.*

**PREP TIME:** 10 minutes
**COOK TIME:** 30 minutes

**INGREDIENTS | SERVES 4**

¼ cup jarred green curry paste

2 cups vegetable broth

1 large sweet potato, peeled and cut into ½" cubes

¼ pound green beans, stems removed

8 ounces sliced button mushrooms

8 ounces fresh spinach leaves

Juice from 1 medium lime

1 (14-ounce) can coconut milk

1. Place a 6- or 8-quart Dutch oven over medium heat. Once it is heated, add curry paste and vegetable broth and stir to combine.

2. Stir in sweet potato cubes, cover, and cook 15–20 minutes or until you can pierce them with a fork. Stir the contents occasionally to keep them from sticking. Turn heat to medium-high and remove the lid. Add remaining vegetables and cook 5–7 minutes, stirring frequently.

3. Once liquid has reduced, lower the heat to medium-low and add lime juice and coconut milk. Keep coconut milk from boiling and cook 2–3 minutes. Serve.

# Lentils with Roasted Root Vegetables

*Beets can be tricky to work with, as their juice can stain your hands and counter. Be sure to wear gloves and use a plastic cutting board to avoid any unwanted stains!*

**PREP TIME:** 40 minutes
**COOK TIME:** 1 hour

**INGREDIENTS | SERVES 8**

2 medium carrots, peeled and cut into ½" pieces

1 medium turnip, scrubbed and cut into ½" cubes

1 medium beet, peeled and cut into ½" cubes

1 medium sweet potato, peeled and cut into ½" pieces

2 tablespoons olive oil, divided

1 tablespoon honey

½ teaspoon salt

½ teaspoon freshly cracked black pepper

2 cups green lentils

4 cups water

1 clove garlic, peeled and smashed

2 sprigs fresh thyme

1 bay leaf

2 tablespoons fresh chopped parsley

1. In a large bowl add carrot, turnip, beet, sweet potato, 1 tablespoon olive oil, honey, salt, and pepper. Toss to coat, then let stand at room temperature 30 minutes.

2. Heat oven to 425°F.

3. Spread vegetables out on a baking sheet in a single layer. Roast until vegetables are tender, about 25–30 minutes. Remove from oven and let cool.

4. In a 6- or 8-quart Dutch oven combine lentils, water, garlic, thyme, and bay leaf. Bring mixture to a simmer over medium heat, then reduce the heat to medium-low and cook lentils at a bare simmer until they are tender, adding additional water if needed to keep them covered, about 30 minutes. Drain lentils, discard garlic, thyme, and bay leaf, and return lentils to the Dutch oven.

5. Add remaining olive oil and roasted vegetables to lentils and toss to combine. Garnish with chopped parsley. Serve warm or room temperature.

## Perfect Lentils

For perfectly cooked lentils remember these tips. First, do not boil your lentils, or they will become mushy. Second, season with salt and acids—like lemon juice—after the lentils have finished cooking. Salt and acid make the lentils tough when added too early in the cooking process. Green and brown lentils tend to be firmer after cooking than red and orange lentils, so save them for soups and stews rather than salads.

# Truffle Risotto

*Want to impress dinner guests? This dish will do the trick! Risotto takes a little time to cook and isn't the place for shortcuts. Take the time; it is well worth it!*

**PREP TIME:** 15 minutes
**COOK TIME:** 1 hour 5 minutes

**INGREDIENTS | SERVES 8**

8 cups vegetable broth

2 tablespoons unsalted butter

1 tablespoon olive oil

1 medium onion, peeled and finely chopped

2 cloves garlic, peeled and minced

2½ cups Arborio rice

½ cup white wine

2 teaspoons black truffle oil

½ teaspoon salt or truffle salt

¼ freshly cracked black pepper

½ cup grated Parmesan cheese

## What's in Your Truffle Oil?

Truffle oil has become very popular as a way to add the flavor and aroma of truffles to food without the extreme cost. When buying truffle oil look for oil that is actually infused with truffles, not oil that is flavored with chemicals to imitate the flavor of truffles. This oil will cost more—but not nearly as much as fresh truffles cost—and is superior in flavor and aroma to any chemically enhanced oil.

1. In a medium saucepan bring broth to a simmer.

2. In a 6- or 8-quart Dutch oven over medium heat add butter and oil. Once butter melts and starts to foam add onion and cook, stirring often, until tender, about 5 minutes. Add garlic and cook until fragrant, about 30 seconds.

3. Add rice to the Dutch oven and cook, stirring frequently, until rice is coated in the fat and is lightly toasted, about 5 minutes. Add white wine and cook, stirring constantly, until wine is absorbed, about 2 minutes.

4. Begin ladling in broth ½ cup at a time, stirring frequently, allowing broth to be absorbed by rice after each addition, about 45–50 minutes.

5. Once all broth is absorbed stir in truffle oil, salt, and pepper. Fold in cheese and serve immediately.

# Pad Thai with Tofu

*Fried tofu is available ready-fried at most Asian markets, but if you can't find it you can make it yourself by frying cubes of extra-firm tofu in vegetable oil until golden brown.*

**PREP TIME:** 1 hour 10 minutes
**COOK TIME:** 20 minutes

**INGREDIENTS | SERVES 4**

12 ounces dried, thin rice stick noodles

½ cup brown sugar

¼ cup tamarind paste

2 tablespoons white sugar

2 tablespoons vegetarian fish sauce, or soy sauce

2 tablespoons vegetable oil

½ medium onion, peeled and minced

3 large eggs

2 (8-ounce) packages fried tofu squares, sliced

½ teaspoon red chili flakes

3 cups bean sprouts, divided

1 cup sliced green onion tops, cut into 2" pieces, divided

½ cup crushed roasted peanuts, for garnish

Lime wedges, for garnish

1. Place the rice noodles into a large bowl and cover with cold water. Soak for 1 hour then drain well. Set aside.

2. Make the sauce by mixing brown sugar, tamarind paste, white sugar, and fish sauce in a medium saucepan. Simmer over low heat until sugar is dissolved, about 3 minutes. Set aside to cool.

3. Heat an 8-quart Dutch oven over medium heat, add oil, and cook onion until fragrant, about 30 seconds.

4. Crack eggs into the pan and break the yolks. Let the eggs fry 2 minutes without stirring, then use a spatula to break up eggs and scramble them. Mix in tofu and chili flakes and cook until heated through, about 1 minute.

5. Turn heat to high and add the noodles. Stir-fry 3–5 minutes, turning the noodles until they are soft and become translucent and brown in color. Add prepared sauce and toss to coat noodles. Cook until sauce is mostly absorbed, about 1 minute.

6. Add 2 cups of bean sprouts and ¾ cup of the green onion tops, reserving the rest for garnish, and cook another 30 seconds.

7. Serve topped with crushed peanuts, green onion tops, bean sprouts, and a wedge or two of lime.

# Cauliflower with Chickpeas and Mustard Seeds

*This dish makes a lot of food but the leftovers can easily be substituted for mashed potatoes in recipes such as Cottage Pie (Chapter 8).*

**PREP TIME:** 10 minutes
**COOK TIME:** 15 minutes

**INGREDIENTS | SERVES 6–8**

1 medium white onion, peeled and chopped

1 tablespoon olive oil

5 tablespoons yellow or black mustard seeds

1 head cauliflower, divided into florets

Pinch salt

1 (15-ounce) can chickpeas, drained and rinsed

¼ cup white wine

1. Place a 6-quart Dutch oven over medium heat. Once the Dutch oven is heated add onion, olive oil, and mustard seeds. Stir frequently and let onion cook until it starts to turn brown, about 8 minutes.

2. Add the cauliflower florets to the Dutch oven with a sprinkle of salt.

3. Stir to combine and cook 4 minutes. Add chickpeas to the Dutch oven with white wine. Stir to combine.

4. Cover the Dutch oven and cook 3–4 minutes. Remove the lid and let liquid evaporate. Serve when cauliflower is fork tender.

# Spicy Black Bean Bisque

*Jalapeño peppers carry most of their heat in the seeds and inner ribs. If you want a milder soup, split the pepper in half and remove the seeds before using.*

**PREP TIME:** 15 minutes
**COOK TIME:** 10 minutes

**INGREDIENTS | SERVES 3–4**

2 (15-ounce) cans black beans, drained and rinsed, divided

1 medium jalapeño pepper, chopped

1 cup half and half

1 teaspoon cumin

¼ teaspoon salt

¼ teaspoon freshly cracked black pepper

⅓ cup sour cream or crème fraîche

Chopped fresh cilantro or green onion, for garnish

1. Reserve ½ cup black beans for later use. Place remaining beans, jalapeño, and half and half in blender. Pulse until blended. Add cumin and blend until puréed.

2. Pour purée into a 4- or 6-quart Dutch oven and cook over medium heat until just bubbling at the sides of the pot, about 5 minutes. Stir in reserved beans, salt, and pepper. Ladle into bowls garnished with sour cream or crème fraîche and chopped cilantro or green onion.

# Moussaka

*Classic Moussaka is made vegetarian by using meatless protein crumbles instead of ground beef.*

**PREP TIME:** 15 minutes
**COOK TIME:** 1 hour 50 minutes

**INGREDIENTS | SERVES 10**

2 large eggplants, peeled and cut into ½"-thick slices

1½ teaspoons salt, divided use

2 tablespoons olive oil

2 medium onions, peeled and chopped

4 cloves garlic, peeled and minced

1 (12-ounce) package meatless crumbles

1 (6-ounce) can tomato paste

1 (8-ounce) can tomato sauce

1 teaspoon dried oregano leaves

½ teaspoon cinnamon

1 teaspoon dried basil leaves

2 tablespoons unsalted butter

2 tablespoons all-purpose flour

⅛ teaspoon white pepper

1½ cups milk

½ cup sour cream

2 large eggs

1 cup grated Romano cheese

¼ cup grated Parmesan cheese

¼ cup dried bread crumbs

1. Sprinkle eggplant slices with ½ teaspoon of the salt. Let stand in a colander while preparing rest of recipe.

2. In an ovenproof 6- or 8-quart Dutch oven heat olive oil over medium heat. Add onions and garlic and cook until tender, about 5 minutes. Stir in meatless crumbles and tomato paste and let brown 5 minutes. Stir in tomato sauce, oregano, cinnamon, basil, and ½ teaspoon salt. Let mixture simmer over low heat 30 minutes, then transfer to a bowl to cool. Wipe out the Dutch oven.

3. For cream sauce, place the Dutch oven back over medium heat and add butter. Once it melts and starts to foam add flour, ½ teaspoon salt, and white pepper. Cook, stirring constantly, until bubbly. Whisk in milk and sour cream, and cook until thick, about 5 minutes. Remove from heat and beat in eggs and Romano cheese. Transfer mixture to a bowl to cool slightly.

4. Heat the broiler in the oven. Clean out the Dutch oven and lightly spray with nonstick cooking spray.

5. Rinse eggplant, pat dry, and broil on a baking sheet for 7–8 minutes, turning once, until browned.

6. Heat oven to 350°F.

7. Place a layer of eggplant in bottom of the Dutch oven. Top with tomato sauce and remaining eggplant. Pour cream sauce over eggplant and top with a mixture of Parmesan cheese and bread crumbs. Bake 40–50 minutes until top is golden brown. Cool 10 minutes, then cut into squares to serve.

# Chickpea Curry

*Cauliflower and curry powder is one of the best anticancer combinations in the food world. And it's delicious!*

**PREP TIME:** 10 minutes
**COOK TIME:** 25 minutes

**INGREDIENTS | SERVES 6**

2 tablespoons olive oil
1 medium onion, peeled and chopped
4 cloves garlic, peeled and minced
2 tablespoons minced gingerroot
1 tablespoon curry powder
1 head cauliflower, cut into florets
½ teaspoon salt
⅛ teaspoon cayenne pepper
⅓ cup water
1 (14.5-ounce) can diced tomatoes, drained
1 (15-ounce) can chickpeas, drained
½ cup coconut milk

1. In a 6- or 8-quart Dutch oven over medium heat add olive oil. Add onion, garlic, gingerroot, and curry powder and cook 4–5 minutes.

2. Add cauliflower, salt, cayenne pepper, and water. Bring to a simmer, cover, reduce heat to low, and simmer 5–8 minutes, or until cauliflower is crisp-tender.

3. Add tomatoes, chickpeas, and coconut milk and bring back to a simmer. Simmer uncovered, stirring frequently, 5–8 minutes until mixture is blended.

# Green Rice

*This could be the main dish for a vegetarian meal. Serve with a fresh corn salad and some brownies for dessert.*

**PREP TIME:** 10 minutes
**COOK TIME:** 1 hour

**INGREDIENTS | SERVES 6**

2 tablespoons olive oil
1 medium onion, peeled and chopped
3 cloves garlic, peeled and minced
1 (10-ounce) package frozen chopped spinach, thawed and drained
3 cups cooked long-grain rice
1 cup light cream
2 large eggs, beaten
⅓ cup chopped flat-leaf parsley
1 cup shredded Swiss cheese
½ teaspoon salt
⅛ teaspoon pepper
¼ cup grated Romano cheese

1. Heat oven to 350°F.

2. In an ovenproof 4- or 6-quart Dutch oven heat olive oil over medium heat. Once oil shimmers add onion and garlic and cook until tender, about 5 minutes. Add spinach and cook until any liquid evaporates. Remove from heat and cool 10 minutes.

3. Combine remaining ingredients except Romano cheese in the Dutch oven. Top with Romano cheese. Bake 45–55 minutes until casserole is hot and bubbling.

# Paneer Masala

*Paneer is a firm, nonmelting cheese that is from South Asia. It is available at most gourmet cheese shops and some grocery stores. If you can't find paneer, or want to make this recipe vegan, use diced firm tofu in its place.*

**PREP TIME:** 10 minutes
**COOK TIME:** 25 minutes

**INGREDIENTS | SERVES 4**

¼ cup vegetable oil, divided

14 ounces paneer, or firm tofu, cut into ½" cubes

1 medium onion, peeled and chopped

2 cloves garlic, peeled and chopped

2 teaspoons fresh grated ginger

1 tablespoon tomato paste

1 tablespoon garam masala

1 teaspoon cumin

1 teaspoon coriander

¼ teaspoon fenugreek

1 (28-ounce) can tomato sauce

2 teaspoons sugar

1 teaspoon salt

⅔ cup heavy cream or cashew cream

¼ cup chopped cilantro

## Cashew Cream

If you are looking for a vegan alternative to heavy cream why not try cashew cream? The cream takes on the flavor of the food you cook it with, but it still adds richness and creaminess. You can make it by covering 1 cup raw cashews with ½ cup water and letting them soak 3 hours. Once soaked put the cashews and water into a blender and purée until very smooth. For savory recipes you can add a pinch of salt. For sweet recipes feel free to add a little sweetener and some vanilla.

1. In a 6- or 8-quart Dutch oven over medium-high heat add 3 tablespoons oil. Once oil shimmers add half the paneer and fry until golden. Remove from the Dutch oven to a paper towel–lined plate to drain and fry remaining paneer. Set aside.

2. In the work bowl of a food processor or blender combine onion, garlic, ginger, tomato paste, garam masala, cumin, coriander, and fenugreek. Process until the mixture is smooth and no lumps remain.

3. Heat the Dutch oven over medium heat and add remaining oil. Once it shimmers add onion and spice mixture. Cook until spices are fragrant, about 3 minutes. Add tomato sauce, sugar, and salt and stir well to combine. Bring mixture to a boil, then reduce heat to low and let sauce simmer until thickened, about 10 minutes.

4. Stir in cream and fried paneer and bring back to a simmer to heat the paneer, about 5 minutes. Garnish with chopped cilantro before serving.

# Mixed Bean Vegetarian Chili

*Even if you aren't a vegetarian you'll enjoy this healthful and economical dish. You can use either canned or home-cooked dried beans for this chili. Serve alone or with rice.*

**PREP TIME:** 10 minutes
**COOK TIME:** 1 hour 5 minutes

**INGREDIENTS | SERVES 8**

2 tablespoons olive oil
1 large onion, peeled and diced
1 small green bell pepper, seeded and diced
1 jalapeño pepper, minced
2 cloves garlic, peeled and minced
2 cups cooked black beans
2 cups cooked small red beans
2 cups cooked navy beans
2 cups cooked pinto beans
1 (28-ounce) can crushed tomatoes, undrained
1 (14-ounce) can tomato sauce
1 teaspoon balsamic vinegar
3 tablespoons chili powder
1 teaspoon cumin
2 cups water
½ teaspoon salt
½ teaspoon freshly cracked black pepper

1. In a 6- or 8-quart Dutch oven over medium-high heat add oil. Once hot add onion, peppers, and garlic and cook until onions and peppers are soft, about 5 minutes.

2. Add remaining ingredients to the Dutch oven and stir well. Bring mixture to a boil, then reduce heat to medium-low and simmer 1 hour, adding more water if needed. Serve.

# French Lentil Chili

*Serve this chili as a vegetarian alternative to meat-based chilies
or as a spicy alternative to ordinary lentil soup.*

**PREP TIME:** 15 minutes
**COOK TIME:** 1 hour 5 minutes

**INGREDIENTS | SERVES 4**

2 tablespoons olive oil

1 medium onion, peeled and diced

2 cloves garlic, peeled and minced

1 pound dried green lentils

6 cups water or vegetable broth

2 (14-ounce) cans diced tomatoes, undrained

1 tablespoon chili powder

1 teaspoon cumin

Pinch thyme

½ teaspoon salt

¼ teaspoon freshly cracked black pepper

¼ cup minced parsley

1. In a 6- or 8-quart Dutch oven over medium heat add the oil, and once it is hot and begins to shimmer add the onion and garlic. Cook until vegetables just start to soften, about 3 minutes.

2. Place lentils in strainer and rinse well. Pick out any bits of debris or discolored lentils. Add lentils to the Dutch oven along with water or broth. Reduce heat to medium and cook until lentils are half cooked, about 30 minutes.

3. Add tomatoes, chili powder, cumin, and a pinch of thyme. Continue cooking 30 minutes, or until lentils are tender and chili reaches your desired consistency.

4. Add salt and pepper and garnish with parsley.

# Okra, Corn, and Tomato Stew

*For best flavor, make this dish during the summer with corn cut from the cob and just-picked tomatoes and okra. Serve this as a side dish or over rice as an entrée.*

**PREP TIME:** 15 minutes
**COOK TIME:** 30 minutes

**INGREDIENTS | SERVES 4**

3 tablespoons oil or unsalted butter

1 medium onion, peeled and finely diced

1 small green bell pepper, seeded and finely diced

1 stalk celery, finely diced

2 cloves garlic, peeled and minced

2 cups sliced okra

2 cups diced ripe tomatoes

2 cups fresh corn kernels

1 cup water or vegetable broth

¼ teaspoon cayenne

1 green onion, sliced

2 tablespoons minced fresh parsley

½ teaspoon salt

¼ teaspoon freshly cracked black pepper

1. In a 6- or 8-quart Dutch oven, heat oil or butter over medium-high heat. Add onion, green pepper, celery, and garlic, and cook until tender, about 5 minutes.

2. Add okra and cook, stirring constantly, 3 minutes or until okra begins to release thick liquid.

3. Add tomatoes, corn, and water or broth. Bring to a boil then reduce heat to medium-low and simmer, stirring often and adding more liquid if needed, 20 minutes, or until corn is tender.

4. Stir in cayenne, green onion, parsley, salt, and pepper. Remove the Dutch oven from heat. Serve.

# Ratatouille

*This savory vegetable stew makes a great vegetarian entrée
when served over whole-wheat couscous or rice.*

**PREP TIME:** 1 hour 10 minutes
**COOK TIME:** 25 minutes

**INGREDIENTS | SERVES 4–6**

1 medium eggplant, diced

2 teaspoons salt, divided

2 tablespoons olive oil

1 small onion, peeled and diced

1 large green bell pepper, seeded
and diced

3 cloves garlic, peeled and minced

1 large zucchini, diced

2 medium yellow squash, diced

4 ounces white mushrooms, quartered

1 (28-ounce) can crushed tomatoes

1 teaspoon dried Italian seasoning mix

¼ teaspoon freshly cracked
black pepper

¼ cup chopped fresh basil leaves

1. Sprinkle eggplant with 1½ teaspoons salt and leave in a colander 1 hour.

2. Rinse eggplant well and pat dry with paper towels.

3. In a 6- or 8-quart Dutch oven heat olive oil over medium-high heat. Once oil shimmers add onion, bell pepper, and garlic. Cook until just tender, about 3 minutes.

4. Add eggplant, zucchini, squash, and mushrooms to the Dutch oven. Pour in crushed tomatoes and Italian seasoning, then reduce heat to medium and simmer 10–15 minutes or until eggplant is tender.

5. Season with remaining salt and pepper and then stir in fresh basil. Remove the Dutch oven from the heat and allow to stand 5 minutes before serving.

# CHAPTER 13

# Dutch Oven Pot Pies

# Cheeseburger Pie

*This is everything you love about cheeseburgers baked under a buttery pastry crust!*
*If you like you can use ground turkey, chicken, or buffalo in this recipe.*

**PREP TIME:** 20 minutes
**COOK TIME:** 1 hour 10 minutes

**INGREDIENTS | SERVES 8**

1 tablespoon unsalted butter

1 pound 85/15 ground beef

1 medium onion, peeled and chopped

1/4 cup dill pickle relish

1/2 teaspoon salt

1/2 teaspoon freshly cracked black pepper

2 tablespoons all-purpose flour

1/2 cup milk

1/4 cup yellow mustard

1/4 cup ketchup

1 1/2 cups shredded Cheddar cheese, divided

1 recipe All-Butter Pastry Crust for Pot Pies (Chapter 3)

## Make the Pie Pretty!

If you want to make your pot pies really pretty for a party use an egg wash to add shine and enhance the golden brown color. Just beat 1 egg until it is uniform in color, then add 1 tablespoon water and whisk to combine. Just before you place your pot pie in the oven lightly brush the egg mixture over the crust. Keep an eye on the crust while baking, and if it is getting too dark lay a sheet of foil over the Dutch oven to shield the crust.

1. Heat oven to 375°F.

2. In an ovenproof 3½- or 4-quart Dutch oven over medium heat add butter. Once it melts and starts to foam add ground beef and cook until well browned. Drain off excess fat.

3. Return the Dutch oven to heat and add onion, relish, salt, and pepper. Cook until onions begin to soften, about 3 minutes, then add flour and cook until flour is just turning golden in color, about 3 minutes. Stir in milk and bring mixture to a boil and cook, stirring often, until mixture begins to thicken, about 5 minutes. Remove from heat and allow the mixture to cool 10 minutes.

4. Once cooled spread meat so it is flat in the Dutch oven. Spread mustard and ketchup over meat, then top with shredded cheese.

5. Place pastry crust directly on cheese and crimp the crust around the edge of the Dutch oven. Using a paring knife cut small vents around crust to let steam escape.

6. Bake 25–30 minutes, or until crust is golden brown and filling is bubbling. Remove from oven and let stand 20 minutes before serving.

# Beef Wellington Pie

*Beef Wellington is a very fancy old-fashioned dish. This recipe takes all the best flavors of a beef Wellington but transforms it into a creamy, easy-to-make pie!*

**PREP TIME:** 20 minutes
**COOK TIME:** 2 hours 50 minutes

**INGREDIENTS | SERVES 8**

¼ pound cubed pancetta, or chopped thick-cut unsmoked bacon

½ cup all-purpose flour

1 teaspoon salt

1 teaspoon freshly cracked black pepper

2 pounds boneless beef short ribs, cut into 1" pieces

4 tablespoons unsalted butter

1 pound button or cremini mushrooms, cleaned and quartered

½ teaspoon dry thyme

½ cup red wine

2 cups beef stock

1 cup water

1 cup pearl onions

1 bay leaf

1 recipe All-Butter Pastry Crust for Pot Pies (Chapter 3)

1 large egg, beaten

1. Heat a 3½- or 4-quart Dutch oven over medium heat. Once hot add pancetta and cook until pancetta is crisp, about 5 minutes. Remove pancetta and set aside to drain on a paper towel–lined plate.

2. In a large zip-top bag add flour, salt, and pepper. Shake to combine, then add half the beef to the bag and shake to coat. Place coated beef pieces into pancetta drippings and brown well on all sides, about 3 minutes per side. Remove to a plate to rest while you coat and brown remaining beef. Add second batch of beef to the first and set aside. Reserve any remaining flour.

3. Add butter to the Dutch oven. Once it starts to foam add mushrooms and thyme. Cook, stirring often, until mushrooms are tender, about 8 minutes. Add any remaining flour used for coating beef and cook 3 minutes. Add red wine and scrape any browned bits from the bottom of the pan. Add beef stock and water and continue to scrape. The sauce should thicken slightly.

4. Add pancetta, beef cubes, pearl onions, and bay leaf. Boil, then reduce to medium-low, cover, and simmer 2 hours. Remove from heat and discard bay leaf.

5. Heat oven to 400°F.

6. Place pastry crust on a lightly floured surface. Using a knife, cut 1" vents in a circle pattern in the center of crust. Brush the edge of the pot with water and brush pastry with beaten egg. Place pastry egg-washed side up over the Dutch oven and press the edges to seal. Trim the pastry so it has a 1" overhang.

7. Bake the pie until pastry crust is golden brown, about 20–25 minutes. Let pie rest 10 minutes.

# Chili with Cheesy Jalapeño Cornbread

*Chili and cornbread are a natural combination, so why not avoid extra cleanup and just bake your cornbread on top of the chili? This dish is great for potluck suppers, parties, and anytime you want an easy dinner!*

**PREP TIME:** 20 minutes
**COOK TIME:** 35 minutes

**INGREDIENTS | SERVES 8**

1 recipe Texas Red Chili (Chapter 5), or 8 cups of your favorite canned chili

½ cup yellow cornmeal

½ cup all-purpose flour

2 teaspoons baking powder

1 teaspoon sugar

¼ teaspoon salt

¼ cup buttermilk

1 large egg

4 tablespoons unsalted butter, melted, divided

½ cup shredded sharp Cheddar cheese

2 tablespoons finely chopped pickled jalapeño slices

1. Heat oven to 375°F.

2. In an ovenproof 4-quart Dutch oven add chili. Warm chili over medium-low heat until it starts to simmer, about 10 minutes. Reduce heat to low, cover and let simmer while you prepare the topping.

3. In a large bowl combine cornmeal, flour, baking powder, sugar, and salt.

4. In a medium bowl add buttermilk, egg, and 3 tablespoons melted butter. Whisk until completely combined. Pour the wet ingredients into the dry ingredients and mix until just combined and no large lumps of dry ingredients remain, about 8 strokes. Add the Cheddar and jalapeño and fold to combine, about 4 strokes.

5. Remove the lid from the Dutch oven and use a spatula to clean the sides of the Dutch oven if chili has splattered. Brush exposed sides of the Dutch oven with remaining butter. Spoon cornbread mixture on top of the hot chili, and gently spread so it covers the surface. Bake 20–25 minutes, or until cornbread is golden brown and chili is bubbling underneath. Cool 10 minutes before serving.

# Tamale Pie

*This hearty casserole feeds a crowd. The spicier the sausage, the spicier the casserole. If you like it really hot, add more jalapeño peppers.*

**PREP TIME:** 15 minutes
**COOK TIME:** 1 hour 35 minutes

**INGREDIENTS | SERVES 8**

2 cups chicken broth

1 cup water

1 cup yellow cornmeal

1½ pounds spicy pork sausage

2 medium onions, peeled and chopped

4 cloves garlic, peeled and minced

2 jalapeño peppers, minced

1 medium green bell pepper, seeded and chopped

1 medium red bell pepper, seeded and chopped

2 (14-ounce) cans diced tomatoes, undrained

1 (15-ounce) can black beans, drained

1 tablespoon chili powder

1 teaspoon cumin

½ teaspoon salt

⅛ teaspoon pepper

1 cup shredded Muenster cheese

¼ cup grated Cotija cheese

1. In an ovenproof 4- or 6-quart Dutch oven bring broth and water to a boil over high heat. Lower heat to medium and whisk in cornmeal. Cover with the lid and simmer 15–20 minutes, stirring frequently, until thick. Transfer to a bowl and set aside. Clean out the Dutch oven.

2. Return the Dutch over to medium heat and cook sausage with onion, garlic, and jalapeño peppers until sausage is brown, about 8–10 minutes. Drain well, then add bell peppers and cook 5 minutes longer.

3. Add tomatoes, beans, chili powder, cumin, salt, and pepper, and simmer 15 minutes.

4. Heat oven to 400°F.

5. Stir Muenster cheese into cornmeal mixture. Spread cornmeal mixture over sausage mixture and top with Cotija cheese.

6. Bake 30–40 minutes or until casserole is bubbling and cornmeal topping is golden brown. Let stand 5 minutes, then serve.

# Tex-Mex Taco Pie

*This is a taco-flavored take on the classic chili pie. The taco meat is topped with layers of corn chips and shredded cheese, and then baked until it is bubbling and hot. Top each serving with lots of cool sour cream!*

**PREP TIME:** 15 minutes
**COOK TIME:** 1 hour

**INGREDIENTS | SERVES 8**

1 tablespoon unsalted butter

1 medium onion, peeled and chopped

1 medium jalapeño, seeded and minced

2 cloves garlic, peeled and minced

2 pounds ground beef

2 packets taco seasoning (or 2 recipes of Homemade Taco Seasoning in the sidebar for Crunchy Topped Taco Mac, Chapter 6)

3 (10-ounce) cans diced tomatoes with green chilies, undrained

1 cup shredded sharp Cheddar cheese, divided

1 cup shredded queso quesadilla cheese, divided

1 cup shredded Colby-jack cheese, divided

2 cups corn chips (such as Fritos)

1 cup sour cream, for garnish

1. Heat oven to 375°F.

2. In an ovenproof 4-quart Dutch oven over medium heat melt butter, and once it foams add onion and cook until tender, about 5 minutes. Add jalapeño and garlic and cook until fragrant, about 1 minute.

3. Add ground beef and cook until well browned, about 10 minutes. Stir in taco seasoning and mix until beef is well coated, then stir in tomatoes with green chilies along with the liquid. Cook, stirring frequently, until mixture thickens and only a little liquid remains, about 10 minutes. Remove the Dutch oven from heat.

4. Add ½ of the shredded cheeses, and stir to combine. Spread the corn chips over the meat and top with the remaining cheese.

5. Bake 20–25 minutes, or until the cheese is golden brown and the mixture is bubbling. Cool 10 minutes before serving.

## Make It Extra Creamy

Want a creamy meat filling for this pie? Mix 1 cup of evaporated milk with 1 beaten egg and whisk well. Once the seasoned meat is cooked remove it from the heat for 10 minutes, and then stir in the milk mixture and the shredded cheese. Proceed as directed, adding an additional 5–10 minutes to the baking time, or until the filling is bubbling and hot.

# Mushroom and Onion Pie

*This pie is hearty, savory, and makes a very filling main meal, but you can also serve this as a side dish with grilled steaks or roast beef. Be sure to use a mix of mushrooms for the best flavor.*

**PREP TIME:** 40 minutes
**COOK TIME:** 1 hour
**INGREDIENTS | SERVES 8**

1 ounce dry mushrooms

2 cups boiling water

8 tablespoons unsalted butter

4 pounds mixed fresh mushrooms, such as button, oyster, chanterelle, shitake, or maitake, cleaned and roughly chopped

2 medium onions, peeled and thinly sliced

½ teaspoon salt

½ teaspoon freshly cracked black pepper

2 cloves garlic, peeled and minced

1 teaspoon fresh minced rosemary needles

⅓ cup all-purpose flour

2 cups chicken stock

½ cup heavy cream

¼ teaspoon grated Parmesan cheese

1 recipe All-Butter Pastry Crust for Pot Pies (Chapter 3)

1 large egg, beaten

1. In a medium bowl combine the dry mushrooms with the boiling water. Allow to stand until the mushrooms are rehydrated, about 30 minutes. Strain the mushrooms, reserving the liquid, and coarsely chop. Set aside.

2. In an ovenproof 4-quart Dutch oven over medium heat add butter. Once it is melted and starts to foam add chopped rehydrated mushrooms, fresh mushrooms, onions, salt, and pepper. Cook, stirring often, until mushrooms are tender, about 10 minutes. Add garlic and rosemary and cook until fragrant, about 1 minute.

3. Sprinkle flour over mushroom mixture and cook, stirring constantly, 3 minutes or until flour is cooked through, then slowly stir in chicken stock, 1 cup reserved mushroom soaking liquid, and heavy cream. Bring mixture to a boil, then reduce heat to medium-low and simmer stirring constantly until sauce is thick, about 10 minutes. Remove from heat and stir in grated cheese.

4. Heat oven to 400°F.

5. Place pastry crust on a lightly floured work surface. Using a sharp knife, cut 1" vents in a circle pattern in the center of crust. Brush the edge of the pot with water and brush pastry with the egg mixture. Place pastry egg-washed side up over the Dutch oven and press the edges to seal. Trim the edge of pastry so it has a 1" overhang.

6. Bake pie until the pastry crust is golden brown all over, about 20–25 minutes. Let the pie rest 10 minutes before serving.

# Creamy Beef and Mushroom Pie

*This pie packs a lot of flavor, and is great for cold winter evenings when a hot, hearty bowl of comfort food is called for. Serve this with some creamy mashed potatoes!*

**PREP TIME:** 20 minutes
**COOK TIME:** 3 hours 20 minutes

**INGREDIENTS | SERVES 8**

2 pounds beef chuck steak, cut into 1" cubes

½ cup all-purpose flour

½ teaspoon salt

½ teaspoon freshly cracked black pepper

4 tablespoons unsalted butter, divided

2 pounds cremini mushrooms, cleaned and quartered

1 medium onion, peeled and thinly sliced

2 cloves garlic, peeled and minced

2 cups chicken stock

1 cup water

½ cup heavy cream

1 bay leaf

1 recipe All-Butter Pastry Crust for Pot Pies (Chapter 3)

1 large egg, beaten

1. In a large zip-top bag combine beef, flour, salt, and pepper. Seal the bag and shake to coat. Set aside.

2. In a 4-quart Dutch oven over medium heat add 1 tablespoon butter. Once it starts to foam add half the beef cubes. Brown well on all sides, about 3 minutes per side, then remove to a plate. Add 1 tablespoon butter to the pot, and once it foams brown remaining beef. Place second batch of beef with first and set aside. Reserve any remaining flour.

3. Add remaining butter and once it starts to foam add mushrooms and onions. Cook, stirring often, until mushrooms are tender, about 10 minutes. Add garlic and cook, about 30 seconds. Sprinkle any reserved flour over mushrooms and cook 3 minutes.

4. Add stock and scrape up any browned bits from the bottom of the Dutch oven. Add water, cream, and bay leaf, and bring mixture to a boil, then reduce heat to medium-low, cover, and simmer 2 hours, or until meat is tender. Uncover pot and let simmer, stirring frequently, until sauce is thick, about 30 minutes. Remove from heat and discard bay leaf.

5. Heat oven to 400°F.

6. Place the pastry crust on a floured surface. Using a knife, cut 1" vents in a circle pattern in the center of crust. Brush the edge of the pot with water and brush pastry with egg mixture. Place pastry egg-washed side up over the Dutch oven and press the edges to seal and trim the edge so it has a 1" overhang.

7. Bake until the pastry crust is golden brown, about 20–25 minutes. Let the pie rest 10 minutes before serving.

# Beef and Potato Pie

*If you love a hearty beef stew then this pie is for you! Under the buttery crust is a mixture of tender beef, potatoes, and carrots. If you want you can add ½ cup of red wine to the pot for a little extra flavor.*

**PREP TIME:** 20 minutes
**COOK TIME:** 2 hours 40 minutes
**INGREDIENTS | SERVES 8**

2 pounds chuck steak, cut into 1" cubes

½ cup all-purpose flour

1 teaspoon salt

1 teaspoon freshly cracked black pepper

1 stick unsalted butter, divided

1 medium onion, peeled and diced

1 stalk celery, chopped

2 cloves garlic, peeled and minced

2 teaspoons chopped fresh rosemary

1 teaspoon chopped fresh thyme

3 cups beef stock

1 cup water

2 medium carrots, peeled and cut into ½" pieces

2 russet potatoes, peeled and cut into 1" cubes

1 recipe All-Butter Pastry Crust for Pot Pies (Chapter 3)

1 large egg, beaten

## Why Brown the Beef?

Many soups, stews, and pot pies made with cubed beef call for browning it before cooking. Browning the beef before simmering or braising does two things. First, it makes the beef more attractive when you serve it. No one wants a stew made with gray bits of boiled meat. Second, browning adds flavor and helps render the fat in the meat. The brown color comes from the amino acids and sugar in the beef caramelizing, and that gives the beef a satisfying roasted flavor. Browning is an important step and should not be skipped if you want the best flavor in your beef dish!

1. In a large zip-top bag combine beef, flour, salt, and pepper. Seal the bag and shake to coat the meat. Set aside.

2. In an ovenproof 4-quart Dutch oven over medium heat add 1 tablespoon butter. Once it starts to foam add half the beef cubes. Brown well on all sides, about 3 minutes per side, then remove to a plate. Add 1 tablespoon butter to the pot, and once it foams brown remaining beef. Place second batch of beef with first and set aside. Reserve any remaining flour.

3. Add remaining butter and once it starts to foam add onion and celery. Cook, stirring often, until vegetables are tender, about 5 minutes, then add garlic, rosemary, and thyme and cook, about 30 seconds. Sprinkle on any reserved flour and cook 3 minutes.

4. Stir in beef stock and water, and scrape any browned bits off the bottom of the Dutch oven. Add carrots and potatoes and bring mixture to a boil, then reduce heat to medium-low, cover with the lid, and simmer 2 hours or until beef is tender. Remove the Dutch oven from heat.

5. Heat oven to 400°F.

6. Place pastry crust on a lightly floured work surface. Using a sharp knife, cut 1" vents in a circle pattern in the center of crust. Brush the edge of the pot with water and brush pastry with egg mixture. Place pastry egg-washed side up over the Dutch oven and press the edges to seal. Trim the edge of pastry so it has a 1" overhang.

7. Bake until the pastry crust is golden brown, about 20–25 minutes. Let rest 10 minutes before serving.

# Lobster Pie

*This pie is rich, and perfect for lobster lovers! If lobster is out of your budget you can replace half of the lobster with more fresh shrimp. You will still get the delectable lobster flavor but at a price that is easier on the pocketbook.*

**PREP TIME:** 20 minutes
**COOK TIME:** 55 minutes

**INGREDIENTS | SERVES 8**

4 tablespoons unsalted butter

1 medium onion, peeled and finely chopped

2 stalks celery, finely chopped

½ teaspoon dry thyme

½ teaspoon seafood seasoning, such as Old Bay

½ teaspoon salt

½ teaspoon freshly cracked black pepper

½ cup white wine

½ cup all-purpose flour

2 cups seafood stock

⅓ cup heavy cream

1 pound cooked lobster meat, cut into ½" pieces

1 pound cooked peeled, deveined shrimp, roughly chopped

2 cups frozen peas

1 recipe All-Butter Pastry Crust for Pot Pies (Chapter 3)

1 large egg, beaten

## Buying Lobster

Have you ever looked at a lobster tank and wondered how to pick the best lobster? Well, you need to look for a few things. First, look for a tank that is clean and not overcrowded. You want the lobsters to have plenty of room. Second, look for lobsters that are active and holding their claws up in the water rather than hanging limp. Third, look at the tail and be sure it is straight and not curled. Finally, many people think the females have a better flavor. If you want to verify the sex yourself, look for feathery, soft swimmerets on the underside of the tail.

1. In an ovenproof 4-quart Dutch oven over medium heat add butter. Once it melts and starts to foam add onion, celery, thyme, seafood seasoning, salt, and pepper. Cook, stirring often, until vegetables are tender, about 5 minutes. Add white wine and cook until wine has reduced to 2 tablespoons, about 5–8 minutes.

2. Sprinkle flour over the vegetables and cook 3 minutes, or until flour is just turning golden brown, then whisk in seafood stock, working out any lumps. Bring mixture to a boil and let sauce thicken, about 5 minutes. Reduce heat to medium-low and stir in heavy cream, lobster, shrimp, and peas. Once shrimp are cooked through, about 3 minutes, remove the pot from heat.

3. Heat oven to 400°F.

4. Place pastry crust on a lightly floured work surface. Using a sharp knife, cut 1" vents in a circle pattern in the center of crust. Brush the edge of the pot with water and brush pastry with egg mixture. Place pastry egg-washed side up over the Dutch oven and press the edges to seal. Trim the edge of pastry so it has a 1" overhang.

5. Bake pie until pastry crust is golden brown all over, about 20–25 minutes. Let the pie rest 10 minutes before serving.

# Creamy Seafood Pie

*Fresh seafood is best for this pie, and you can use any blend of seafood you prefer. You can also add a link of diced smoked sausage to this pie to add some extra flavor.*

**PREP TIME:** 20 minutes
**COOK TIME:** 1 hour

**INGREDIENTS | SERVES 8**

2 strips thick-cut smoked bacon, chopped

4 tablespoons unsalted butter

1 medium russet potato, peeled and cut into ¼" pieces

1 medium onion, peeled and finely chopped

1 pint sliced mushrooms

2 cloves garlic, peeled and minced

½ teaspoon dry thyme

½ teaspoon smoked paprika

½ teaspoon salt

½ teaspoon freshly cracked black pepper

⅓ cup all-purpose flour

2 cups milk

1 cup half and half

1 pound fresh peeled, deveined shrimp, roughly chopped

1 pound fresh bay scallops

12 ounces lump crabmeat, picked through for shells

1 recipe Biscuit Topping for Savory Stews (Chapter 3)

1. In 4-quart Dutch oven over medium heat add chopped bacon and cook, stirring frequently, until crisp. Remove bacon from the Dutch oven and drain on a paper towel–lined plate. Set aside.

2. Add butter to the Dutch oven. Once butter foams add potato, onion, and mushrooms. Cook, stirring constantly, until potatoes become tender, about 10 minutes. Add garlic, thyme, paprika, salt, and pepper and cook until fragrant, about 1 minute.

3. Sprinkle flour over the vegetables and cook until flour is just turning golden brown, about 3 minutes. Slowly stir in milk and half and half, working out any lumps, and bring mixture to a simmer, stirring constantly, until sauce thickens, about 5–8 minutes.

4. Add shrimp, scallops, and crabmeat. Cook for 2 minutes then remove the pan from heat and cool slightly. Stir in crisp bacon.

5. Top with Biscuit Topping for Savory Stews. Bake 25–30 minutes or until biscuits are brown and filling is bubbling. Cool 10 minutes before serving.

# Cajun-Style Crawfish Pie

*If you like okra you can add 1–2 cups sliced fresh or frozen and thawed to this pie. A little andouille sausage would be lovely here as well.*

**PREP TIME:** 20 minutes
**COOK TIME:** 1 hour

**INGREDIENTS | SERVES 8**

2 strips bacon, chopped

3 tablespoons unsalted butter

2 stalks celery, diced

1 medium onion, peeled and diced

1 medium green bell pepper, seeded and diced

1 clove garlic, peeled and minced

½ teaspoon salt

1 teaspoon Cajun seasoning blend

¼ cup all-purpose flour

2 cups seafood stock

1 (10-ounce) can diced tomatoes and green chilies, drained

1 pound fresh peeled, deveined shrimp, roughly chopped

1 pound cooked crawfish meat, thawed if frozen

1 recipe All-Butter Pastry Crust for Pot Pies (Chapter 3)

1 large egg, beaten

## Thawing Seafood

Frozen seafood is common, and good to have on hand for quick meals, but you need to be careful when thawing. It is popular to thaw frozen seafood in a bowl of warm water, but that can be very dangerous and promote bacterial growth. If you are thawing seafood you should place the seafood in the refrigerator overnight to thaw. If you need the seafood quickly you can place the seafood in a bowl and run cold water over it until thawed. Be sure to use your thawed seafood immediately.

1. In an ovenproof 4-quart Dutch oven over medium heat add bacon and fry until it is crisp and the fat has been rendered. Add butter and melt until it foams then add celery, onion, and bell pepper. Cook, stirring frequently, until vegetables are tender, about 8 minutes, then add garlic, salt, and Cajun seasoning and sauté until fragrant, about 30 seconds.

2. Sprinkle flour over the top of vegetable mixture and cook until flour is just turning golden brown, about 3 minutes. Stir in stock and diced tomatoes with green chilies and bring to a boil, then reduce the heat to medium-low and simmer until mixture thickens, about 10 minutes.

3. Add shrimp and simmer until just cooked, about 3 minutes. Remove the Dutch oven from heat and fold in crawfish meat.

4. Heat oven to 400°F.

5. Place pastry crust on a lightly floured work surface. Using a sharp knife, cut 1" vents in a circle pattern in the center of crust. Brush the edge of the pot with water and brush pastry with egg. Place pastry egg-washed side up over the Dutch oven and press the edges to seal. Trim the edge of pastry so it has a 1" overhang.

6. Bake pie until pastry crust is golden brown all over, about 20–25 minutes. Let the pie rest 10 minutes before serving.

# Vegetable Pot Pie

*Want to get more vegetables into your diet? This pot pie is a great way to do so, and makes a great "Meatless Monday" main dish!*

**PREP TIME:** 20 minutes
**COOK TIME:** 55 minutes

**INGREDIENTS | SERVES 8**

4 tablespoons unsalted butter

1 pint button mushrooms, cleaned and quartered

1 pint cremini mushrooms, cleaned and quartered

2 medium carrots, peeled and diced

1 large onion, peeled and chopped

1 stalk celery, chopped

½ teaspoon salt

½ teaspoon freshly cracked black pepper

½ cup all-purpose flour

4 cups vegetable broth

2 russet potatoes, peeled and cut into ½" pieces

2 cups broccoli florets, cut into ½" pieces

2 cups cauliflower florets, cut into ½" pieces

1 recipe All-Butter Pastry Crust for Pot Pies (Chapter 3)

1 large egg, beaten

## Puff Pastry Option

Any pot pie recipe in this book that calls for the All-Butter Pastry Crust for Pot Pies recipe can be made with store-bought frozen puff pastry. Let the puff pastry thaw according to the package directions. Once thawed, roll it out on a lightly floured work surface, then use a pizza cutter to cut a circle that is about 1" wider than the Dutch oven you need to cover. Use a fork to pierce a few holes in the pastry so it does not puff too high. Bake according to the package directions. For a shiny finish you can brush the top with beaten egg.

1. In an ovenproof 4-quart Dutch oven over medium heat melt butter until it foams. Add mushrooms, carrots, onions, celery, salt, and pepper. Cook until softened, about 10 minutes.

2. Sprinkle flour over vegetables and cook until it is just turning golden brown, about 3 minutes, then stir in vegetable broth, potatoes, broccoli, and cauliflower. Bring mixture to a boil, then reduce heat to medium-low and simmer, stirring constantly, until sauce thickens and potatoes are tender, about 10 minutes. Remove the Dutch oven from heat.

3. Heat oven to 400°F.

4. Place pastry crust on a lightly floured work surface. Using a sharp knife, cut 1" vents in a circle pattern in the center of crust. Brush the edge of the pot with water and brush pastry with egg mixture. Place pastry egg-washed side up over the Dutch oven and press the edges to seal. Trim the edge of pastry so it has a 1" overhang.

5. Bake pie until pastry crust is golden brown all over, about 20–25 minutes. Let pie rest 10 minutes before serving.

# Chicken Pot Pie

*This pot pie uses a shortcut—rotisserie chicken. If you want to use up fresh chicken, simply season with salt and pepper and roast until thoroughly cooked. Cool and shred. You will need approximately 4 cups of shredded chicken for this recipe.*

**PREP TIME:** 20 minutes
**COOK TIME:** 55 minutes

**INGREDIENTS | SERVES 8**

2 tablespoons unsalted butter

1 large onion, peeled and chopped

3 stalks celery, finely chopped

3 medium carrots, peeled and diced

1 teaspoon fresh thyme

½ teaspoon salt

½ teaspoon freshly cracked black pepper

½ cup all-purpose flour

3 cups chicken stock

1 bay leaf

½ cup heavy cream

1 (3–4 pound) rotisserie chicken, cooled and shredded

1 recipe All-Butter Pastry Crust for Pot Pies (Chapter 3)

1 large egg, beaten

1. In an ovenproof 4-quart Dutch oven over medium heat add butter. When it has melted and starts to foam add onion, celery, and carrots and cook until they begin to soften, about 5 minutes. Add thyme, salt, and pepper and cook 3 minutes more, or until herbs are fragrant.

2. Sprinkle flour over vegetables and cook until flour is just turning golden brown, about 3 minutes. Stir in chicken broth, bay leaf, cream, and chicken meat and bring mixture to a boil, then reduce heat to medium-low and simmer, stirring often, until sauce has thickened, about 10 minutes. Remove the Dutch oven from heat and discard bay leaf.

3. Heat oven to 400°F.

4. Place pastry crust on a lightly floured work surface. Using a sharp knife, cut 1" vents in a circle pattern in the center of crust. Brush the edge of the pot with water and brush pastry with egg mixture. Place pastry egg-washed side up over the Dutch oven and press the edges to seal. Trim the edge of pastry so it has a 1" overhang.

5. Bake pie until pastry crust is golden brown all over, about 20–25 minutes. Let pie rest 10 minutes before serving.

# Leftover Turkey and Dressing Pie

*Thanksgiving leftovers are a gift and a curse. A gift because you have a refrigerator full of food for days!
A curse because the same old meal can get a bit boring.
Here is a way to use the leftovers in a fun new way!*

**PREP TIME:** 10 minutes
**COOK TIME:** 1 hour

**INGREDIENTS | SERVES 8**

2 cups leftover Cornbread Dressing (Chapter 7), or other bread dressing

1 large egg, beaten

3 cups chicken broth, divided

3 tablespoons unsalted butter

1 medium onion, peeled and chopped

2 stalks celery, chopped

2 medium carrots, peeled and diced

1 pint sliced mushrooms

½ teaspoon salt

½ teaspoon freshly cracked black pepper

⅓ cup all-purpose flour

4 cups shredded roasted turkey meat

## Cooking with Leftovers

When cooking new meals with your leftovers it is important to keep a few things in mind. First, be sure your leftovers were properly cooled, meaning they were chilled to under 40°F within 2 hours of cooking. Also, if they are older than 3 days they should probably be discarded. Second, you need to get your leftovers dish hot, hot, hot! Be sure that the food comes to a boil or reaches a minimum of 165°F to make sure any bacteria are killed. Third, your new meal should be consumed within 1 day, and any leftovers discarded after 24 hours.

1. In a large bowl combine dressing, egg, and ¼ cup broth. Mix until dressing is moist and easy to spread or dollop. Set aside.

2. Heat oven to 375°F.

3. In an ovenproof 4-quart Dutch oven over medium heat add butter. Once it melts and starts to foam add onion, celery, carrots, mushrooms, salt, and pepper. Cook, stirring often, until vegetables are tender, about 5 minutes.

4. Sprinkle flour over vegetables and cook until flour is just turning golden brown, about 3 minutes. Stir in remaining chicken broth and turkey meat and bring mixture to a boil, then reduce heat to medium-low and simmer, stirring often, until sauce has thickened, about 10 minutes. Remove the Dutch oven from heat.

5. Spread or scoop dollops of the dressing mixture over the top of turkey mixture. Bake 30–40 minutes, or until the topping is firm and golden brown and the filling is bubbling. Cool 10 minutes before serving.

# Chicken and Biscuits

*This dish is simple—easy enough for a quick weeknight dinner—and very satisfying! When possible, it is best to reheat any leftovers in an oven to keep the biscuits tasting fresh!*

**PREP TIME:** 20 minutes
**COOK TIME:** 1 hour 10 minutes

**INGREDIENTS | SERVES 8**

4 tablespoons unsalted butter, divided

2 pounds boneless, skinless chicken thighs, cut in half

1 medium onion, peeled and finely chopped

2 stalks celery, finely chopped

1 medium carrot, peeled and finely chopped

½ teaspoon salt

½ teaspoon freshly cracked black pepper

¼ teaspoon crushed red pepper flakes

½ cup all-purpose flour

2 cups chicken broth

1 cup whole milk

1 recipe Biscuit Topping for Savory Stews (Chapter 3)

1. In an ovenproof 4-quart Dutch oven over medium heat add 1 tablespoon butter. Once butter melts and starts to foam add half the chicken. Brown well on both sides, about 5 minutes per side. Remove browned chicken from the Dutch oven and repeat with remaining chicken. Set aside.

2. To the Dutch oven add remaining butter. Once it melts and starts to foam add onion, celery, carrot, salt, pepper, and red pepper flakes. Cook until vegetables are tender, about 10 minutes.

3. Sprinkle flour over the vegetables and cook until flour is just starting to turn golden brown, about 3 minutes. Stir in browned chicken, chicken broth, and milk, being sure to work out any lumps, and bring to a boil. Reduce heat to medium-low and simmer until the mixture is very thick, about 12 minutes. Remove the Dutch oven from heat and cool slightly.

4. Heat oven to 375°F.

5. Top with Biscuit Topping for Savory Stews and bake 25–30 minutes, or until biscuits are golden brown and the filling is bubbling. Cool 10 minutes before serving.

# Pizza Pot Pie

*Kids will love this pizza-flavored pot pie, and parents will love that it is packed with vegetables. This pie is a great place for leftover roasted or grilled vegetables!*

**PREP TIME:** 20 minutes
**COOK TIME:** 1 hour

**INGREDIENTS | SERVES 8**

½ pound bulk Italian sausage, sweet or hot

2 tablespoons olive oil

1 medium onion, peeled and sliced

1 medium red bell pepper, seeded and cut into ½" pieces

1 medium green bell pepper, seeded and cut into ½" pieces

2 pints sliced mushrooms

2 cloves garlic, peeled and minced

1 (28-ounce) can diced tomatoes, drained

1 teaspoon ground fennel

½ teaspoon dried oregano

¼ teaspoon thyme

¼ teaspoon crushed red pepper flakes

4 ounces turkey pepperoni slices

2 cups shredded mozzarella cheese

1 recipe All-Butter Pastry Crust for Pot Pies (Chapter 3)

1 large egg, beaten

2 tablespoons shredded Parmesan cheese

1. In an ovenproof 4-quart Dutch oven over medium heat add Italian sausage. Cook, stirring frequently, until sausage is browned and crumbled, about 8 minutes. Remove sausage from the Dutch oven and set aside. Drain off the fat.

2. Return the Dutch oven to medium heat and add olive oil. Once oil shimmers add onion, bell peppers, and mushrooms. Cook, stirring frequently, until vegetables are tender, about 10 minutes. Add garlic and cook until fragrant, about 30 seconds. Add diced tomatoes, fennel, oregano, thyme, and red pepper flakes and cook until the spices are fragrant, about 3 minutes. Remove the Dutch oven from heat.

3. Fold cooked sausage and pepperoni slices into vegetable mixture, then use a spatula to smooth the top. Spread mozzarella cheese over filling in an even layer.

4. Heat oven to 400°F.

5. Place pastry crust on a lightly floured work surface. Using a sharp knife, cut 1" vents in a circle pattern in the center of crust. Brush the edge of the pot with water and brush pastry with egg mixture. Place pastry egg-washed side up over the Dutch oven and press the edges to seal. Trim the edge of pastry so it has a 1" overhang. Sprinkle top with shredded Parmesan cheese.

6. Bake pie until pastry crust is golden brown all over, about 20–25 minutes. Let pie rest 10 minutes before serving.

# Cheesy Sausage Pie

*Bulk Italian sausage is usually available in your grocery store's meat department, or in the freezer section. If you can't find it, you can use fresh sausages with the casings removed.*

**PREP TIME:** 20 minutes
**COOK TIME:** 50 minutes

**INGREDIENTS | SERVES 8**

1 pound bulk hot Italian sausage

1 medium onion, peeled and chopped

1 medium green bell pepper, seeded and finely chopped

2 pints sliced button mushrooms

2 cloves garlic, peeled and minced

1 cup shredded Fontina cheese

1 cup shredded mozzarella cheese

1 recipe Biscuit Topping for Savory Stews (Chapter 3)

2 tablespoons butter, melted

¼ cup shredded Parmesan cheese

## Homemade Italian Sausage

Want to make your own Italian sausage at home? In a medium bowl simply mix 1 pound ground pork, 1 teaspoon ground fennel, ½ teaspoon dried oregano, ½ teaspoon smoked paprika, ¼ teaspoon dried thyme, ¼ teaspoon crushed red pepper flakes, and a pinch of salt and pepper. Cover and refrigerate at least 2 hours, or overnight. This will allow the flavors to penetrate the meat, giving your homemade sausage more flavor!

1. Heat a 4-quart Dutch oven over medium heat. Once hot add sausage and cook, stirring often, until sausage is browned and crumbled, about 10 minutes. Remove sausage from the Dutch oven to a paper towel–lined plate to drain.

2. Return the Dutch oven to medium heat and add onion, bell pepper, and mushrooms. Cook, stirring often, until vegetables are just tender, about 5 minutes. Add garlic and cook until fragrant, about 30 seconds. Remove the Dutch oven from heat.

3. Add browned sausage back to the Dutch oven and stir to combine, then add shredded cheese and stir to incorporate. Top with biscuit topping. Brush biscuits with melted butter and sprinkle on Parmesan cheese.

4. Bake 25–30 minutes, or until biscuits are golden brown all over. Cool 10 minutes before serving.

# Meat Lovers Deep Dish Pizza

*While pizza is not technically a pie, this deep dish pizza certainly looks the part! Serve this pizza pie at your next big game party, or anytime you want an ooey-gooey, super meaty pizza!*

**PREP TIME:** 15 minutes
**COOK TIME:** 45 minutes

**INGREDIENTS | SERVES 8**

1 recipe Dutch Oven Pizza Crust (Chapter 3)

8 ounces sliced whole milk mozzarella cheese

8 ounces bulk hot Italian sausage, cooked and crumbled

8 ounces ground beef, cooked and crumbled

6 strips thick-cut bacon, cooked crisp and chopped

½ cup diced Canadian bacon

4 ounces sliced pepperoni

1 cup store-bought or homemade pizza sauce

½ cup fresh grated Parmesan cheese

1. Heat oven to 450°F.

2. Roll out pizza crust and line the inside of an ovenproof 12-inch Dutch oven, making sure the crust comes at least 1" up the sides of the pot.

3. Inside the pizza crust layer remaining ingredients in the order listed. Bake 10 minutes, then reduce heat to 350°F and bake another 20–25 minutes, or until pizza is bubbling and the crust is golden brown. Cool 10 minutes before serving.

# Potato Salmon Pie

*This hearty pie is good for a cold winter night. You can use leftover mashed potatoes; use about 4 cups.*

**PREP TIME:** 20 minutes
**COOK TIME:** 1 hour 15 minutes

**INGREDIENTS | SERVES 8**

2 tablespoons olive oil

1 large onion, peeled and chopped

3 cloves garlic, peeled and minced

1 medium green bell pepper, seeded and chopped

1 cup frozen baby peas

1 (23-ounce) package refrigerated mashed potatoes

3 large eggs, beaten

½ teaspoon salt

⅛ teaspoon freshly ground black pepper

½ cup grated Romano cheese

1 (14-ounce) can red salmon, drained and flaked

1 recipe All-Butter Pastry Crust for Pot Pies (Chapter 3)

2 tablespoons butter

1. Heat oven to 350°F.

2. In an ovenproof 6- or 8-quart Dutch oven over medium heat, warm olive oil. Once it shimmers add onion and garlic and cook until tender, about 5 minutes. Add bell pepper and peas, and cook until tender, about 4–5 minutes longer. Remove the Dutch oven from heat.

3. Place potatoes in a large bowl and beat in eggs, salt, pepper, and cheese. Add salmon, then transfer mixture into the Dutch oven and stir well. Place pastry crust on top of mixture and cut slits to vent steam.

4. Place little pieces of butter into the slits in the pastry crust. Bake 55–65 minutes until crust is brown. Let stand 10 minutes, then slice to serve.

# Steak and Kidney Pie

*This dish is an acquired taste, but if you don't like organ meats, you can always substitute more beef or chopped sausage.*

**PREP TIME:** 20 minutes
**COOK TIME:** 3 hours

**INGREDIENTS | SERVES 4**

3 tablespoons butter

1 pound round steak, thinly sliced

¼ pound lamb kidneys, trimmed and cut into small dice

1 shallot, peeled and minced

2 cloves garlic, peeled and minced

4 ounces mushrooms, sliced

2 tablespoons all-purpose flour

3 cups beef broth

1 tablespoon tomato paste

1 teaspoon Worcestershire sauce

¼ teaspoon thyme

¼ teaspoon cayenne

¼ teaspoon salt

¼ teaspoon freshly cracked black pepper

1 recipe All-Butter Pastry Crust for Pot Pies (Chapter 3)

1. In an ovenproof 6- or 8-quart Dutch oven melt butter over medium-high heat. Working in batches, brown steak and kidneys then remove to a platter. Add shallot, garlic, and mushrooms and cook until tender, about 5 minutes.

2. Sprinkle flour over the vegetables and cook until flour is just turning golden, about 3 minutes. Add broth and stir until no lumps remain. Add tomato paste, Worcestershire, thyme, and cayenne. Bring to a boil, then reduce heat to medium. Return steak and kidneys to pot and simmer 2 hours, or until meat is very tender. Add salt and pepper, then remove the Dutch oven from heat.

3. Heat oven to 375°F.

4. Cover meat mixture with pastry crust and cut a few slits to vent. Bake 40 minutes or until pie crust is browned and filling is bubbly. Let stand 10 minutes before serving.

# Chicken under a Bread Crust

*Thawed frozen bread dough works perfectly well with this recipe and eliminates a lot of time and mess.*

**PREP TIME:** 1 hour
**COOK TIME:** 1 hour

**INGREDIENTS | SERVES 4**

½ pound frozen bread dough, thawed
2 tablespoons butter
1 small onion, peeled and diced
1 large stalk celery, diced
1 large carrot, peeled and diced
1 pound mushrooms, sliced
2 tablespoons all-purpose flour
1½ cups chicken broth
1 cup heavy cream
¼ cup chopped fresh herbs such as a mix of thyme, oregano, dill, chives, and parsley
2 cups diced cooked chicken
½ teaspoon salt
½ teaspoon freshly cracked black pepper

1. Place bread dough in a large bowl, cover loosely with plastic wrap, and allow to rise until double in bulk, about 40 minutes. Punch dough down and set aside.

2. In an ovenproof 6- or 8-quart Dutch oven over medium-high heat melt butter. Add onion, celery, and carrot and cook until just tender, about 3 minutes. Add mushrooms and cook until soft, about 5 minutes.

3. Sprinkle flour over the vegetable mixture and cook until flour is just turning golden brown, about 3 minutes. Add broth and bring mixture to a boil, then reduce heat to medium-low and simmer 15 minutes, allowing broth to reduce by ⅓.

4. Add cream, herbs, chicken, salt, and pepper, and simmer 5 minutes, then remove the Dutch oven from heat.

5. Heat oven to 350°F.

6. Lightly butter hands and shape bread dough into roll-sized balls about 1" in diameter. Place dough balls over chicken, spacing dough evenly. Bake until bread crust is browned and firm, about 30 minutes.

# CHAPTER 14

# International Flavors

# Char Siu Pork Ribs

*These ribs are sticky, moist, and very tender. If you want you can finish these ribs on the grill rather than under the broiler.*

**PREP TIME:** 4–12 hours
**COOK TIME:** 1 hour 40 minutes

**INGREDIENTS | SERVES 4–6**

2 slabs baby back ribs, cut into 3–4 rib sections
½ cup hoisin sauce
¼ cup Shaoxing wine or sherry
¼ cup light soy sauce
1 tablespoon minced fresh ginger
2 cloves garlic, peeled and minced
1 teaspoon Chinese five spice powder
1 (8-ounce) jar char siu sauce, divided

## What Is Char Siu?

Char siu is a Cantonese style of barbecue. It is usually boneless cuts of pork that are marinated in a mixture of hoisin sauce, spices, and rice wine, and then roasted on long metal forks with a sweet red sauce until tender. The name "char siu" literally translates into "fork roast." In Chinese restaurants you will often find char siu pork stuffed into steamed buns, or served over steamed rice. Char siu sauce can be found in most well-stocked grocery stores, in most Asian markets, and is available online.

1. In a large zip-top bag add ribs. In a small bowl whisk together hoisin sauce, Shaoxing wine, soy sauce, ginger, garlic, and five spice powder. Pour marinade over ribs, seal the bag, and gently massage so all ribs are coated. Refrigerate at least 4 hours, or overnight.

2. Heat oven to 375°F.

3. Pour half the char siu sauce into a bowl and reserve.

4. Remove ribs from marinade and place into an ovenproof 6- or 8-quart Dutch oven. Pour remaining char siu sauce over ribs and coat them evenly. Cover Dutch oven with a lid and bake 1½ hours, rotating ribs every 20 minutes and basting with sauce from the bottom of the Dutch oven. Once ribs are tender and meat is shrinking back from the bones remove the pot from oven and heat the broiler.

5. Remove ribs from the Dutch oven and place onto a baking rack over a baking sheet meat-side down. Glaze back side of the ribs with reserved sauce. Broil back side of ribs 3–5 minutes, or until sauce is bubbling, then turn ribs meat-side up, baste with more sauce, and broil 5–8 minutes, or until ribs are bubbling and slightly charred. Cool slightly before serving.

# Egg Drop Soup

*The secret to this recipe is adding the eggs to the boiling broth very slowly, resulting in smooth ribbons of egg throughout the soup.*

**PREP TIME:** 10 minutes
**COOK TIME:** 20 minutes

**INGREDIENTS | SERVES 4**

6 cups chicken broth

¼ teaspoon grated fresh ginger or dash ground ginger

2 large eggs, beaten

1 tablespoon minced green onion or chives

1 tablespoon cornstarch dissolved in 2 tablespoons cold water

¼ teaspoon salt

¼ teaspoon freshly cracked black pepper

1. In a 6- or 8-quart Dutch oven bring broth and ginger to a rolling boil over high heat. Reduce heat to medium, then drizzle in the beaten eggs in a thin stream. While egg streams drip into pot, gently stir broth with your other hand using a fork or a pair of chopsticks. Continue until all egg is in soup.

2. Stir in green onion or chives and cornstarch dissolved in water. Stir and continue to cook until the soup is slightly thickened, about 1–2 minutes. Season with salt and pepper before serving.

# German Red Cabbage with Sausages

*This cabbage is also a great side dish with fried pork cutlets (schnitzel) and buttered spaetzle.*

**PREP TIME:** 10 minutes
**COOK TIME:** 1 hour 10 minutes

**INGREDIENTS | SERVES 6**

2 pounds bratwurst or knackwurst

2 tablespoons unsalted butter

6 cups shredded red cabbage

1 Granny Smith apple, peeled, cored, and thinly sliced

⅓ cup apple cider vinegar

¼ cup water

¼ cup sugar

2 teaspoons salt

½ teaspoon freshly cracked black pepper

1. In a 6- or 8-quart Dutch oven over medium-high heat add sausage and brown on both sides, about 5 minutes per side. Remove from the Dutch oven and set aside.

2. To the Dutch oven add butter. Once it melts add remaining ingredients and stir well to combine. Bring mixture to a boil, then reduce heat to medium-low, cover with a lid, and simmer 30 minutes.

3. Add sausages to the pot, cover again, and simmer another 30–40 minutes, or until cabbage is tender and sausages are cooked through. Serve hot.

# Tom Kha Gai (Thai Chicken Soup)

*If you don't have access to lemongrass, lime leaves, and galangal, you can still make this soup. Just buy prepared Tom Kha Gai seasoning paste at the supermarket.*

**PREP TIME:** 10 minutes
**COOK TIME:** 45 minutes

**INGREDIENTS | SERVES 4**

4 cups chicken broth

3 stalks lemongrass, white part only, bruised with back of a knife

4 kaffir lime leaves

2 slices galangal root

2 cloves garlic, pressed

3 Thai chili peppers, halved lengthwise

2 tablespoons lime juice

1 tablespoon fish sauce

1 pound boneless, skinless chicken breasts, diced

4 ounces white or straw mushrooms, quartered

1 small onion, peeled and cut in strips

½ medium red bell pepper, seeded and cut in strips

1 (14-ounce) can coconut milk

¼ teaspoon salt

¼ teaspoon freshly cracked black pepper

⅓ cup fresh cilantro leaves

1. Pour broth into a 6- or 8-quart Dutch oven along with lemongrass, lime leaves, galangal, garlic, and chilies. Bring to a boil over high heat then reduce heat to medium, cover, and simmer 20 minutes. Strain broth.

2. Return broth to the Dutch oven and add lime juice, fish sauce, chicken, mushrooms, onion, and bell pepper. Simmer over medium heat, stirring often, until chicken is cooked and vegetables are just tender, about 10 minutes.

3. Stir in coconut milk, salt, pepper, and cilantro. Simmer 5 minutes before serving.

# Thai Mussamun Curried Beef

*Mussamun is a type of Thai curry paste that is popular in Southern Thailand, especially among those who are Muslim. It is an intensely flavored but lightly spicy curry paste. Serve this dish over jasmine rice.*

**PREP TIME:** 10 minutes
**COOK TIME:** 30 minutes

**INGREDIENTS | SERVES 4**

2 tablespoons peanut oil
1 large yellow onion, peeled and sliced
1 teaspoon dried chili powder
1 teaspoon ground coriander
1 teaspoon ground cumin
½ teaspoon black pepper
½ teaspoon ground nutmeg
1" piece ginger, peeled and shredded
1 serrano or Thai chili, thinly sliced
1 lemongrass stalk
1 (15-ounce) can coconut milk
½ pound beef sirloin, cut into cubes
1 teaspoon soy sauce
2 teaspoons sugar

1. Place a 6- or 8-quart Dutch oven over medium heat and once it's heated add oil and onion. Stir frequently and cook 7–9 minutes or until onion is lightly browned. Stir in dried spices, ginger, and chili and cook 3–5 minutes, or until spices are fragrant.

2. Remove outer leaves from lemongrass stalk. Cut off base end and top dried portion. Cut stalk in half lengthwise and then into 1" chunks. Stir lemongrass and coconut milk into the pot.

3. Add cubed beef, soy sauce, and sugar to the Dutch oven. Stir to combine and cook 7–10 minutes. Serve.

## Thai Curry Dishes versus Indian Curry Dishes

Even though both cuisines call their dishes curry, they're fairly different. Thai dishes use a paste made mostly from fresh ingredients and vegetables and usually involve coconut milk. Indian dishes are usually flavored with a dried spice mixture. Indian curries can be either dry or cooked with tomato sauce or broth and clarified butter.

# Panang Curry

*This Thai specialty is rich and spicy, and perfect with a side of steamed white rice. Panang curry paste is available in sealed packets or tubs in most Asian markets or gourmet shops. Serve this dish hot with rice.*

**PREP TIME:** 10 minutes
**COOK TIME:** 45 minutes

**INGREDIENTS | SERVES 6**

2 (13.5-ounce) cans full-fat coconut milk, refrigerated and unshaken

½ cup Panang curry paste

2 pounds sliced boneless, skinless chicken breast

2 tablespoons fish sauce

2 tablespoons light brown sugar

6 torn kaffir lime leaves, or the juice of 1 lime

2 medium red bell peppers, seeded and cut into 1" pieces

2 ripe tomatoes, cut into wedges

1 cup Thai basil

1. Do not shake coconut milk. Open cans and scoop out thick coconut cream and put it into a 4- or 6-quart Dutch oven. Reserve remaining liquid.

2. Heat the Dutch oven over medium heat. Once coconut cream starts to melt add Panang curry paste and bring mixture to a boil, then reduce heat to low and simmer until fragrant and mixture looks a little oily, about 5 minutes.

3. Add chicken, fish sauce, brown sugar, lime leaves, and bell pepper to the Dutch oven along with reserved coconut milk. Increase heat back to medium and bring mixture to a boil, then reduce heat to medium-low, cover, and let simmer 20 minutes.

4. Uncover and simmer 10–15 minutes more to thicken the sauce. Stir in tomatoes and basil and turn off the heat. Serve hot.

# Thai Shrimp Curry

*Packaged Thai curry pastes, available in most supermarket Asian-food sections,
bring the exotic flavors of galangal root, kaffir lime leaves, lemongrass, and
chilies to your kitchen without all the shopping and chopping.*

**PREP TIME:** 20 minutes
**COOK TIME:** 25 minutes

**INGREDIENTS | SERVES 8**

2 tablespoons olive oil

3 tablespoons Thai green curry paste

2 (14-ounce) cans coconut milk

1 tablespoon fish sauce

1 medium sweet onion, peeled and cut into 8 wedges

1 medium red bell pepper, diced

2 small Asian eggplants, diced

3 pounds shrimp, peeled and deveined

1 tablespoon lime juice

½ cup fresh sweet basil leaves

¼ teaspoon salt

¼ teaspoon freshly cracked black pepper

4 cups cooked jasmine rice

Chopped peanuts or cashews, for garnish

1. In a 6- or 8-quart Dutch oven heat oil over medium-high heat. Add curry paste and cook until fragrant, stirring constantly, about 1 minute.

2. Slowly add coconut milk and fish sauce, then reduce heat to medium. Whisk to incorporate the curry paste into coconut milk.

3. When sauce starts to simmer add onion, pepper, and eggplant. Cook 15 minutes.

4. Add shrimp and continue cooking until shrimp turn opaque, about 3 minutes.

5. Stir in lime juice, basil leaves, salt, and pepper. Serve with steamed jasmine rice and garnish with chopped peanuts or cashews.

# Malaysian Sambal Chicken

*In its purest form, sambal sauce is ground chilies and salt. From that base, other ingredients have been added to make a wide array of dishes. Serve this dish with steamed rice.*

**PREP TIME:** 40 minutes
**COOK TIME:** 25 minutes

**INGREDIENTS | SERVES 4**

4 dried hot chilies, stems removed

½ teaspoon kosher salt

1 slice fresh ginger

1 piece lemongrass, white part

3 tablespoons olive oil, divided

1 pound chicken breast halves, sliced crosswise

1 medium onion, peeled and diced

2 cloves garlic, peeled and minced

3 plum tomatoes, diced

½ teaspoon turmeric

1 cup coconut milk

½ teaspoon cardamom

⅓ cup minced cilantro

½ teaspoon salt

1. Place hot chilies in a small bowl. Add enough warm water to cover and soak 30 minutes. Drain water, reserving 1 teaspoon. Place soaking water, chilies, salt, ginger, and lemongrass in food processor. Pulse to grind, about 10–15 pulses.

2. In a 6- or 8-quart Dutch oven heat 2 tablespoons oil over high heat. Brown chicken pieces well on both sides, about 5 minutes per side. Transfer chicken to a platter to rest. Add remaining oil and chili mixture and cook until fragrant, about 1–2 minutes.

3. Add onion, garlic, and tomatoes and cook until vegetables are just tender, about 3 minutes.

4. Reduce heat to medium. Add turmeric and coconut milk and stir well. Add chicken and cardamom and simmer until chicken is cooked through, about 10–15 minutes. Add cilantro and salt. Serve.

# Baked Bratwurst in Beer

*This makes a great football night supper for those times when you're watching the game at home. It's an easy recipe to double or triple. Simply increase the size of the pan. The baking times won't change. Serve with a salad or coleslaw.*

**PREP TIME:** 10 minutes
**COOK TIME:** 1 hour 15 minutes

**INGREDIENTS | SERVES 4**

4 bratwurst

4 medium red potatoes, peeled and quartered

1 (2-pound) bag sauerkraut, rinsed and drained

1 large yellow onion, peeled and roughly chopped

1 (12-ounce) can of beer, room temperature

4 hot dog buns

Stone-ground or Bavarian-style mustard, for garnish

## Baked Bratwurst in Beer for a Crowd

If you'll be serving the bratwurst for a casual meal with potato chips on the side, omit the potatoes. There will be enough sauerkraut for 8–12 sandwiches. Add the desired amount of bratwurst and otherwise follow the baking instructions.

1. Heat oven to 425°F.

2. Lightly spray an ovenproof 6- or 8-quart Dutch oven with nonstick cooking spray and lay bratwurst in the pan. Bake uncovered 15 minutes.

3. Remove the Dutch oven from oven and arrange potato wedges around meat. Add sauerkraut and onion over potatoes and meat. Pour beer into the pan, being careful that it doesn't foam up. Cover and bake 45 minutes. Remove the lid and bake an additional 15 minutes, or until potatoes are tender and much of beer has evaporated.

4. Serve the bratwurst on buns generously spread with mustard; add some drained sauerkraut and onions to each sandwich. Serve potatoes and additional sauerkraut on the side.

# German Chicken and Spaetzle Soup

*Some cooks like to boil the spaetzle in a separate pot of water to avoid clouding the chicken broth.*

**PREP TIME:** 10 minutes
**COOK TIME:** 40 minutes

**INGREDIENTS | SERVES 6**

2 tablespoons olive oil

1 small onion, peeled and diced

1 large stalk celery, diced

1 large carrot, peeled and diced

8 cups chicken broth

½ teaspoon red wine vinegar

1 teaspoon sugar

1 pound chicken breast halves, diced

1½ cups all-purpose flour

½ teaspoon salt

¼ teaspoon freshly ground black pepper

2 large eggs, beaten

½ cup milk

¼ cup minced parsley or chives

1. In a 6- or 8-quart Dutch oven over medium-high heat add oil. Once it shimmers add onion, celery, and carrot. Cook until just tender, about 5 minutes.

2. Add broth, vinegar, and sugar. Bring to a boil; reduce heat to medium. Simmer 10 minutes. Add chicken and simmer 10 minutes.

3. In the work bowl of a stand mixer, or in a medium bowl with a hand mixer, combine flour, salt, pepper, eggs, and milk. Mix on medium-low speed until smooth, then stir in parsley or chives.

4. Bring soup to a boil over high heat. Drop spaetzle dough into soup, using about ½ teaspoon of dough for each dumpling. Reduce heat to medium and stir gently. When the spaetzle float to top of soup, about 2–3 minutes, the soup is ready to serve.

## Noodles versus Dumplings

Sometimes it's hard to tell the difference between pasta and dumplings. (In fact, in some corners, spaetzle is known as "noodle dumplings.") The truth is, the ingredients are virtually identical—it's all a matter of how they're treated. If the dough is wet, minimally handled, and dropped in boiling liquid in dollops or pieces, it's a dumpling. Roll it out thin, cut and shape it, and it's a noodle.

# Cassoulet

*This French dish is named for the earthenware pot that this dish was originally made in, but a Dutch oven has a similar shape and cooks food the same way. Ducks legs are available frozen in most grocery stores, or fresh in Asian markets and specialty food stores. This dish can also be made with goose and mutton.*

**PREP TIME:** 8–12 hours
**COOK TIME:** 5 hours
**INGREDIENTS | SERVES 6–8**

1 pound dried cannellini beans
Water, as needed
4 duck legs, about 4–6 ounces each
1 pound garlic flavored sausage
1 pound lamb shoulder, cubed
½ pound bacon, cut into strips
2 ham hocks
1 large onion, peeled and roughly chopped
2 large carrots, peeled and roughly chopped
2 large celery stalks, roughly chopped
7 cloves garlic, peeled and minced, divided
2 quarts chicken broth
2 tablespoons tomato paste
2 bay leaves
2 tablespoons fresh thyme, or 2 teaspoons dried
1 tablespoon sweet or smoked paprika
½ teaspoon salt
2 cups bread crumbs
6 tablespoons chopped parsley
2 tablespoons melted butter

1. Sort cannellini beans and remove any debris. Cover with water by several inches in a large bowl and soak overnight.

2. Place a 6- or 8-quart Dutch oven over medium-high heat. Place duck legs skin side down in the pan and cook each side 3–4 minutes. Remove duck and add sausage, browning each side, about 2 minutes per side. Remove sausage and add lamb, cooking 4–5 minutes per side until browned. Remove lamb and add bacon. Cook until it starts to render its fat, about 10 minutes. Add ham hocks and cook until browned on all sides, about 4–5 minutes per side. Remove the hocks; leave bacon in pan.

3. Add onion, carrot, and celery to bacon. Cook 10 minutes, or until vegetables have softened and bacon is crispy. Add 5 minced garlic cloves and cook 1 minute.

4. Add broth, tomato paste, bay leaves, and thyme. Stir until blended. Increase heat and bring to a boil. Add beans and all meat. Cover and reduce heat to low. Simmer 3–4 hours. Turn off heat.

5. Remove meat from the pan. Cut sausage into chunks and set aside. Remove ham and duck meat from the bones and set aside. Skim the fat from the stew and add paprika and salt. Return meat to the pan.

6. Turn on broiler and set an oven rack in second lowest position.

7. Combine bread crumbs, parsley, and remaining garlic in a small bowl and spread over the pan. Drizzle butter on top. Place the pan under the broiler and cook until browned. Serve warm.

# Irish Lamb Stew

*This stew freezes well and is a great way to introduce lamb to friends and family who think they don't like it.*

**PREP TIME:** 10 minutes
**COOK TIME:** 2 hours 25 minutes

**INGREDIENTS | SERVES 6–8**

6 strips bacon

⅓ cup all-purpose flour

1½ teaspoons kosher salt, divided

1 teaspoon freshly ground black pepper

½ teaspoon garlic powder

¼ teaspoon paprika

3 pounds boneless lamb shoulder, trimmed of fat and cut into 1½" cubes

2 medium onions, peeled and diced, divided

2 cloves garlic, peeled and minced

4 cups beef or lamb broth, divided

1 teaspoon sugar

1 cup stout ale

2 bay leaves

½ teaspoon dried thyme leaves

1 large leek, trimmed and sliced

3 pounds white potatoes, peeled and cut into chunks

3 cups thickly sliced carrots

1½ cups green peas, frozen or shelled fresh

¼ teaspoon freshly cracked black pepper

⅓ cup minced fresh parsley

1. In a 6- or 8-quart Dutch oven over medium heat, cook bacon until crisp then remove from the pot to drain on a paper towel–lined plate.

2. In a zip-top bag combine flour, 1 teaspoon salt, pepper, garlic powder, and paprika. Add lamb pieces and shake to coat.

3. Working in batches, brown lamb cubes in bacon fat over medium-high heat, about 3 minutes per side. Remove to plate with bacon to rest.

4. Add the onions to the Dutch oven and cook until browned, about 8–10 minutes. Add garlic and 1 cup broth and, with a wooden spoon or heatproof rubber spatula, scrape the browned bits from bottom of pot. Add bacon and browned lamb along with remaining broth, sugar, ale, bay leaves, and thyme.

5. Increase heat to high and bring mixture to a boil. Reduce heat to medium and cook, stirring occasionally, until the lamb is tender, about 1½ hours. Add additional broth or water if needed.

6. Add leek, potatoes, carrots, and peas, then cover with a lid and cook until potatoes are tender, about 20–30 minutes.

7. Remove from heat and add remaining salt, pepper, and parsley. Serve in shallow bowls with broth.

# Stacked Chicken Enchiladas with Mole

*Rolling enchiladas individually can take a long time, but stacking them makes your prep fast!*

**PREP TIME:** 10 minutes
**COOK TIME:** 1 hour

**INGREDIENTS | SERVES 8**

1 tablespoon vegetable oil

1 medium onion, peeled and finely chopped

2 tablespoons chopped fresh cilantro

1 clove garlic, peeled and minced

1 teaspoon cumin

½ teaspoon smoked paprika

4 cups shredded cooked chicken breast or rotisserie chicken meat

3 cups shredded queso quesadilla cheese, divided

2 (8.25-ounce) jars mole sauce, such as Doña María

16 corn tortillas

½ cup sour cream, for garnish

1. In an ovenproof 6- or 8-quart Dutch oven over medium heat add oil. Once it shimmers add onion and cook until just tender, about 3 minutes. Add cilantro and cook until fragrant, about 1 minute. Add garlic, cumin, and smoked paprika and cook until spices and garlic are fragrant, about 1 minute. Remove the Dutch oven from heat.

2. In a medium bowl add chicken and cooked onion mixture. Toss well to combine. Add 2 cups shredded cheese and mix to combine. Set aside.

3. Heat oven to 350°F. Wipe out the Dutch oven then lightly spray with nonstick cooking spray.

4. In a medium saucepan over medium heat add both jars of mole sauce. Once mole is hot and starting to simmer, reduce heat to low.

5. Working in batches, dip four tortillas into mole 10 seconds to soften and then layer them into bottom of the prepared Dutch oven. Spread ⅓ of chicken mixture over tortillas, then drizzle 1–2 tablespoons of warm mole sauce over chicken. Repeat this process, ending with tortillas.

6. Spread ¼ cup of the remaining warm mole over top of tortillas, discarding the rest, and spread reserved cheese evenly over the top. Cover Dutch oven with the lid and bake 25–30 minutes.

7. Remove lid and bake 10–15 minutes more, or until the cheese on top is bubbling and melted. Cool 10 minutes, then serve with dollops of sour cream on top of each serving.

# Sour Cream Chili Bake

*Because of the tomato sauce in this dish, this isn't a good recipe for an un-enameled Dutch oven. Tomato sauces can remove seasoning from bare cast iron and discolor aluminum.*

**PREP TIME:** 10 minutes
**COOK TIME:** 50 minutes

**INGREDIENTS | SERVES 4–6**

1 pound lean ground chicken

½ small onion, peeled and finely chopped

1 teaspoon ground cumin

1 (10-ounce) can enchilada sauce

1 (8-ounce) can tomato sauce

1 (15-ounce) can pinto beans, drained and rinsed

6 ounces crushed tortilla chips

2 cups shredded Cheddar cheese, divided

½ teaspoon salt

6 ounces tortilla chips

1 cup sour cream

## Spice It Up!

This is a weeknight-easy dish that can be made to suit your family's spice level. Mild enchilada sauce will result in a tame dish. You can also use spicy enchilada sauce, or double the mild sauce and leave out the tomato sauce. You could also substitute 1 cup salsa for the plain tomato sauce to add even more flavor and texture to the dish.

1. Heat oven to 350°F. Place an ovenproof 6- or 8-quart Dutch oven over medium heat.

2. When the Dutch oven has warmed, crumble ground chicken into it, breaking meat into chunks. Cook for 5 minutes using a wooden spoon or spatula to cut and toss meat.

3. Sprinkle in onion and cumin. Continue stirring and chopping until meat is more brown than pink, about 3 minutes. Drain any excess fat. Add enchilada sauce, tomato sauce, beans, crushed chips, and 1½ cups cheese. Stir to combine so cheese melts evenly, then season with salt.

4. Place the Dutch oven in the middle of oven and bake 30 minutes.

5. When edges of casserole are crispy and mixture is lightly bubbling, sprinkle remaining cheese across the top and bake 2–3 minutes longer or until cheese melts.

6. Serve with chips and sour cream as a garnish.

# Carne Guisada

*"Carne guisada" means "stewed beef" in Spanish. Every region of Central America and many of the Spanish-speaking islands have their own version of this dish. This one isn't spicy, but some are. It's best to serve this version with white rice in bowls.*

**PREP TIME:** 10 minutes
**COOK TIME:** 3 hours 40 minutes

**INGREDIENTS | SERVES 6**

2 tablespoons vegetable oil

1½ pounds beef stew meat, trimmed and cut into 1" cubes

1 large onion, peeled and cut into eighths

1 large red bell pepper, seeded and sliced

4 cloves garlic, peeled and minced

1 celery stalk, chopped

8 ounces button mushrooms, sliced

1 cup beer

1 (14-ounce) can stewed tomatoes

2 fresh jalapeño peppers, stemmed, seeded, and diced

1 teaspoon ground cumin

2 cups beef broth

1. Place a 6- or 8-quart Dutch oven over medium-high heat. Add oil and beef and cook 5 minutes so all sides are browned. Remove beef and set aside.

2. Add onion and peppers and cook 5 minutes while stirring frequently. Add garlic, celery, and mushrooms and cook 5 minutes. Once celery has softened, add beer. Stir to loosen the brown bits on the bottom of the pot.

3. Add tomatoes, jalapeños, cumin, and beef broth. Return meat to the pan and stir until everything is well combined. Turn heat to lowest setting and cover. Cook 3–3½ hours. The meat should fall apart when you pick it up. Serve immediately.

# Ragu Bolognese

*Ragu Bolognese usually contains lots of different types of meat.*
*This easier version is still rich and delicious.*

**PREP TIME:** 10 minutes
**COOK TIME:** 1 hour

**INGREDIENTS | SERVES 8**

3 slices bacon
2 tablespoons butter
1 medium onion, peeled and chopped
4 cloves garlic, peeled and minced
½ cup chopped carrots
½ cup chopped celery
½ teaspoon salt
⅛ teaspoon freshly ground black pepper
1¼ pounds ground beef
1 (26-ounce) jar pasta sauce
¼ cup dry red wine
½ cup beef stock
1 (16-ounce) package linguine
½ cup heavy cream

1. In a 6- or 8-quart Dutch oven cook bacon until crisp. Drain on paper towels, crumble, and set aside. Drain fat from pan but do not wipe out.

2. Add butter and once it melts add onions, garlic, carrots, and celery. Cook until tender, about 6–7 minutes. Add salt and pepper.

3. Add beef and bacon, and stir to break up meat. Once meat has browned, about 10 minutes, drain off the excess fat, add pasta sauce, wine, and stock and bring to a simmer. Cook, stirring frequently, 30–40 minutes.

4. Cook pasta according to the package directions in salted water.

5. Add cream to meat sauce and simmer 3 minutes.

6. Drain pasta and place on serving plate and top with meat mixture. Serve immediately.

# Palak Paneer: Indian Spinach with Fresh Cheese

*This Indian dish may also be called saag paneer. "Palak" and "saag" are often used to mean "spinach" or similar green. Paneer is an unsalted and unaged cheese. If you can't find paneer you can substitute feta or firm tofu. Serve this dish over cooked basmati rice.*

**PREP TIME:** 20 minutes
**COOK TIME:** 25 minutes

**INGREDIENTS | SERVES 4 AS A SIDE, 2 AS AN ENTRÉE**

1 tablespoon vegetable oil

1 small yellow onion, peeled and chopped

½ teaspoon ground turmeric

1 teaspoon ground cumin

1 teaspoon garam masala powder

1 pound frozen spinach, thawed, squeezed, and chopped

1 green jalapeño (optional), seeded and chopped

1 clove garlic, peeled and minced

1 small tomato, chopped

¼ cup chopped cilantro

1 teaspoon salt

12 ounces chicken broth

1 cup plain Greek yogurt

2 (8-ounce) packages paneer cheese, cut into ½" cubes

1. Place a 6- or 8-quart Dutch oven over medium heat. Once it is warm, add oil and onion. Stir frequently 4–5 minutes, or until translucent.

2. Add dried spices and stir continually 2 minutes. The spices should be very fragrant.

3. Add spinach to the Dutch oven and stir, scraping any bits of spice off the bottom if necessary. Add jalapeño, garlic, tomato, and cilantro. Cook 10 minutes.

4. Add salt and broth to the pot and stir to combine. Let liquid evaporate before stirring in yogurt and cheese. Stir 1–2 minutes until cheese and yogurt are warmed. Serve immediately.

# Indian-Style Lamb Curry

*It is rare to see dishes in India called curries. The British settlers in India adopted the Tamil word kari, which means "sauce for rice" to refer to any dish with a sauce that was served over rice.*

**PREP TIME:** 2 hours 20 minutes
**COOK TIME:** 2 hours 10 minutes

**INGREDIENTS | SERVES 4–6**

1 small yellow onion, peeled and halved, one half minced

1 small clove garlic, peeled

½ cup Greek-style yogurt

2 teaspoons lemon juice

1 teaspoon ground coriander

½ teaspoon salt

½ teaspoon cumin

½ teaspoon ground cloves

½ teaspoon ground cardamom

½ teaspoon freshly ground black pepper

¼ teaspoon ground ginger

¼ teaspoon ground cinnamon

½ teaspoon olive oil

1½ teaspoons cornstarch

1 pound boneless lamb, cut into 1" cubes

1 tablespoon butter

1 tablespoon vegetable oil

1 cayenne pepper, whole

1. Purée onion half with garlic, yogurt, and lemon juice in a blender.

2. Place a dry skillet over medium heat. Once it's heated, add dry spices and shake every few seconds. Cook 2 minutes. Add spices to a blender container with olive oil and cornstarch and blend.

3. Pour yogurt mixture over lamb cubes in a sealable container. Toss so meat is coated. Leave the meat at room temperature 2 hours, or marinate overnight in the refrigerator.

4. Place a 6- or 8-quart Dutch over medium heat and once it's heated add butter and vegetable oil. Once butter stops foaming add minced onion and cook until tender, about 5 minutes. Add meat and marinade and bring to a simmer. Add whole cayenne pepper.

5. Reduce heat to low; cover and simmer 2 hours. Stir occasionally to keep sauce from sticking. After 1 hour, taste the sauce. As soon as it seems spicy enough, remove cayenne pepper. Serve.

# Indian Chicken Vindaloo

*If some members of your family like white meat and others like dark, you can substitute a quartered and skinned 3½-pound chicken for the thighs. This makes a rich, spicy stew you can serve over cooked rice or cooked diced potatoes.*

**PREP TIME:** 20 minutes
**COOK TIME:** 1 hour 25 minutes

**INGREDIENTS | SERVES 4–8**

¼ cup ghee

8 chicken thighs, skin removed

3 cloves garlic, peeled and minced

2 large yellow onions, peeled and diced

2 tablespoons fresh ginger, grated

2 teaspoons ground cumin

2 teaspoons yellow mustard seeds, crushed

1 teaspoon ground cinnamon

½ teaspoon ground cloves

1 tablespoon turmeric

1½ teaspoons cayenne pepper, or to taste

1 tablespoon paprika

1 tablespoon tamarind paste

2 teaspoons fresh lemon juice

2 tablespoons white vinegar

1 teaspoon light brown sugar

1–2 teaspoons salt

2 cups water

1. In a 6-quart Dutch oven over medium heat add the ghee. Once the ghee has melted and starts to shimmer add chicken pieces and fry until browned, about 5 minutes each side. Remove chicken from the Dutch oven and keep warm.

2. Add garlic and onion to pan and sauté until golden brown, about 8 minutes. Stir in the ginger, cumin, mustard seeds, cinnamon, cloves, turmeric, cayenne, and paprika; sauté for a 3 minutes. Stir in tamarind paste, lemon juice, vinegar, brown sugar, salt, and water.

3. Add chicken pieces. Bring to a boil; cover, lower heat, and simmer 45 minutes, or until chicken is tender.

4. Remove the cover and continue to simmer another 15 minutes, or until sauce thickens.

## Cucumber Salad with Yogurt

Indian Chicken Vindaloo is good with a simple cucumber salad. Thinly slice 2 cucumbers; dress the slices with 2 tablespoons fresh lemon juice, ¼ cup extra-virgin olive oil, 1 tablespoon chopped fresh dill, and ¼ teaspoon each salt and freshly cracked black pepper. Add a dollop of plain yogurt to each serving of the salad.

# Lebanese Baked Kibbe

*Serve with a Greek salad or Cucumber Salad with Yogurt (see sidebar in Indian Chicken Vindaloo recipe in this chapter). If you are serving the cucumber salad, omit the dill and garnish it with chopped fresh mint.*

**PREP TIME:** 40 minutes
**COOK TIME:** 1 hour 20 minutes
**INGREDIENTS | SERVES 8**

2 cups fine-grain bulgur

¼ cup dried onion flakes

4 cups water

2½ pounds ground lamb, divided

2 teaspoons dried parsley

1 teaspoon salt, divided

¼ teaspoon ground allspice

¼ teaspoon ground cinnamon

1 teaspoon dried mint

¼ cup cold water

2 tablespoons butter

¼ cup pine nuts

1 medium yellow onion, peeled and chopped

⅛ teaspoon ground cinnamon

⅛ teaspoon ground allspice

½ teaspoon freshly cracked black pepper

5 tablespoons extra-virgin olive oil, divided

1. In a medium bowl mix bulgur and onion flakes together; add 4 cups water and set aside to soak 30 minutes.

2. Drain bulgur and mix it with 2 pounds ground lamb and parsley, ½ teaspoon salt, ¼ teaspoon allspice, ¼ teaspoon cinnamon, mint, and cold water.

3. Melt butter in an ovenproof 4-quart Dutch oven. Add the remaining ½ pound ground lamb, pine nuts, onion, ⅛ teaspoon cinnamon, ⅛ teaspoon allspice, ½ teaspoon salt, and pepper. Sauté until onions are tender, about 5 minutes. Remove meat mixture from the pan and set aside.

4. Heat oven to 400°F.

5. Coat the bottom of the Dutch oven with 2 tablespoons olive oil. Press half of bulgur-lamb mixture into the pan. Evenly spread the sautéed lamb mixture over bulgur-lamb mixture. Spoon remaining bulgur-lamb mixture on top and use the back of a spoon or a spatula to press it down evenly over sautéed mixture. Drizzle remaining 3 tablespoons olive oil over top of casserole.

6. Bake 20 minutes; reduce oven temperature to 300°F and bake another 30 minutes, or until golden brown. To serve, cut into 8 wedges; use a spatula to remove each wedge from pan.

# Moroccan Chicken and Vegetables

*This is an adaptation of a chicken tagine recipe. It's traditionally served in deep soup bowls over cooked rice, noodles, or couscous.*

**PREP TIME:** 20 minutes
**COOK TIME:** 45 minutes

**INGREDIENTS | SERVES 4–8**

3 tablespoons extra-virgin olive oil

4 (4-ounce) chicken thighs, skin removed

2 (6-ounce) chicken breasts, halved and skin removed

1 large yellow onion, peeled and diced

3 cloves garlic, peeled and minced

1 large eggplant, cut into 1" pieces

3 cups chicken broth

2 (2") cinnamon sticks

1 teaspoon curry powder

1 teaspoon ground cumin

¼ teaspoon turmeric

¼ teaspoon freshly cracked black pepper

2 large carrots, peeled and diced

1 large zucchini, diced

1 large white turnip, peeled and diced

1 small red pepper, seeded and diced

2 cups diced tomatoes

½ cup golden raisins

2 tablespoons fresh chopped cilantro, divided

1. Add oil to a 6- or 8-quart Dutch oven over medium-high heat. Once the oil is hot and starts to shimmer add chicken pieces in batches, starting with the thighs, and brown on both sides, about 2–3 minutes per side. Remove from pan and keep warm.

2. Reduce heat to low and add onion, garlic, and eggplant. Sauté 5–10 minutes, or until onion is transparent. Increase heat to medium-high; stir in broth, cinnamon sticks, curry powder, cumin, turmeric, and black pepper and bring to a boil. Reduce heat and simmer 10 minutes.

3. Add chicken thighs, carrots, zucchini, turnip, and red pepper. Cover and simmer 10 minutes. Add chicken breasts, tomato, raisins, and half of cilantro; cover and simmer 10 minutes, or until chicken is cooked through. Garnish with remaining cilantro.

### Eggplant Matters

Some people find the taste of eggplant to be bitter unless it's first salted and allowed to sit for 20 minutes. If you take that step, drain off any liquid after 20 minutes, then rinse the eggplant and let it drain well again.

# Chicken in Harissa Sauce

*This Tunisian-inspired recipe can be made in stages, refrigerating the harissa sauce and cooked chicken until you're ready to put it all together. Serve this dish over couscous.*

**PREP TIME:** 30 minutes
**COOK TIME:** 1 hour 45 minutes
**INGREDIENTS | SERVES 6**

**Harissa:**
10 dried red hot peppers, stemmed
3 cloves garlic, peeled
1 teaspoon cumin
½ teaspoon caraway seeds
¼ teaspoon cloves
½ teaspoon kosher salt
½ cup olive oil, divided

**Chili:**
1 (3-pound) chicken
Water, as needed
2 cinnamon sticks
1 large orange, quartered
2 tablespoons olive oil
1 large onion, peeled and diced
1 large green bell pepper, seeded and diced
1 tablespoon all-purpose flour
6 tomatoes, peeled, seeded, and diced
½ cup coarsely chopped black olives
½ cup minced parsley

1. To make the harissa, soak red peppers in enough hot water to cover for 20 minutes, then drain well. Combine hot peppers, garlic, cumin, caraway seeds, cloves, and salt in a food processor. Pulse until it forms a coarse paste. With the processor running, slowly add 5 tablespoons olive oil. Scrape harissa into a small container. Pour remaining olive oil over top.

2. Place chicken in a 6- or 8-quart Dutch oven with enough water to cover. Add cinnamon sticks and quartered orange. Place the Dutch oven over high heat and bring to a boil, then reduce heat to medium-low and simmer, uncovered, 1 hour. After 1 hour turn off heat and allow chicken to cool in broth, about 15 minutes.

3. Remove chicken from broth; reserve broth. Pull chicken meat from bones, discarding skin, and shred meat. Place meat in a medium bowl. Strain reserved broth, and add, if needed, enough water to make 2 cups. Pour 1 cup broth over shredded chicken.

4. In a 6- or 8-quart Dutch oven heat 2 tablespoons olive oil over high heat. Add onion and bell pepper and cook until tender, about 3 minutes. Sprinkle with flour and cook until flour turns golden, about 3 minutes.

5. Slowly add remaining broth, working out any lumps. Add tomatoes and 3 tablespoons of prepared harissa sauce. Bring mixture to a boil, then reduce heat to medium and cook until thickened, about 10 minutes.

6. Add reserved shredded chicken, olives, and parsley. Simmer 5 minutes, or until heated through. Serve.

# CHAPTER 15

# Desserts

# Baked Apples

*Be sure to use a firm apple for this recipe. Softer apples are great for eating out of hand, but they can get a little mushy after baking. A scoop of vanilla ice cream would be a lovely accompaniment to these apples!*

**PREP TIME:** 15 minutes
**COOK TIME:** 50 minutes

**INGREDIENTS | SERVES 6**

½ cup packed light brown sugar

¼ cup finely chopped pecans

½ teaspoon cinnamon

¼ teaspoon allspice

6 Granny Smith or Pink Lady apples, cored

3 tablespoons unsalted butter

¼ cup apple juice

## How to Core an Apple

There are different ways you can core an apple. The method you select depends on how you plan to use the apple. For apples that need to stand, slice off the bottom of the apple then use an apple corer to remove the center of the apple. This will leave you with a whole apple with an empty central tube. If you do not have an apple corer, you can slice the apples in half and use a melon baller or teaspoon to scoop out the core. Be sure to also remove the stem and blossom end of the apple.

1. Heat oven to 350°F.

2. In a small bowl combine brown sugar, pecans, cinnamon, and allspice.

3. Place apples into a 6- or 8-quart Dutch oven. Spoon brown sugar mixture into the center of each apple, pressing down as needed to fit more filling in. Top each apple with ½ tablespoon butter, then pour apple juice into the bottom of the Dutch oven.

4. Cover the Dutch oven with a lid and bake 45–50 minutes, or until apples are tender and a paring knife is easily inserted into the apples. Cool 5 minutes before serving.

# Apple Cashew Toffee Crisp

*Cashews and toffee bits add fabulous flavor and texture to the candy-like topping of this classic crisp recipe.*

**PREP TIME:** 15 minutes
**COOK TIME:** 1 hour 45 minutes

**INGREDIENTS | SERVES 12**

7 large Granny Smith apples, peeled, cored, and sliced into ¼"-thick slices

2 tablespoons lemon juice

¼ cup apple juice

½ cup sugar

2½ cups brown sugar, divided

2 cups plus 2 tablespoons all-purpose flour, divided

1 teaspoon cinnamon

¼ teaspoon nutmeg

2 cups quick-cooking oatmeal

½ teaspoon baking soda

1 cup butter, melted

1 cup English toffee bits

½ cup chopped cashews

## Party Fun

You can use different types of apples in this easy dessert recipe. But make sure that you choose apples that hold their shape after baking. Those apples include Cortland, Empire, Golden Delicious, Granny Smith, Jonathan, McIntosh, and Winesap. Also try different nuts—chopped walnuts or pecans would be delicious.

1. Heat oven to 350°F.

2. Place apples in a medium bowl with lemon juice, apple juice, sugar, ½ cup brown sugar, 2 tablespoons flour, cinnamon, and nutmeg and toss to coat.

3. In a large bowl, combine oatmeal, 2 cups brown sugar, 2 cups flour, and baking soda and mix well. Add melted butter and mix until crumbs form. Stir in toffee bits and cashews.

4. Place half of oatmeal mixture in an ovenproof 6- or 8-quart Dutch oven. Top with apple mixture, then remaining oatmeal mixture. Bake 45–55 minutes or until topping is browned and apples are tender when pierced with a fork. Let cool 1 hour, then serve.

# Fried Fruit Pies

*These fried pies are filled with a sweet fresh apple filling, but you can substitute
your favorite fruit pie filling or canned filling if you prefer!*

**PREP TIME:** 2 hours 20 minutes
**COOK TIME:** 20 minutes

**INGREDIENTS | SERVES 8**

2 Granny Smith apples, peeled, cored,
and finely chopped

½ teaspoon cinnamon

¼ cup packed light brown sugar

2 tablespoons cornstarch

2 recipes All-Butter Pastry Crust for Pot
Pies (Chapter 3)

1 large egg, beaten

Oil, for frying

½ cup powdered sugar, for garnish

## Chill Out

Before frying any fruit pie it is a good idea
to let the made-up pies chill in the refrigerator for at least an hour or two. This will
allow the butter or fat in the crust to get
nice and cold, so when it hits the hot oil it
will form steam and make the crust very
crisp and slightly puffed. If you skip the
chilling step you may end up with a soggy,
greasy pie because the butter will just
melt away!

1. In a medium bowl combine apples, cinnamon, sugar, and cornstarch. Mix well, then let stand at room temperature 10 minutes.

2. Trim pastry crusts into rough squares, then cut crusts into 4 pieces each. Place about ¼ cup of filling into center of each square, then brush the edges of pastry lightly with beaten egg and fold dough over filling. Crimp the edges of pies with a fork, then transfer to a parchment-lined baking sheet and chill 2 hours.

3. In a 6- or 8-quart deep Dutch oven heat 3" oil over medium-high heat to 350°F, making sure there is at least a 3" air gap at the top of the pot.

4. Fry pies 2 at a time until they are golden brown and lightly puffed on both sides, about 3–5 minutes. Transfer fried pies to a wire rack over a baking sheet to drain. Dust with powdered sugar before serving. Serve warm.

# Salted Caramel Apple Crumble

*The sweet and salty bite the salted caramel sauce gives the apple filling makes this crumble irresistible!*

**PREP TIME:** 15 minutes
**COOK TIME:** 50 minutes
**INGREDIENTS | SERVES 8**

2 cups sugar, divided

2 tablespoons water

2 tablespoons light corn syrup

¾ cup heavy cream

4 tablespoons unsalted butter

1½ teaspoons sea salt

8 Granny Smith or Pink Lady apples, peeled, cored, and cut into ½" wedges

¼ cup cornstarch

1 teaspoon vanilla

½ teaspoon cinnamon

¼ teaspoon nutmeg

1 cup all-purpose flour

8 tablespoons (1 stick) unsalted butter, cubed

## Silky Smooth Caramel Sauce

When making caramel sauce there are a few things to keep in mind. First, never stir the caramel. Stirring encourages the creation of sugar crystals, and that will lead to a gritty sauce. Second, brush the edges of the pot with a little water. This will melt any sugar crystals that have clung to the side that could make the sauce gritty. Third, use a deep pot. When you add your butter and cream the sauce will bubble up. If you do not use a deep pot the sauce could boil over.

1. In a medium saucepan with deep sides add 1 cup sugar, water, and corn syrup. Place the pot over medium heat and, swirling but never stirring, bring mixture to a boil. Brush the sides of the pan with a wet pastry brush if any sugar crystals cling to the edge of the pot. Allow mixture to boil until it is a deep amber color and smells like dark caramel, about 6 minutes.

2. Remove pot from the heat and, very carefully as it will bubble up, whisk in heavy cream, butter, and salt. Once butter is melted let caramel cool to room temperature.

3. In an ovenproof 6- or 8-quart Dutch oven combine apples, cornstarch, vanilla, cinnamon, and nutmeg until all apples are evenly coated. Pour in ½ cup salted caramel sauce and mix to combine. Set aside.

4. Heat oven to 350°F.

5. In a medium bowl combine remaining sugar, flour, and butter. With your fingers rub butter into the flour and sugar until mixture is crumbly and well combined. Spread mixture evenly over apples and bake 30–40 minutes, or until apples are fork tender and crumble topping is golden brown.

6. Cool 10 minutes before serving. Drizzle each serving with a little of remaining caramel sauce.

# Very Berry Cobbler

*This cobbler uses a biscuit topping to mimic the look of a cobbled street, hence the name cobbler!*

**PREP TIME:** 20 minutes
**COOK TIME:** 45 minutes

**INGREDIENTS | SERVES 8**

2 cups frozen dark sweet cherries, thawed and drained

2 cups fresh blueberries

2 cups fresh raspberries

2 cups fresh strawberries, hulled and quartered

1 cup sugar, divided

¼ cup cornstarch

1 teaspoon vanilla

½ teaspoon cinnamon

1 recipe Biscuit Topping for Savory Stews (Chapter 3)

4 tablespoons unsalted butter, melted and cooled

1. Heat oven to 350°F and lightly spray an ovenproof 6- or 8-quart Dutch oven with nonstick cooking spray.

2. In a large bowl combine cherries, blueberries, raspberries, strawberries, ¾ cup sugar, cornstarch, vanilla, and cinnamon. Mix until everything is evenly distributed, then pour into the prepared Dutch oven.

3. Scoop biscuit topping over fruit mixture, then brush each biscuit with melted butter and sprinkle with remaining sugar.

4. Bake 35–40 minutes, or until biscuits are golden brown and fruit filling is bubbling. If biscuits are getting too brown place a layer of aluminum foil loosely over the Dutch oven. Cool 10 minutes before serving. Enjoy warm or at room temperature.

# Warm Ambrosia

*Fresh fruit makes all the difference in this new take on an old classic.*

**PREP TIME:** 10 minutes
**COOK TIME:** 5 minutes

**INGREDIENTS | SERVES 4**

1 cup diced fresh pineapple

1 cup fresh clementine orange slices, pith removed

½ cup drained maraschino cherries

¼ cup flaked sweetened coconut

1 cup coconut milk

1 cup miniature marshmallows

Whipped cream

1. Combine pineapple, oranges, cherries, coconut, and coconut milk in a 4- or 6-quart Dutch oven. Gently warm ingredients over medium heat until fruit is heated through, about 5 minutes.

2. Serve in bowls topped with miniature marshmallows and whipped cream.

# Stone Fruit Stew with Shortbread

*Although you can serve this stew as a dessert in its own right, it really works well as a sauce for pound cake or ice cream.*

**PREP TIME:** 30 minutes
**COOK TIME:** 25 minutes

**INGREDIENTS | SERVES 6–8**

1 cup seeded diced plums
1 cup seeded diced peaches
1 cup seeded diced nectarines
1 cup seeded diced apricots
1 cup seeded cherries
1 cup sugar
1 cup water
¼ cup orange juice
1 recipe shortbread (see sidebar)

1. Combine all fruits in a 4- or 6-quart Dutch oven. Sprinkle with sugar and let stand 20 minutes.

2. Add water and orange juice. Over medium-high heat, bring mixture to a boil, stirring constantly. Reduce heat to medium-low and simmer 15 minutes, stirring frequently.

3. Remove from heat. Serve warm with shortbread.

## How to Make Shortbread

Shortbread is about the simplest cookie to make. Recipes abound, but you can't go wrong by combining 2 cups cold butter with 4 cups flour and 1 cup brown sugar. Just work the mixture together as you would a pie crust. Sprinkle up to ½ cup more flour over the soft dough to make it easy to handle, then roll it into a rectangle. Score the shortbread diagonally in both directions, then bake at 325°F for 20 minutes. Cool, break apart, and serve.

# Warm Apple Cranberry Stew

*Think of this stew as apple cobbler without the crust. The sugar can be replaced with an equivalent amount of artificial sweetener. Serve this stew warm with cookies, ice cream, or cake.*

**PREP TIME:** 10 minutes
**COOK TIME:** 30 minutes

**INGREDIENTS | SERVES 4**

2 Granny Smith apples, peeled, cored, and diced

2 Fuji or McIntosh apples, peeled, cored, and diced

1 cup dried sweetened cranberries

½ cup sugar

1 teaspoon cinnamon

1 cup apple or cranberry-apple juice

1. Combine all ingredients in a 4- or 6-quart Dutch oven. Stirring constantly, bring to a boil over medium-high heat. Reduce heat to low and simmer 20 minutes or until apples are tender.

2. Let mixture stand at least 10 minutes then serve.


# Stewed Cherries with Almonds

*This super-simple stewed fruit dish tastes best with fresh cherries, but frozen will do in a pinch. Serve this over ice cream or pound cake.*

**PREP TIME:** 10 minutes
**COOK TIME:** 25 minutes

**INGREDIENTS | SERVES 4**

½ cup water

½ cup sugar

1 teaspoon almond extract

3 cups pitted fresh cherries

1 tablespoon cherry brandy

⅓ cup toasted slivered almonds

1. Combine water and sugar in a 4-quart Dutch oven and bring to a boil over medium-high heat, stirring constantly until sugar is dissolved.

2. Remove from heat and carefully add almond extract and cherries. Return to medium-high heat and bring to a boil. Reduce heat to medium-low and simmer 5 minutes.

3. Stir in cherry brandy then remove from heat. Sprinkle with toasted almonds and serve.

# Port-Poached Pears with Vanilla

*Poached pears make an elegant finish to a fancy dinner. Serve these pears with
a little freshly whipped cream or some good-quality vanilla ice cream!*

**PREP TIME:** 10 minutes
**COOK TIME:** 1 hour 10 minutes

**INGREDIENTS | SERVES 6**

1½ cups port wine

1 cup sugar

2 tablespoons fresh grated orange zest

1 cinnamon stick

4 whole cloves

6 Bosc pears, bottom cut off, peeled,
stems attached

Water, for covering pears

1. In a 6- or 8-quart Dutch oven combine port, sugar, orange zest, cinnamon stick, and cloves.

2. Place pears cut side down into the Dutch oven and fill with enough water to just cover pears. Bring mixture to a boil then reduce heat to medium-low. Simmer 50–55 minutes or until a paring knife slides easily into the thickest part of pears.

3. Remove Dutch oven from the heat and let pears cool to room temperature. Transfer pears to serving plates. Drizzle a little of cooking liquid over them, if desired.

# Easy Cherry Dump Cake

*Yes, this is made with cake mix and canned pie filling, and it is really, really
good! You can add chopped nuts to this recipe if you like.*

**PREP TIME:** 5 minutes
**COOK TIME:** 1 hour 10 minutes

**INGREDIENTS | SERVES 12**

2 (20-ounce) cans cherry pie filling

1 (15.25-ounce) package yellow cake mix

8 tablespoons (1 stick) butter, sliced

1. Heat oven to 350°F and lightly spray an ovenproof 10- or 12-inch Dutch oven with nonstick cooking spray.

2. In the prepared Dutch oven add cherry pie filling. Sprinkle cake mix over filling then lay butter slices over cake mix.

3. Bake 50–55 minutes, or until top is browned and filling is bubbling. Cool 20 minutes before serving.

# Warm Chocolate Pudding Cake

*This cake has a moist, pudding-like texture and a decadent chocolate sauce on the bottom. It is fantastic served with fresh whipped cream and fresh berries!*

**PREP TIME:** 20 minutes
**COOK TIME:** 1 hour

**INGREDIENTS | SERVES 10**

1 cup all-purpose flour
1½ cups sugar, divided
½ cup Dutch-processed cocoa powder, divided
2 teaspoons baking powder
½ teaspoon salt
¾ cup whole milk
½ cup butter, melted and cooled
2 teaspoons vanilla
½ cup packed light brown sugar
1¼ cups hot water

1. Heat oven to 350°F and lightly spray an ovenproof 8- or 10-inch Dutch oven with nonstick cooking spray.

2. In a large bowl combine flour, ¾ cup sugar, ¼ cup cocoa powder, baking powder, and salt. Whisk to mix, then add milk, butter, and vanilla. Mix until just combined, about 12 strokes. Spread this mixture into the prepared Dutch oven.

3. In a small bowl combine remaining sugar, cocoa powder, and brown sugar. Sprinkle this mixture evenly over the batter. Pour hot water over top. Do not stir.

4. Bake 35–40 minutes, or until the center of cake is just set.

5. Cool 20 minutes before serving. Be sure to scoop all the way to the bottom of the Dutch oven to get the warm sauce that will be there.

# Broiled S'mores Casserole

*Be sure not to overbake the filling. You want it to be soft and gooey, just like a melted chocolate bar!*

**PREP TIME:** 10 minutes
**COOK TIME:** 45 minutes

**INGREDIENTS | SERVES 10**

1¼ cups graham cracker crumbs

1½ sticks unsalted butter, melted, divided

2 large eggs

1 cup sugar

1 teaspoon vanilla

½ cup all-purpose flour

⅓ cup Dutch-processed cocoa powder

¼ teaspoon salt

1 cup semisweet chocolate chips

1 (10-ounce) bag miniature marshmallows

1. Heat oven to 350°F and lightly spray an ovenproof and broilerproof 10-inch Dutch oven with nonstick cooking spray.

2. In a medium bowl combine graham cracker crumbs with ½ cup melted butter. Mix until graham cracker crumbs are completely coated, then press into the bottom of the Dutch oven. Bake 10 minutes, then set aside to cool.

3. In a small bowl combine remaining butter with eggs, sugar, and vanilla. Mix until thoroughly combined.

4. In a medium bowl combine flour, cocoa powder, and salt. Whisk to combine.

5. Pour wet ingredients into dry ingredients and mix until dry ingredients are just moistened, about 12 strokes. Fold in chocolate chips, then pour batter over the graham cracker base.

6. Bake 25–30 minutes, or until filling is just set around the edges.

7. Pour marshmallows over the top of chocolate filling. Heat the broiler and broil until marshmallows are golden brown and puffed. Cool 10 minutes before serving.

# Rice Pudding

*A big pot of rice pudding is perfect for a cold day! Feel free to use any kind of dried fruit in this recipe if raisins do not appeal to you.*

**PREP TIME:** 10 minutes
**COOK TIME:** 1 hour 5 minutes

**INGREDIENTS | SERVES 8**

3 large eggs
1 large egg yolk
2 cups whole milk
1 cup half and half
1 cup sugar
½ teaspoon fresh grated nutmeg
Pinch of cinnamon
3 cups cooked rice
½ cup raisins

1. Heat oven to 375°F.

2. In a medium bowl whisk together eggs and egg yolk until well combined. Add milk, half and half, sugar, nutmeg, and cinnamon. Mix in rice and then pour into an ovenproof 4- or 6-quart Dutch oven. Stir in raisins.

3. Bake 45–50 minutes, or until the center of rice pudding jiggles slightly when the Dutch oven is moved and a paring knife inserted into the center comes out clean. Cool 20 minutes before serving.

# Coconut Mango Sticky Rice

*This rice is sticky because it is made with short-grain rice, also known as sushi rice. If you only have medium or long-grain rice you can still make this dish; it will just be a little thinner.*

**PREP TIME:** 10 minutes
**COOK TIME:** 15 minutes

**INGREDIENTS | SERVES 10**

4 cups cooked short-grain rice
1 (15-ounce) can coconut milk
1 cup whole milk
½ cup sugar
2 tablespoons butter
¼ teaspoon cardamom
2 teaspoons vanilla
1 cup diced fresh mango
1 cup shredded sweetened coconut, toasted

1. In a 6- or 8-quart Dutch oven combine rice, coconut milk, milk, sugar, butter, and cardamom. Heat mixture over medium heat until it comes to a boil.

2. Reduce heat to medium-low and simmer until the mixture is very thick, about 5 minutes.

3. Remove the Dutch oven from heat and add vanilla, mango, and toasted coconut. Fold to combine. Serve warm.

# Chocolate Caramel Rice Pudding

*This decadent recipe is a great combination of comfort food and elegance.*

**PREP TIME:** 7 hours
**COOK TIME:** 50 minutes

**INGREDIENTS | SERVES 8**

4 cups water
2 cups milk
½ teaspoon salt
½ cup brown sugar
1 cup long-grain white rice
1 cup semisweet chocolate chips
1 cup heavy cream
2 tablespoons powdered sugar
2 teaspoons vanilla
½ cup caramel ice-cream topping

1. In 6- or 8-quart Dutch oven bring water, milk, salt, and sugar to a boil over medium-high heat. Stir in rice, reduce heat to low, then cover and cook 40–50 minutes, or until rice is very soft. Stir gently twice during cooking time.

2. Stir in chocolate chips until melted, then transfer to large bowl and chill until cold, about 4 hours.

3. In small bowl, beat cream with powdered sugar and vanilla. Fold into rice mixture and place in serving cups. Drizzle with caramel ice-cream topping. Chill 2–3 hours before serving.

# Chocolate Chip Skillet Cookie

*If you prefer, you can bake this in a 10- to 12-inch cast-iron skillet or cake pan for 45 minutes.*

**PREP TIME:** 10 minutes
**COOK TIME:** 50 minutes

**INGREDIENTS | MAKES 1 (10-INCH) COOKIE**

2 cups all-purpose flour
1 teaspoon baking soda
½ teaspoon salt
¾ cup plus 1 teaspoon unsalted butter, softened, divided
½ cup sugar
¾ cup packed brown sugar
1 large egg
2 teaspoons vanilla extract
1½ cups chocolate chips

1. Heat oven to 350°F.

2. Combine the flour, baking soda, and salt in a bowl. Use the paddle attachment of a stand mixer, or a use a handheld mixer, to cream ¾ cup butter and sugars until they're light and fluffy. Add egg and vanilla and blend on low until combined. Add flour mixture and beat on low until it is just combined. Stir in chocolate chips by hand.

3. Grease an ovenproof 10-inch or 4-quart Dutch oven with 1 teaspoon butter. Press dough evenly over the bottom of the Dutch oven. Bake 30 minutes, or until the edges are brown and the top is golden. Leave in the pan and rest on a wire rack 20 minutes to cool. Cut and serve.

# Chocolate Poke Cake

*This rich chocolate cake is smothered while still hot with a dulce de leche mixture that soaks into the cake and makes it very, very moist.*

**PREP TIME:** 10 minutes
**COOK TIME:** 5 hours 25 minutes
**INGREDIENTS | SERVES 8**

8 tablespoons (1 stick) butter, at room temperature
¾ cup sugar
1 large egg
1½ teaspoons vanilla, divided
1 cup cake flour
⅓ cup Dutch-processed cocoa powder
½ teaspoon baking powder
¼ teaspoon baking soda
½ cup whole milk
1 cup dulce de leche
1¼ cup heavy cream, divided
2 tablespoons powdered sugar

1. Heat oven to 350°F and spray an ovenproof 9- or 10-inch Dutch oven with nonstick cooking spray.

2. In a large bowl cream together butter and sugar until well combined and somewhat lighter in color. Add egg and 1 teaspoon vanilla and mix until well combined.

3. In a medium bowl sift together flour, cocoa powder, baking powder, and baking soda. Alternately add flour mixture and milk into butter mixture in three additions, beginning and ending with flour.

4. Pour mixture into the prepared Dutch oven and spread so the batter is even. Bake 20–25 minutes, or until cake springs back when gently pressed in the center and edges of the cake pull away from the sides of the Dutch oven. Do not overbake.

5. While cake is baking combine dulce de leche and ¼ cup heavy cream in a small saucepan. Heat over low heat until smooth and runny, about 5 minutes. Cover and keep warm while cake finishes baking.

6. Once cake comes out of oven immediately poke holes into it with the end of a large wooden spoon. Pour warm dulce de leche over cake. Cool on the counter 1 hour, then cover with the lid and chill at least 4 hours or overnight.

7. Just before serving prepare the topping: In a stand mixer or a large bowl with a hand mixer combine 1 cup cream, powdered sugar, and ½ teaspoon vanilla. Whip until mixture forms soft peaks, about 2 minutes. Spread whipped cream over cake. Serve immediately.

# Dutch Oven Brownies

*Fudgy, moist, and super rich, these brownies will satisfy even the most hardcore chocolate lovers!*

**PREP TIME:** 15 minutes
**COOK TIME:** 30 minutes

**INGREDIENTS | SERVES 10**

½ cup all-purpose flour

½ cup cocoa powder

1 teaspoon baking powder

¼ teaspoon salt

½ cup butter

1 cup chocolate chips, divided

1 cup sugar

1 teaspoon vanilla

2 large eggs

2 tablespoons honey

1 cup chopped walnuts or pecans

## Honey for Fudgy Brownies

If you want moist, fudgy brownies you should use a little honey. Honey is a hygroscopic sugar and attracts moisture from the air around it. When added to cakes, brownies, and other sweet batters it helps to retain moisture while baking and to keep baked goods moist by absorbing moisture from the air. Brownies made with honey will stay fresh longer—if they are not devoured right away! Other hygroscopic sugars include molasses, golden syrup, and cane syrup.

1. Heat oven to 350°F and lightly spray an ovenproof 10-inch Dutch oven with nonstick cooking spray.

2. In a large bowl combine flour, cocoa powder, baking powder, and salt. Set aside.

3. In a microwave-safe bowl combine butter with ½ cup chocolate chips. Microwave for 30-second intervals, stirring after each interval, until the butter and chips are melted and smooth.

4. Transfer chocolate mixture to a medium bowl along with sugar, vanilla, eggs, and honey. Whisk until smooth and well combined.

5. Pour the wet ingredients into the dry and mix until just combined, about 10 strokes, then add remaining chocolate chips and nuts and fold to combine, about 3–4 strokes more.

6. Pour batter into the prepared Dutch oven and bake 25–35 minutes or until the brownies are set around the edges and slightly jiggly in the center. Enjoy warm from the Dutch oven, or cool completely and cut into wedges.

# Butterscotch Crumble Cake

*This cake is great for snacking, or to serve with cups of coffee in the afternoon as a pick-me-up.*

**PREP TIME:** 20 minutes
**COOK TIME:** 30 minutes

**INGREDIENTS | SERVES 10**

1½ cups all-purpose flour, divided

1¼ cups packed light brown sugar, divided

½ teaspoon baking powder

½ teaspoon baking soda

¼ teaspoon salt

2 large eggs

½ cup buttermilk

⅓ cup vegetable or coconut oil

1 teaspoon vanilla

1 (12-ounce) package butterscotch chips, divided

4 tablespoons unsalted butter

1. Heat oven to 350°F and lightly spray an ovenproof 10-inch Dutch oven with nonstick cooking spray.

2. In a large bowl combine 1 cup flour, ¾ cup sugar, baking powder, baking soda, and salt. Whisk until well combined.

3. In a medium bowl combine eggs, buttermilk, oil, and vanilla. Whisk until smooth.

4. Pour the wet ingredients into the dry and mix until just combined, about 8 strokes, then add half the butterscotch chips and fold to combine, about 3–4 strokes more. Pour batter into the prepared Dutch oven.

5. In a medium bowl combine remaining flour, sugar, and butter. With your fingers rub butter into flour and sugar until mixture is crumbly and well combined. Spread mixture evenly over cake batter, then sprinkle remaining butterscotch chips over top.

6. Bake 25–35 minutes, or until the cake springs back in the center when gently pressed and a toothpick inserted into center of cake comes out clean. Cool to room temperature before serving.

# Chocolate Cookie Brownies

*This recipe uses a mix of crumbled chocolate chip and chocolate sandwich cookies in the center of the brownies. If you want to use one type, or something different like peanut butter sandwich cookies, feel free!*

**PREP TIME:** 15 minutes
**COOK TIME:** 35 minutes

**INGREDIENTS | SERVES 10**

½ cup all-purpose flour
½ cup cocoa powder
1 teaspoon baking powder
¼ teaspoon salt
½ cup butter
½ cup chocolate chips
1 cup sugar
1 teaspoon vanilla
2 large eggs
2 tablespoons honey
12 chocolate sandwich cookies, broken into large pieces
12 chocolate chip cookies, broken into large pieces

1. Heat oven to 350°F and lightly spray an ovenproof 10-inch Dutch oven with nonstick cooking spray.

2. In a medium bowl combine flour, cocoa powder, baking powder, and salt. Set aside.

3. In a microwave-safe bowl combine butter with chocolate chips. Microwave for 30-second intervals, stirring after each interval, until butter and chips are melted and smooth.

4. Transfer chocolate mixture to a medium bowl along with sugar, vanilla, eggs, and honey. Whisk until smooth and well combined.

5. Pour the wet ingredients into the dry and mix until just combined, about 12–13 strokes. Pour half batter into the prepared Dutch oven, sprinkle broken cookies onto batter, and pour remaining batter over the top. Use a spatula to evenly cover cookie pieces.

6. Bake 25–35 minutes, or until brownies are set around the edges and slightly jiggly in the center. Cool completely and cut into wedges.

# Pineapple Upside-Down Cake

*This retro classic is a welcome addition to any potluck, barbecue, or party!*

**PREP TIME:** 25 minutes
**COOK TIME:** 50 minutes

**INGREDIENTS | SERVES 12**

1 cup butter, melted, divided

1⅔ cups packed light brown sugar, divided

1 (14-ounce) can pineapple rings, drained, juice reserved

Maraschino cherries, to put in the center of the pineapple rings

1½ cups all-purpose flour

1½ teaspoons baking soda

½ teaspoon salt

¾ cup milk

1 large egg

## Pineapple Right-Side-Up Cake

Want to make this cake even easier? Make the cake mixture and pour it into the pan, then top it with the melted butter, brown sugar, and pineapple rings with cherries in the center. The cake will have a somewhat gooey top, and there will not be a rush to get the warm cake out of the Dutch oven after baking. Along with being a little easier to serve, it tastes just as good!

1. Heat oven to 350°F and lightly spray an ovenproof 10-inch Dutch oven with nonstick cooking spray.

2. Pour ⅓ cup melted butter into the prepared Dutch oven, then sprinkle 1 cup of the brown sugar evenly into butter. Lay pineapple rings into the Dutch oven, as many as will fit in one layer, and place a cherry in the center of each ring. Set aside.

3. In a medium bowl combine flour, baking soda, and salt. Whisk to combine.

4. In a separate bowl add remaining butter, remaining sugar, ¼ cup reserved pineapple juice, milk, and egg. Mix until smooth. Pour the wet ingredients into the dry ingredients and mix until batter is well combined, about 20 strokes. Small lumps are okay.

5. Carefully pour batter over pineapple rings. Spread so it is even. Bake 50–55 minutes, or until the cake springs back when gently pressed and the sides of the cake are starting to pull away from the sides of the Dutch oven.

6. Immediately turn cake out onto a heatproof serving plate, allowing butter and brown sugar sauce to drip over the cake. Be careful—the cake and Dutch oven are very hot. If any of the pineapple rings or cherries stick, loosen them with a fork and place them back on cake. Serve warm or at room temperature.

# Traditional Bread Pudding

*Brioche is a buttery French bread that is available in most grocery store bakeries.
If you can't find it you can substitute challah bread or croissants.*

**PREP TIME:** 15 minutes
**COOK TIME:** 1 hour 45 minutes

**INGREDIENTS | SERVES 8**

6 cups cubed brioche bread, about ½" cubes
2 cups whole milk
1 cup heavy cream
3 large eggs
2 large egg yolks
⅔ cup sugar
1 teaspoon vanilla
¼ teaspoon cinnamon
¼ teaspoon nutmeg

1. Heat oven to 350°F and lightly spray an ovenproof 6- or 8-quart Dutch oven with nonstick cooking spray.

2. Spread cubed bread in the Dutch oven. Set aside.

3. In a large bowl whisk together remaining ingredients until well combined and smooth. Pour over cubed bread and allow to soak at room temperature 10 minutes.

4. Once soaked, bake 45–50 minutes, or until the bread pudding is golden brown and puffed all over. Cool 1 hour before serving.

# Baked Bananas with Rum

*This recipe is the perfect topping for vanilla ice cream. If you want to make
this without rum just add a little pineapple juice instead.*

**PREP TIME:** 10 minutes
**COOK TIME:** 20 minutes

**INGREDIENTS | SERVES 4–6**

6 large bananas, peeled and cut into 1" pieces
½ cup packed light brown sugar
¼ cup light rum
2 tablespoons pineapple juice
2 tablespoons butter, melted
⅛ teaspoon cinnamon

1. Heat oven to 350°F and lightly spray an ovenproof 4- to 6-quart Dutch oven with nonstick cooking spray.

2. Lay banana pieces in the prepared Dutch oven.

3. In a medium bowl whisk together remaining ingredients. Pour sauce over the bananas. Bake 15–20 minutes, spooning the sauce over the bananas every 5 minutes, until the bananas are tender and glazed. Cool 5 minutes before serving.

# Cherry Chocolate Bread Pudding

*This bread pudding is similar to a British bread and butter pudding, but this version is made with sour cherry jam and chocolate hazelnut spread.*

**PREP TIME:** 20 minutes
**COOK TIME:** 1 hour 45 minutes

**INGREDIENTS | SERVES 10**

10 (1") slices of challah or brioche bread
¾ cup sour cherry jam
½ cup chocolate hazelnut spread, such as Nutella
2 cups whole milk
1 cup heavy cream
3 large eggs
½ cup sugar
1 teaspoon vanilla
1 cup frozen dark sweet cherries, thawed and drained
½ cup chocolate chips

1. Heat oven to 350°F and lightly spray an ovenproof 6- or 8-quart Dutch oven with nonstick cooking spray.

2. Lay bread out on a work surface. On half the bread slices spread jam; on the other half spread chocolate hazelnut spread. Combine the two sides, one cherry and one chocolate, into sandwiches. Stand sandwiches up on edge in the bottom of the prepared Dutch oven. Set aside.

3. In a large bowl whisk together remaining ingredients except cherries and chocolate chips until well combined and smooth. Pour over the arranged sandwiches and allow to soak at room temperature 10 minutes. Poke whole cherries in between sandwiches, then sprinkle chocolate chips over the top. Bake 45–50 minutes, or until the bread pudding is golden brown and puffed all over. Cool 1 hour before serving.

# Norwegian Sweet Soup

*Some cooks augment this Christmas soup with Mandarin orange slices. Serve warm soup as is or with a scoop of vanilla ice cream.*

**PREP TIME:** 10 minutes
**COOK TIME:** 35 minutes

**INGREDIENTS | SERVES 6**

6 cups water
½ cup sugar
1 tablespoon quick-cooking tapioca
1 cinnamon stick
1 cup halved dried apricots
½ cup diced dried apples
½ cup diced dried pears
1 cup dry-packed prunes
1 cup golden raisins
1 cup fresh or frozen pitted cherries
1 teaspoon grated lemon zest
1 teaspoon vanilla

1. In a 4- or 6-quart Dutch oven combine water, sugar, and tapioca. Bring to a boil over medium-high heat, stirring constantly. Add cinnamon stick, apricots, apples, pears, prunes, and raisins. Reduce heat to medium, cover with the lid, and simmer 20 minutes, or until the fruit is plump and tender.

2. Stir in cherries, lemon zest, and vanilla. Continue to simmer 5 minutes, then remove from heat. Remove cinnamon stick and serve warm.

# Glossary

**Anodize:** To coat something, often metal such as aluminum, with a protective film.

**Bake:** A dry-heat method of cooking in which food is surrounded by heat at an even temperature.

**Braise:** A cooking method that uses both moist and dry heat. Typically the food is seared then cooked in a covered pot with liquid that covers ½–⅔ of the food. Also referred to as pot-roasting.

**Brine:** A liquid mixture that usually combines sugar, salt, and other spices and is used to season meat by soaking it before cooking.

**Boil:** Cooking method in which liquid is heated until it begins to change into a vapor.

**Broil:** A dry-heat method of cooking in which food is placed directly under a heat source.

**Butcher's twine:** Thick cotton string used to truss meats, roasts, or tie boquet garni, before cooking. Also referred to as kitchen twine.

**Casserole:** Any of a variety of deep dish cooking vessels that can used in the oven. This term also refers to the food cooked in these vessels.

**Cast iron:** Iron, typically pig iron and other alloying elements, which are melted down and then poured into a mold.

**Chili pepper:** The fruit of plants that are members of the nightshade family. Chili peppers come in many varieties, in heat levels from mild to very hot, and can be purchased fresh, dried, pickled, or powdered.

**Chop:** To cut food into small, uniform pieces ⅛"–¼" in size.

**Creaming:** The process of working food into a smooth paste. In baking it refers to blending butter and sugar into a uniform, often slightly fluffy, mixture.

**Curry:** A combination of spices used for cooking that can be a dry powder or paste. The types of spices vary depending on the type of cuisine.

**Deep-fry:** A cooking method in which food is cooked in heated oil.

**Dice:** To cut food into small, uniform cubes that can range in size from ¼" to ¾" depending on the recipe.

**Disher:** A round scoop with a release mechanism that portions soft foods or dough. Also referred to as an ice-cream scoop.

**Enamel:** A glossy protective coating that is bonded to the surface of metal or pottery.

**Ghee:** Clarified butter commonly used in Indian cooking and for deep-frying.

**Kaffir lime leaves:** The fragrant leaves of the kaffir lime tree, which is native to India and Southeast Asia.

**Mince:** To finely chop food so that it is in pieces smaller than 1/8" in size.

**Mole:** A sauce or stew originating from Mexico and Latin America that is made with a variety of spices and other ingredients. Mole varies by region, with each region having a specific blend of spices and ingredients.

**Oxidation:** The process by which oxygen combines with an element to change the appearance of that element.

**Panko bread crumbs:** Japanese-style bread crumbs that have a larger, flakier texture than traditional Western-style bread crumbs.

**Quart:** A unit of liquid measurement in the United States that is equal to 2 pints or .946 liters.

**Quinoa:** An edible seed that is a good source of protein, fiber, and other nutrients.

**Roast:** A dry-heat cooking method in which hot air is used to cook the food. The heat can come from an oven, open flame, or other heat source.

**Sear:** The process of browning food by exposing it to high heat.

**Slow cooking:** A cooking method in which food is cooked for a long period of time at a moderate temperature. Often used for soups, stews, and tough cuts of meat.

**Stainless steel:** A steel alloy that does not corrode or rust.

**Shaoxing wine:** A traditional Chinese rice wine that is popular in Chinese cooking.

**Tofu:** A food made from coagulated soy bean milk.

**Simmer:** The temperature of a liquid while cooking that is just below the boiling point.

**Wholemeal flour:** Flour that is coarsely ground, giving it a toothsome texture. Popular in Irish baking. The grind can range from very coarse to fine.

# Standard U.S./Metric Measurement Conversions

## VOLUME CONVERSIONS

| U.S. Volume Measure | Metric Equivalent |
| --- | --- |
| ⅛ teaspoon | 0.5 milliliter |
| ¼ teaspoon | 1 milliliter |
| ½ teaspoon | 2 milliliters |
| 1 teaspoon | 5 milliliters |
| ½ tablespoon | 7 milliliters |
| 1 tablespoon (3 teaspoons) | 15 milliliters |
| 2 tablespoons (1 fluid ounce) | 30 milliliters |
| ¼ cup (4 tablespoons) | 60 milliliters |
| ⅓ cup | 90 milliliters |
| ½ cup (4 fluid ounces) | 125 milliliters |
| ⅔ cup | 160 milliliters |
| ¾ cup (6 fluid ounces) | 180 milliliters |
| 1 cup (16 tablespoons) | 250 milliliters |
| 1 pint (2 cups) | 500 milliliters |
| 1 quart (4 cups) | 1 liter (about) |

## WEIGHT CONVERSIONS

| U.S. Weight Measure | Metric Equivalent |
| --- | --- |
| ½ ounce | 15 grams |
| 1 ounce | 30 grams |
| 2 ounces | 60 grams |
| 3 ounces | 85 grams |
| ¼ pound (4 ounces) | 115 grams |
| ½ pound (8 ounces) | 225 grams |
| ¾ pound (12 ounces) | 340 grams |
| 1 pound (16 ounces) | 454 grams |

## OVEN TEMPERATURE CONVERSIONS

| Degrees Fahrenheit | Degrees Celsius |
| --- | --- |
| 200 degrees F | 95 degrees C |
| 250 degrees F | 120 degrees C |
| 275 degrees F | 135 degrees C |
| 300 degrees F | 150 degrees C |
| 325 degrees F | 160 degrees C |
| 350 degrees F | 180 degrees C |
| 375 degrees F | 190 degrees C |
| 400 degrees F | 205 degrees C |
| 425 degrees F | 220 degrees C |
| 450 degrees F | 230 degrees C |

## BAKING PAN SIZES

| American | Metric |
| --- | --- |
| 8 x 1½ inch round baking pan | 20 x 4 cm cake tin |
| 9 x 1½ inch round baking pan | 23 x 3.5 cm cake tin |
| 11 x 7 x 1½ inch baking pan | 28 x 18 x 4 cm baking tin |
| 13 x 9 x 2 inch baking pan | 30 x 20 x 5 cm baking tin |
| 2 quart rectangular baking dish | 30 x 20 x 3 cm baking tin |
| 15 x 10 x 2 inch baking pan | 30 x 25 x 2 cm baking tin (Swiss roll tin) |
| 9 inch pie plate | 22 x 4 or 23 x 4 cm pie plate |
| 7 or 8 inch springform pan | 18 or 20 cm springform or loose bottom cake tin |
| 9 x 5 x 3 inch loaf pan | 23 x 13 x 7 cm or 2 lb narrow loaf or pate tin |
| 1½ quart casserole | 1.5 liter casserole |
| 2 quart casserole | 2 liter casserole |

# INDEX